A Woman Alone

Travel Tales From Around the Globe

Edited by
Faith Conlon,
Ingrid Emerick and
Christina Henry de Tessan

SEAL PRESS

Published by Seal Press
An Imprint of Avalon Publishing Group Incorporated
161 William Street, 16th Floor, New York, NY 10038
sealpress@sealpress.com

Cover design by Trina Stahl
Text design by Christina Henry de Tessan
Cover photograph by Theo Allofs courtesy Tony Stone

"For Your Kind Information and Necessary Action, Please," from *Beyond the Sky and the Earth* by Jamie Zeppa, copyright © 1999 by Jamie Zeppa. Used by permission of Riverhead Books, a division of Penguin Putnam, Inc.

"Moonlight and Vodka," from *Wall to Wall: From Berlin to Beijing by Rail* by Mary Morris, copyright © 1991 by Mary Morris. Used by permission of Doubleday, a division of Random House, Inc.

"Don't Rely on Maps," from *Tracks* by Robyn Davidson, copyright © 1980 by Robyn Davidson. Used by permission of Pantheon Books, a division of Random House, Inc.

"In the Ladies' Compartment," from *A Journey of One's Own: Uncommon Advice for the Independent Woman Traveler, 2nd Edition* by Thalia Zepatos, copyright © 1996 by Thalia Anastasia Zepatos. Reprinted by permission of Eighth Mountain Press.

"The End of the Road," from *A Woman's World* by Marybeth Bond, copyright © 1995 by Marybeth Bond (Travelers' Tales, 1995). Used by permission of the author.

"The Truth About Italian Men," by Dawn Comer Jefferson, copyright © 1997 by Dawn Comer Jefferson, first appeared as "A Black Broad Abroad," in *Go Girl* (Eighth Mountain Press, 1997). Used by permission of the author.

"Pretty Enough to be a Showgirl" by Chelsea Cain first appeared in a slightly different form in *Grand Tour: the Journal of Travel Literature* (Spring 1997).

"Table for One" by Susan Spano first appeared as "Two's a Crowd" in the July 20, 1997 issue of the *New York Times* Travel section. Published here by permission of the author.

Printed in Canada
First printing, November 2001
Distributed to the trade by Publishers Group West
In Canada: Publishers Group West Canada, Toronto, Ontario
In the United Kingdom, Europe and South Africa: Hi Marketing, London
In Asia and the Middle East: Michelle Morrow Curreri, Beverly, MA

10   9   8   7   6   5   4   3

A woman alone: travel tales from around the globe/edited by Faith Conlon, Ingrid Emerick, and Christina Henry de Tessan.
          p.cm.
ISBN: 1-58005-059-X (alk. paper)
1. Women travelers--Anecdotes. 2. Voyages and travels--Anecdotes. I. Conlon, Faith, 1955- II. Emerick, Ingrid. III. De Tessan, Christina Henry.

G465 .W643 2001
910.4'082--dc21   2001049708

For Edythe Van Rees Conlon
and the myriad women travelers
whose stories inspire us

Acknowledgments

We're grateful to our families for their patience and enthusiasm during the editing of this collection. Thanks to our colleagues at Seal Press for their creative brainstorming during the early stages of the book and for their level-headed assistance while we dashed to the finish line—Rosemary Caperton, Ellen Carlin, Anne Mathews, Leslie Miller, Lucie Ocenas, Lynn Siniscalchi, Anitra Sumaya Grisales and Cassandra Greenwald.

Contents

Introduction

Why go alone? This is the oft-asked question solo travelers grapple with, whether it springs from deep within or from the lips of curious friends and worried family members. "Why aren't you going with someone?" they ask. "Wouldn't it be safer, easier, less intimidating to travel with a companion?" Why, indeed?

When the three of us began talking about our own travels, we found we were most curious about each other's solo trips—where did we go, how did we do it, and, of course: Why did we go? In the casual swapping of our stories and those of our friends, we realized that the reasons for going alone are as many and varied as the travelers themselves. For some of us, the first solo trip is less a personal choice than a last resort: Family and friends couldn't commit, partners were too busy or didn't exist. For others, traveling alone fulfilled a long-held dream, sometimes years in the making. But whether propelled by fierce independence or circumstance, each of us found that the urge to travel had simply become too strong to ignore any longer. Facing down assorted worries—loneliness, vulnerability, fear of the unknown—we packed our bags and headed out on our own.

While traveling alone can be challenging, it is also liberating; for many women, especially those of us who've been told that "we shouldn't," learning to navigate the inevitable ups and downs of solo adventure without the safe harbor of companionship quickly evolves from unnerving to satisfying. Every obstacle overcome is all the more exhilarating, each happy surprise—the meal you hope you've ordered actually appears on your table—more gratifying. With each misadventure and triumph, we learn that the world reveals itself in startling and vivid ways when experienced without the filter of someone else's viewpoint. Perhaps this is why we experience our solitary trips with such intensity and remember them in remarkable detail.

Then too is the pleasure of simply being free to go wherever we want, whenever we want, untied to the whims, schedules and expectations of others. When you travel by yourself, you do what *you* want to do, be it to wander all day in an obscure town or to sit and read a book when the mood strikes. We come to rely on ourselves, and this greater self-confidence fuels us as we tackle each day. Through the sometimes-hilarious process of trial and error, we learn a great deal about ourselves along the way. Perhaps most important of all, we learn to be good and reliable companions to ourselves.

Knowing how many of our women friends had traveled on their own —or at least talked about giving it a try—we were surprised to find that no volume of women's solo travel stories existed. Certainly the travel literature sections overflow with stories by men, and there exist several wonderful single-author accounts of solo adventure by women such as Robyn Davidson or Mary Morris. But we wanted a book that would present a wide array of experiences and shine a light on the growing numbers of women who are exploring every corner of the globe. We wanted to inspire other women to listen to the inner voice urging them on, to put their fears on hold. And we wanted stories that told it straight: What went wrong, what went right, what was it *really* like?

Working on this book was an inspiring and exciting process as we read through all the wonderful, wild, strange, poignant and funny stories. Certainly we hoped for tales of adventure and independence—and we got those in spades, from scorching African deserts to rain-chilled islands in the North Atlantic—but we were also intrigued by the stories that focused on cross-cultural connection and friendship. Interestingly it seems that traveling solo opens wide the possibility for connecting with others, perhaps because we must rely on the kindness of strangers or simply because we are at liberty to interact in new ways. Over and over we read about memorable, if fleeting, bonds made during the course of a trip, whether on a crowded train through India, a quiet wood in Ireland or a bustling village in Senegal. Women are often cautioned about the dangers of traveling alone, but these stories show that warmth and friendliness are common the world over.

Editing *A Woman Alone* made us long to hit the road ourselves, to put down our pens and take off—obviously the stories had cast their spell. We hope you will experience the same feeling as you read, whether you are a seasoned traveler or contemplating your first solo journey. We think you'll find compatriots in this volume, a travel tip or two, a good laugh, a new locale and perhaps a little inspiration.

Faith Conlon, Ingrid Emerick, Christina Henry de Tessan, editors
Seattle, Washington
September 2001

A Woman Alone

Travel Tales From Around the Globe

In the Ladies' Compartment

by Thalia Zepatos

A mango moon ripened as the day's heat drifted into the South Indian night. I fidgeted on the noisy train platform at Ernakulum Junction, alongside the northbound express that was to carry me on the overnight journey up the west coast of the subcontinent to Bombay. Under the watchful eyes of a six-year-old vendor, I drained the last of the *chai*, the pungent cardamom-spiced tea that punctuates the Indian day at regular intervals, and returned the glass to his waiting hands.

The platform buzzed with now-familiar railway station life. Indian travelers lugging parcels of all shapes and sizes picked their way between sleeping figures huddled under shawls. Wealthier travelers paraded before their hired coolies, who calmly balanced metal suitcases and trunks on their red turbans as they followed in single file. Men and women lined up at water stands, washing away the heat and dust of the day. Chai and coffee *wallahs* bellowed their wares, each toting a huge aluminum kettle in one hand, a bucket of repeatedly rinsed glasses in the other. Food vendors chanted their way alongside the train, exchanging fruit and chili-laced snacks for one- and two-rupee notes

3

pushed between the metal bars that crossed each window of the ancient train cars.

Trains in the south provided an unusual treat—a small "ladies' compartment" at the end of each car, designed to carry six or eight women traveling without the protection of a male. They seemed unneeded for these strong Indian women who dealt matter-of-factly with numbing adversity. I was thankful, however, that the Indian Railway system had provided me an exclusive place to meet Indian women without hovering husbands, fathers and brothers edging in to control the conversation. My previous journeys in the "ladies' compartments" had been the scene of some of my most delightful and instructive encounters.

On one twelve-hour ride across the shimmering heat of the Thar desert to the fortress city of Jaisalmer, I was surrounded by fierce-looking, bejeweled, Rajasthani women. They frankly reviewed my foreign looks and dress, their black eyes wandering slowly from my wavy brown hair to my ringless toes.

I returned the interest, pointing to their red and blue patterned skirts and the scores of ivory bracelets that climbed past their elbows and under the sleeves of their tight-fitting bodices. With shy smiles, they admired my silver ankle bracelets and, one by one, displayed theirs. They removed their necklaces and earrings with girlish giggles and adorned me like a doll. Riotous laughter met my polite refusal of a tattooed matron's offer to pierce my nose. Heads shook with approval as a young woman with high cheekbones and a lustrous smile combed and oiled my hair. As we approached Jaisalmer, we scrambled to return jewelry and sandals to their owners.

Days later as I wandered though the walled town, these same women drew me into their houses, painted elaborate designs on my palms and feet with henna that lasted for weeks.

A shrill whistle from the steam locomotive jolted me and urged me inside for the long trip to Bombay. This "ladies' compartment" was crowded, with eight or nine women sharing seats for six. We smiled and nodded greetings in Hindi; no one offered a word of English. As a wiry young woman in a tattered green sari closed the door that separated the compartment from the rest of the train, I glanced around and wondered what new play would unfold during this night's ride.

While the train pulled out of the station, I was preoccupied with the necessity to transfer in Mangalore in the middle of the night. With sign language and a few words, I indicated that I was headed for Bombay. A confident, middle-aged woman with silver streaks highlighting her thick black braid alternately pointed her finger at my chest and hers, repeating "Bombay" with each movement. Yes, yes, we both had the same destination. She then started the process anew, this time saying "Mangalore" while using sign language to pantomime that we would get down and change trains there. I hoisted my pack and followed it up to the overhead bunk. I folded myself into sleep, hoping to keep her in sight during the late-night transfer.

Dozens of jangling bangle bracelets sounded a tinny alarm as a brown hand shook me repeatedly. It was 3:00 A.M. and I struggled awake as the slowing of the train's momentum signaled the approach of Mangalore station. My protector picked up her own small bag, pulled my backpack from the overhead rack, grabbed my hand and hauled me down from my berth. It seemed that keeping her in sight would not be difficult.

We wandered up and down the platform in a zigzag pattern to avoid sleeping travelers. Carrying her cloth bag without trouble, she headed straight for the corner where the red-shirted coolies were dozing and negotiated with one until he accepted her offer. He then led us along an empty track until we came to a spot that looked to me like any other. His fee paid, he floated away as she triumphantly smiled and pulled me down to squat beside her. She indicated that we would wait in that spot for the Bombay train.

I decided to put my faith in her, discarding the notion of finding a railway employee for official verification, and settled down to wait. Other travelers emerged from the night and spread their bundles to claim sections of the platform. Their low murmurs were silenced by the deep rumbling of the approaching train. As the steam-belching locomotive screeched into the station, people and luggage multiplied around us. Suddenly we were at the head of a pulsating crowd. Madame, as I thought of her, firmly stood her ground and barked at anyone who tried to usurp my spot. I knew that none of us transferring from other trains would have reserved seats; now I realized that many might not even make it onto the train.

The air brakes hissed and we bounded up the steps of the car still lumbering slowly before us. I stopped short as we entered the corridor; every spot was already filled, there was simply nowhere to go. Madame propelled me forward as I struggled to keep my pack from battering other passengers. The first compartment we passed had twelve or fourteen women sardined into a space designed for six. As we pushed our way forward I realized that *every* compartment was a ladies' compartment. The entire train was packed with hundreds of Indian women—matrons, teenagers and tiny grandmothers shushing girl and boy children. The ultimate Ladies' Compartment.

My advocate moved ahead of me, regally examined the two benches that faced each other in the next section and parted the women on one bench with a sweep of her mighty arm. She parked me firmly between those on one bench and inserted herself opposite me. A howl went up from women on both sides. Color rose to my face, and I started to relinquish my place, but Madame pushed me back down and answered each argument with a quick retort. A quiet woman wrapped in a blue sari edged in gold brocade murmured in clipped English, "She is informing everyone that you are a visitor to our country and we must show you hospitality." Grateful for a translator, I implored, "Please apologize for me and explain that I will sit in the corridor."

As the argument proceeded, a growing faction seemed to be urging acceptance. To make more room, some of the children were sent to join the luggage in the upper berth. The train moved out of the station, and everyone became resigned to our presence. Arms and parcels were adjusted for the most comfortable fit; several women lifted the ends of their saris over their faces as they prepared for sleep. I tipped my head to get a better view down the corridor; it looked like a refugee train, a scene from a movie where all the men were gone and only women and children remained.

Then a single masculine figure began working his way toward us from the opposite end of the car. A grizzled old man dressed for colder climes in a green wool army-surplus coat, he lumbered down the aisle, a vintage musket resting in the crook of his arm. Stopping before each compartment, he peered nearsightedly at the faces crowded inside and then moved on. As he inspected our section, I questioned the English-speaking woman again. "Who is he?"

"A guard hired to protect the women."

Incredible, I thought, and smiled at him. He stared. Perhaps he didn't encounter too many foreigners in the second-class train.

Then he said something urgent, lifted the gun, and pointed it straight at me. The women around me all started chattering at once, with Madame trying to yell louder than the rest. My translator tilted her head to one side as she listened, and then said in a low voice, "He thinks you are a man and has ordered you out of this car." A moment later, she added, "The others are arguing whether you are a man or a woman."

I laughed briefly at this turn of events, until he jerked the gun at my insolence. I wore neither the long braid, nor the sari or knee-length tunic over trousers of the other women on the train. My close-cropped hair, baggy pants, and collarless white cotton Indian man's shirt were chosen for comfort, ease of travel, and to help me avoid harassment. I stood and rocked unsteadily among the jumbled feet and discarded sandals of my travel-mates in the narrow space between the two facing benches. Momentarily turning my back to the old fellow, I pulled the baggy shirt taut under both arms and showed the women the outline of my chest. They roared in laughter and approval, and pushed the old man and his gun away.

As dawn approached, food and hot chai were produced from among the folds of bags and parcels. The story of the guard and the foreigner passed in waves up and down the train, the punch line always enacted amid gales of laughter. Madame seemed especially proud of me as women and girls craned their necks or shyly walked over to see me in person.

When we reached Bombay, Madame was reluctant to turn me loose. She walked me to the front of the station and negotiated fiercely with the autorick driver for my fare to the General Post Office. Then, she gave me a long lecture in rapid dialect. Her accompanying gestures advised me to be careful of men driving rickshas, on the streets, in buses, or just about anywhere. Despite the language difference, her message was clear. She seemed to be saying that if I got scared or had a problem, I should always rely on women for help.

Table for One

by Susan Spano

A few years ago, in a famous dumpling restaurant in the Chinese city of Xian, the maitre d' told me he couldn't seat me because I was alone. Feeling stubborn—not to mention hungry—I waited around the foyer for forty-five minutes, watching waiters push through the kitchen door carrying oversized bottles of beer, tureens of steaming soup and platters of dumplings so beautifully decorated that they looked like bonbons. Finally a large round table opened up, which I insisted on taking. There I sat, sampling each delicious course as it came, surrounded by seven empty chairs. I was charged twelve dollars for the meal, which would have fed three easily, at four dollars each.

The problem isn't only that the Chinese don't cook for just one. Hardly anyone does. The world is a feast spread—and priced—for two at the very least, aboard cruise ships, at spas and on package tours. Single occupancy is allowed, but usually for the infamous single supplement. And though one does sometimes find hotels with low-priced single rooms, they are usually the dreariest, smallest, worst-situated accommodations in the house—in basements or overlooking air shafts. Furthermore, when you travel à deux you can split ancillary expenses, like car rental—surely the most convincing argument for finding a companion.

Sometimes I do, and not entirely for budgetary reasons. Trips like the bicycle tour of County Clare, Ireland, that I took with my sister two springs ago are simply more doable and fun with another person along. And I'm no daredevil, so I recognize that there are things that I really can't attempt on my own, like backpacking through isolated valleys of the Anti-Atlas Mountains in Morocco. For this reason I joined a tour group headed there last January, without knowing a soul—least of all the Scottish roommate the English tour operator assigned me. Sharing quarters with a stranger struck me as dicey, though because of it I didn't have to pay a single supplement. As luck would have it she turned out to be funny and considerate; I'm happy now to count her as a friend I'd travel with again.

It is nice to have company. This fact was driven home to me in China, on an overnight train from Bejing to Xian. There I met a young American couple, sitting across from me. I arrived in the sleeping compartment minutes before the train pulled out, overheated from lugging my bags down the platform, and discombobulated because I'd gone first to the wrong station. I'd had to pay an outlandish sum to a cabdriver, who gleefully ran red lights all across Bejing while I clutched the dashboard and prayed. When I told Sandy and Brian about it, they said that they'd almost made the same mistake, but Sandy had consulted a guidebook just before leaving the hotel.

The more we talked the more I came to envy the way they worked together as a traveling team. She guarded the bags while he stood in line to buy tickets; he planned the trip, but she held the purse strings. As darkness fell on the passing farm fields of central China, she took off her boots and Brian massaged her feet. The man sitting next to me was a Chinese policeman who spoke no English and didn't look inclined to rub mine.

Still, more often than not I travel by myself—even though it isn't always the most economical way to go and I know there's something silly and sad about sitting alone at a table for eight. I could claim that I do so out of necessity, because I travel so much and because for me travel isn't primarily a recreational pursuit but a job—albeit an immensely pleasurable one. While many of my friends have told me they'd love to come along, I've hesitated to ask because they don't know how wound up I can be in research mode. And I wonder how much fun they'd have doing some of the crazy things I do to get a story—like swimming with dolphins in a frigid pool in New Zealand, or taking endless, uncomfortable bus rides instead of flying just to save a buck.

But the truth is, I started traveling solo before I began writing about travel. Six years ago I took a train from Paris to Rome, stopping in places like Arles, where an Englishman in a café scolded me for being there alone in what I thought was a rather demure black dress; in Florence I spent one long, extremely civil afternoon drinking gin and tonics in the Piazza della Signoria with a retired American businessman, whom I never saw again; on the Ligurian Coast, I followed the treacherous cliff path that links the villages of the Cinque Terre, dreaming dreams out of Percy Bysshe Shelley; and in Rome I breathed exhaust fumes and dodged motor scooters on a jog from the Piazza Navona to the Colosseum. Modest adventures, of a sort I could handle—but ones that wouldn't have happened in quite the same way, if at all, had I been with a companion. Ever since that trip, I've preferred traveling alone.

Above all, it is because I get to be in complete control. I'm not so arrogant as to believe that other people don't have brilliant ideas about where to go and what to see. But I must take my own trips, make my own discoveries, and deal with my own disasters. Last December on a camping expedition in the northern Baja with my older brother, I had no problem letting him arrange the gear, select provisions, even plot our route, because he has expertise in these areas. And when our car got stuck on a dirt road in the mountains, I was more than content to let him get us out of the predicament. But I came away wondering how I'd have managed on my own. I'll never know, though I do know that when I travel with someone I'm not as capable as I am when I'm by myself, just because I don't have to be.

Then, too, trips are precious, delicate things, easily spoiled by bad moods, lapses of good humor and disagreements. Even the best, most affectionate friends sometimes find that they make uncomfortable travel companions, embarrassing each other or arguing over issues that would be of little importance at home. I wouldn't want to alienate a friend—even temporarily—over where to dine in Paris; on the other hand, I wouldn't want to give in and eat *frites* in an indifferent bistro.

A therapist might say that I have control issues. Just so. And I have other issues, as well, which compel me to behave as I do. Travel intensifies the elements of a person's nature—both fine and toxic—making them stand out more starkly than they ever do in the safe, regulated environment of home. When I travel alone, I can give the whole mixed bag full rein, without monitoring myself, making compromises, negotiating, or even talking. I am somehow better able to tap my thoughts and feelings. It is as if the stage clears, the background music fades, and I come forward. At night I dream more vividly. "Alone we can afford to be wholly whatever we are," wrote May Sarton, "and to feel whatever we feel absolutely."

I've noticed this while sunning myself on Mexican beaches, wandering through the Prado, riding crowded buses in Bejing and especially walking in the countryside. For anyone who has yearned to travel alone but felt somehow daunted, I would suggest beginning with a solo walking vacation in a place that is scenically blessed but not too wild for comfort—for instance, the English Lake District, where Romantic poets set a precedent for solitary rambling. Thoreau tramped all over New England alone, ultimately deciding that he "never found a companion so companionable as solitude," and Robert Louis Stevenson documented a 120-mile hike through the mountains of southern France in *Travels with a Donkey in the Cévennes,* a plucky little book that could serve as a primer for all solo travelers.

It is important to start in a place where you feel secure, because fear is a great impediment to solo travelers. After all, the Western world is hardly as safe a place as it was in the days of Wordsworth and Thoreau. This is especially true for budget travelers who tend to seek out edgy, low-priced destinations, take third-class buses and frequent cheap hotels in questionable neighborhoods; budget travelers who also happen to be women face an even higher risk factor, or so I've read. As a result, I've learned to choose my destinations wisely, secure my valuables (in a money belt, usually), watch where I walk, sit near the driver on overnight buses, and check the locks on hotel room doors. I've even fantasized about traveling with a pearl-handled pistol, like something Belle Starr might have tucked into her garter. And I've read with interest the exploits of Sarah Hobson, who some twenty years ago cropped her hair, bound up her breasts, and traveled through Iran as a young man named John.

But I don't really care for guns and gender games. I would rather take a cue from Stevenson, who wrote, "Something might burst in your inside any day of the week, and there would be an end of you, if you were locked into your room with three turns of the key." The worst thing that ever happened to me when traveling alone was being chased by a pack of wild dogs along a jungly path on an island in the South Pacific—which had nothing to do with the fact that I'm a woman, or was alone. And on my own in Sofia, Bulgaria, I met a Canadian filmmaker who was so afraid of having his gear stolen that he asked if he could tour the city with me.

The dangers of traveling alone are far more subtle than robbery, rape and murder, as far as I'm concerned. They can be summed up in Degas's painting *L'Absinthe:* a woman alone in a Paris café, wearing an ugly hat and a dejected expression. She looks lonely, pitiable and much too depressed for the Folies Bergères. This is the way I sometimes feel, and am afraid of appearing when I travel alone. After all, travel is an immensely romantic undertaking, leading people to think that when in Paris or Kuala Lumpur, they should be falling in love or having deep, soulful conversations with significant others. In Mexico, hotel chambermaids have glanced searchingly at my fingers for a wedding band, and the very fact that I was a woman traveling alone so perturbed a pedicab driver in Tiananmen Square that he pinned me with an astonished glare and yelled, "Who are you? How old are you?"

Encounters like this depress me sometimes; but more often than not I am amused and touched by the varied responses I get. By the pool at a hotel in Tahiti, a middle-aged Australian lady with a potbellied husband who'd clearly had too many mai tais once plied me with questions about how she, too, could travel alone. Men on the make in hotel bars can't figure out why I won't let them buy me a drink. And at an elegant restaurant in Paris near the Church of St.-Julien-le-Pauvre, the French couple at the table next to me watched me surreptitiously all through dinner—disapprovingly I thought, until they started talking to me, and wound up asking me to their apartment for drinks the next night.

I've learned a few tricks to ward off loneliness and depression, like taking special care to stay healthy when away from home (it's easy to feel blue when you fall ill), packing plenty of books and keeping photographs of my family and dearest friends in my wallet. If I start to feel low I remind myself that I may never again get a chance to walk where Julius Caesar walked in the Roman Forum, to gaze into Lake Buttermere, or see sheep climbing argan trees in southern Morocco. The place is the thing, not the way I feel. So I make a list of all the sights I've got to see, set out to visit them and get over it.

Prices may be higher for single travelers; people may stare; and maitre d's in dumpling restaurants may hassle me. But life is short, and trips shorter. I've reached a point where I've decided to deal with both on my own terms.

Don't Rely on Maps

by Robyn Davidson

Editor's Note: In the 1970s, Robyn Davidson walked across the scorching deserts of Western Australia with only her dog and four camels for company. The following is an excerpt from her travel memoir Tracks, which recounts this extraordinary 1700-mile journey.

A ll I remember of that first day alone was a feeling of release; a sustained buoyant confidence as I strolled along, Bub's nose-line in my sweaty palm, the camels in a well-behaved line behind me and Goliath bringing up the rear. The muffled tinkling of their bells, the soft crunching of my feet in the sand and the faint twittering of the wood-swallows were the only sounds. The desert was otherwise still.

I had decided to follow an abandoned track that would eventually meet up with the main Areyonga road. Now, the definition of a track in Australia is a mark made across the landscape by the repeated passage of a vehicle, or, if you are very lucky, initially by a bulldozer. These tracks vary in quality from a corrugated, bull-dust covered, well-defined and well-used road to something which you can barely discern by climbing a hill and squinting in the general direction you think the said track may go.

Sometimes you can see where a track is by the tell-tale blossoms of wild-flowers. Those along the track will either be growing more thickly or be of a different type. Sometimes, you may be able to follow the trail by searching for the ridge left aeons ago by a bulldozer. The track may wind around or over hills and ridges and rocky outcroppings, straight into sand-dunes, get swallowed up by sandy creek-beds, get totally lost in stony creek-beds, or fray into a maze of animal pads. Following tracks is most often easy, sometimes frustrating, and occasionally downright terrifying.

When you are in cattle or sheep station country, the following of tracks can be especially puzzling, mainly because one always assumes that a track will lead somewhere. This is not necessarily so since station people just don't think like that. Also there is the problem of choice. When you are presented with half a dozen tracks all leading off in the general direction you want to go, all used within the last year, and none of them marked on the map, which one do you choose? If you choose the wrong one it may simply stop five miles ahead, so that you have to back-track, having lost half a day's travel. Or it may lead you to an abandoned, waterless windmill and bore, or slap-bang into a new fence-line, which, if followed, will begin leading you in exactly the opposite direction to where you thought you wanted to go, only now you're not quite sure because you've made so many turnings and weavings that you are beginning to lose confidence in your sense of direction. Or it might lead you to a gate made by some jackaroo who thought he was Charles Atlas and which you haven't got a hope in hell of opening, or if you can open it without suffering a rupture, then closing it is impossible without using the camels as a winch, which takes half an hour to do and you're already hot and bothered and dusty and all you really want in life is to get to the next watering place and have an aspirin and a cup of tea and a good lie down.

This is complicated further by the fact that whoever those people are who fly in planes and make maps of the area, they need glasses; or perhaps were drunk at the time; or perhaps just felt like breaking free of departmental rulings and added a few little bits and pieces of imaginative topography, or even, in some cases, rubbed out a few features in a fit of solitary anarchic vice. One expects maps to be always but always 100 percent correct, and most of the time they are. It's those other times that can set you into a real panic. Make you doubt even your own senses. Make you think that perhaps that sand-ridge you swore you sat on back there was a mirage. Make you entertain the notion that you are sun-struck. Make you gulp once or twice and titter nervously.

However, that first day held none of these problems. If the track petered out into dust bowls with drinking spots in the middle of them, it was relatively easy to find where it continued on the other side. The camels were going well and behaving like lambs. Life was good. The country I was traveling through held my undivided attention with its diversity. This particular area had had three bumper seasons in succession and was carpeted in green and dotted with white, yellow, red, blue wildflowers. Then I would find myself in a creek-bed where tall gums and delicate acacias cast deep cool shadow. And birds. Everywhere birds. Black cockatoos, sulphur-cresteds, swallows, Major-Mitchells, willy-wagtails, quarrian, kestrels, budgerigar flocks, bronzewings, finches. And there were kungaberries and various solanums and mulga apples and eucalyptus manna to eat as I walked along. This searching for and picking wild food is one of the most pleasant, calming pastimes I know. Contrary to popular belief, the desert is bountiful and teeming with life in the good seasons. It is like a vast untended communal garden, the closest thing to earthly paradise I can imagine. Mind you, I wouldn't want to have to survive on bush-tucker during the drought. And even in the good season, I admit I would prefer my diet to be supplemented by the occasional tin of sardines, and a frequent cup of sweet billy tea.

I had learnt about wild foods from Aboriginal friends in Alice Springs, and from Peter Latz, an ethnobotanist whose passion was desert plant-foods. At first, I had not found it easy to remember and recognize plants after they had been pointed out to me, but eventually the scales fell from my eyes. The Solanaceae especially had me confused. These are a huge family, including such well knowns as potatoes, tomatoes, capsicums, datura and nightshades. The most interesting thing about the group is that many of them form a staple diet for Aboriginal people, while others which look almost identical are deadly poisonous. They are tricky little devils. Peter had done some tests of various species and found that one tiny berry contained more vitamin C than an orange. Since these were eaten by the thousands when Aboriginal people were free to travel through their own country, it stands to reason that their modern-day diet, almost totally devoid of vitamin C, is just one more factor contributing to their crippling health problems.

I was a little nervous my first night out. Not because I was frightened of the dark (the desert is benign and beautiful at night, and except for the eight-inch-long, pink millipedes that sleep under the bottom of the swag and may wish to bite you when you roll it up at dawn, or the careless straying of a scorpion under your sleep-twitching hand, or the lonely slithering of a Joe Blake who may want to cuddle up and get warm under the bedclothes then fang you to death when you wake up, there is not too much to worry about) but because I wondered if I would ever see the camels again. I hobbled them out at dusk, unclogged their bells and tied little Goliath to a tree. Would it work, I asked myself? The answer came back, "She'll be right, mate," the closest thing to a Zen statement to come out of Australia, and one I used frequently in the months ahead.

The process of unloading had been infinitely easier than putting the stuff on. It only took an hour. Then there was wood to be gathered, a fire and lamp to be lit, camels to be checked on, cooking utensils, food and cassette player to be got out, Diggity to be fed, camels to be checked on, food to be cooked and camels' to be checked on. They were munching their heads off happily enough. Except Goliath. He was yelling piggishly for his mother, who, thank god, was taking no notice whatsoever.

I think I cooked a freeze-dried dish that night. A vastly overrated cardboard-like substitute for edible food. The fruit was okay, you could eat that straight like biscuit, but the meat and vegetable dishes were tasteless soggy tack. I fed all my packets to the camels later on, and stuck with what was to be my staple diet: brown rice, lentils, garlic, curry, oil, pancakes made with all manner of cereals and coconut and dried egg, various root vegetables cooked in the coals, cocoa, tea, sugar, honey, powdered milk, and every now and then, the ultimate in luxury, a can of sardines, some pepperoni and Kraft cheese, a tin of fruit, and an orange or lemon. I supplemented this with vitamin pills, various wild foods, and the occasional rabbit. Far from being deficient, this diet had me so healthy, I felt like a cast-iron amazon; cuts and gashes vanished in a day, I could see almost as well at night as I could in sunlight, and I grew muscles on my shit.

After that first lack-luster meal, I built the fire up, checked again on the camels, and put my Pitjantjara learning tapes into the cassette. *Nyuntu palya nyinanyi. Uwa, palyarna, palu nyuntu,* I mumbled repeatedly at the night sky now thick and gorgeous with billions of stars. There was no moon that night.

I nodded off with Diggity snoring in my arms as usual. And from that first night, I developed a habit of waking once or twice to check on the bells. I would wait until I heard a chime, and if I didn't I would call to them so they turned their heads and chimed, and if that didn't work, I would get up and see where they were. They were usually no more than a hundred yards from camp. I would then fall instantly back to sleep and remember waking up only vaguely in the morning. When I woke well before dawn, one fear at least had diminished. The camels were huddled around my swag, as close as they could get without actually crushing me. They got up at the same time I did, that is, over an hour before sun-up, for their early-morning feed.

My camels were all still young and growing. Zeleika, the oldest, I thought was maybe four and a half or five. Dookie was going on four and

Bub was three—mere puppies, since camels can live until they're fifty. So they needed all the food they could get. My routine was built around their needs and never my own. They were carrying what I would consider a lot of weight for young animals though Sallay would have scoffed at such an idea. He had told me how a bull camel had stood up with a ton on its back and that up to half a ton was usually carrying capacity. Getting up and down was the hardest thing for them. Once they were up, carrying the weight was not so difficult. The weight, however, had to be evenly balanced or the saddle would rub, causing discomfort and eventually producing a saddle-sore, so at this stage the process of loading up was fastidiously checked and rechecked. On the second morning I got it down to just under two hours.

I never ate much in the mornings. I would build a cooking fire, boil one or two billies of tea, and fill a small Thermos with what was left. Sometimes I craved sugar and would pile two tablespoons into the billy then wolf down several tablespoons of cocoa or honey. I burnt it up quickly enough.

My main problem now seemed to be whether the gear would hold together, whether the saddles would rub, and how the camels handled the work. I was a little worried over Zeleika. Diggity was doing fine but occasionally got foot-sore. I felt great, if knock-kneed with exhaustion by the end of a day. I decided to cover approximately twenty miles a day, six days a week. (And on the seventh day she rested.) Well, not always. I wanted to keep a fair distance covered in case something went wrong, and I had to sit somewhere for days or weeks. There was a slight pressure on me not to take it as easy as I would have liked. I didn't want to be traveling in summer and I had promised *Geographic* I would be at journey's end before the year was out. That gave me six months of comfortable travel, which I could stretch to eight if needs be.

So, by the time everything was packed away and the fire smothered, the camels would have had a couple of hours of feeding. I would then bring them in nose-line to tail, tie Bub with his halter to the tree and ask them to whoosh down please. The cloths and saddles went on first, front to back, the girths done up, by pushing them underneath the animal and behind the brisket. The nose-lines were taken off the tail and attached to the saddle. Next the loading, first one object, then its equivalent on the other side. It was all checked and checked again, then I asked them to stand up, and the girths were tightened and the holding ropes run through them. All set to go. One more check. Departure. Hey ho.

But wouldn't it be my luck that on the third day, when I was still a puppy, a cub-scout in the ways of the bush, and still believing blindly that all maps were infallible and certainly more reliable than common sense, I found a road that wasn't meant to be there. While the road I wanted to be there was nowhere to be seen.

"You've lost a whole road," I said to myself, incredulously. "Not just a turning or a well or a ridge, but a whole bloody road."

"Take it easy, babe, be calm, she'll be right, mate, settle down settle DOWN."

My little heart felt like a macaw in a canary cage. I could feel the enormity of the desert in my belly and on the back of my neck. I was not in any real danger—I could easily have set a compass course for Areyonga. But I kept thinking, what if this happens when I'm two hundred miles from anywhere? What if, what if. And I felt very small and very alone suddenly in this great emptiness. I could climb a hill and look to where the horizon shimmered blue into the sky and see nothing. Absolutely nothing.

I re-read the map. No enlightenment there. I was only fifteen or so miles from the settlement, and here was this giant dirt highway where there should only be sandstone and rolypoly. Should I follow it or what? Where the hell did it lead? Was it a new mining road? I checked the map for mines but there was nothing marked.

I sat back and watched myself perform. "Okay. First of all, you are not lost, you are merely misplaced, no no, you know exactly where you are so stifle that impulse to scream at the camels and kick Diggity. Think clearly. Then, make camp for the night here, there is plenty of green feed, and spend the rest of the afternoon looking for that goddamn track. If you don't find it, cut across country. Easy enough. Above all, do not flap around like a winged pigeon. Where's your pride? Right."

I did all that, then went off scouting, map in hand, Diggity at foot. I found an ancient trail that wound up through the mountains, not exactly where the map said it should be but close enough for a margin of credibility at least. It went for a couple of miles off course then came out to meet up with, yes, yet another major highway that had no right to exist. "Shit and damnation." This I followed for another half mile in the general direction of Areyonga, until I came across a bullet-ridden piece of tin bent over double and almost rusted away, but with an arrow that pointed at the ground and the letters A ON upon it. I skipped back to camp in the gathering twilight, apologized profusely to my poor dumb entourage, and fixed lesson one firmly in my brain for future reference. When in doubt, follow your nose, trust your instincts, and don't rely on maps.

The Truth About Italian Men

by Dawn Comer Jefferson

My friends thought I was crazy. An African-American woman going to Italy alone, to spend Carnival in Venice. "Oh, the Italian men are horrible. They'll chase you down the street and pinch your butt," warned one friend. "They kidnap women traveling alone and sell them into prostitution rings. Black women are considered exotic, so be careful," another cautioned. Taking their warnings with a grain of salt, I packed my bags and boarded a plane for Italy.

I hadn't traveled alone since college, but I fondly remembered my last solo trip—the freedom to go where I pleased, when I pleased, the ease at meeting other solo travelers, and the daily feelings of accomplishment over the little things, like successfully navigating the streets or conquering a dinner menu written in a foreign tongue. I couldn't wait to explore Italy on my own.

I don't speak Italian, and I had no hotel reservations other than for my first few nights in Venice. After that, I wanted to travel at will, making reservations as I went. I knew I wanted to see Rome, and as a college theater major, I remembered reading about Verona, Padua, and Mantua in Shakespeare, so I thought I might tour those cities as well. With my thirty-second birthday rapidly approaching, and being single, childless, and between jobs, I was sure that this would be the only time in the next couple of years that I could travel extensively on my own. It was an opportunity I was not going to miss.

As a result of late planes, stopovers, and lost luggage, I arrived in Venice thirty-three hours after leaving Los Angeles. I was so exhausted—my body in time zone hell—that my eyes watered from the moment I landed until the next day. But when I stepped off the *vaporetto* (the Venetian version of a city bus, except it's a boat) at the Piazza San Marco, the festivities were in full swing, and I could feel my body thrill to the sights, sounds and smells.

Carnival in Venice, I was to discover, is very different from Mardi Gras in New Orleans or Carnival in Brazil. Pushing crowds, drunkenness and rowdy behavior are the exception, not the norm. It was like an elegant pageant where locals and tourists alike dress in elaborate costumes and masks, parade through the city, and pose for photographers, entertaining the crowds. I took seventy-five photos my first day. The costumes range from Renaissance characters in hoop skirts and white wigs to representations from Greek mythology or Italian folklore. Historically, the masks were worn by nobility so that they could walk the streets unrecognized, behaving in ways that were otherwise unacceptable in the proper society of their time. Most of the costumes were magnificent. Only one young man, a white American, was tasteless enough to dress as his idea of an African native, complete with black face, Afro wig, and a plastic bone piercing his nose.

I saw three Senegalese street vendors and many Japanese people in large tour groups, but as far as I could tell, I was the only African American woman in Venice, and I stood out in the crowds. As I walked the foot paths and bridges of the city, Venetians would approach me and in either Italian or broken English, say, "I saw you on the Rialto Bridge yesterday," or "You were by the Church of San Polo this morning, do you remember me?" It was easy for them to remember me, I was the only black woman in town. Often, they assumed I was Brazilian, Mexican, or from Great Britain. When I corrected them, they'd give me a surprised look and say, "Welcome to Carnival!"

Despite my friends' warnings, my encounters with Italian men were delightfully charming. Not once was I the recipient of a rude catcall or butt-grabbing. I admit that when I started the trip, I made a point of dressing down, wearing no makeup and putting on my New York face ("Don't mess with me, I'm serious"). I wanted to appear strong, independent, capable of handling anything. Men ignored me. But the tough-cookie act is tiring, and after a few days, I lowered my guard. One night, I dressed in fancy duds, did my hair, put on lipstick, and suddenly, things changed. Men smiled as I passed on the street. They gave friendly waves from passing gondolas. I liked the attention. I began to realize that I could take care of myself, be independent and capable, and still interact and enjoy being on my own in Italy. When I went to the world famous Harry's Bar for a taste of their fabled drink, the Bellini (champagne and fresh peaches blended together), it seemed as if all of the waiters in the restaurant were waiting on my table. They rushed to help me with my coat, and when I left, one followed me out and said, "My compliments, you are very beautiful."

Other times, drinks would arrive at my dinner table. A sparkling wine called *Brachetto* was sent several times by waiters. A tumbler of *Grappa* (an after-dinner liqueur) was sent by an admiring customer at another table. Never did these men follow up their offerings with an attempt to join me at my table or talk to me. They would raise their glass in salute, smile, nod, or blow a kiss. They wanted nothing more than to be kind to a stranger abroad. At one restaurant, after several free glasses of Brachetto had been consumed, I spent the evening talking Latin music and American action movies with the waiters as they cleaned up.

My last night in Venice, I became overwhelmed by the crowds in San Marco Square, so I walked down to the waterfront to be alone. Venice has a few hundred thousand people living there, no cars, bikes, or other vehicles, and violent crime is almost nonexistent except for an occasional crime of passion. So at night, I felt safe walking through the narrow paths and back alleys of the city alone. As I stood on the dark dock and looked across the lagoon at the Lido (an island across from Venice and the setting for Thomas Mann's book, *Death in Venice*), a peaceful calm came over me. I'm glad I came alone to Italy, I thought to myself. Just as a child is excited every time she learns a new task, at this time in my life, I needed that same sense of accomplishment at being able to do something new. I needed to take this trip on my own. However, when I looked up and saw ten figures wearing costumes and masks surrounding me, my friends' warnings screamed in my ears. I was certain I'd be mugged, kidnapped, or worse. I clung to my purse. I tried to back away, but they were on three sides and my back was to the canal. As they were closing in, I thought about jumping in the water. I started to panic as they reached for my arms, my shoulders, my waist, until I heard them start to giggle. One of them pulled out a camera. They wanted me to pose with them for a photograph. I started to laugh. The masked man snapped his camera. Then I gave him mine to take another picture.

Yes, the world *can* be dangerous. We all read the papers, live in the neighborhoods. We see and hear about tragedy every day. But for me, the tragedy would be in not going out and exploring the world. Traveling to Italy alone reinforced my belief in my own ability to make my way through life. And if I hadn't been alone, I never would have been ambushed by Carnival revelers in search of a picture with a black broad abroad.

Halibut Woman

by Barbara Sjoholm

My knees shook. My stomach lurched. The uneasiness that came over me at my first sight of the Faroe Islands, pin points of unnecessary punctuation in a vast uncaring sea, would creep up on me again and again during my time there. It seemed as if they could not really be anchored to the ocean floor; it seemed as if they might break loose and float off into the widening mid-Atlantic rift, helpless to hold on in spite of their Danish infrastructure of highways and bridges and tunnels, in spite of the imported weight of petrol stations, supermarkets and cultural centers.

I'd boarded the Faroese-owned car ferry, the *Norröna,* at two-thirty in the morning in the Shetland Islands. Only a handful of passengers embarked with me and, as the ship glided slowly past Lerwick's stately granite buildings, the tallest windows shimmering gold with the first rays of sunrise, it was easy to believe I was still among Scottish friends. To wake somewhat groggily six hours later was to wake into a different country. The cafeteria of the Scottish-owned ferry *St. Sunniva* had served oatmeal and eggs and bacon, marmalade and cold toast; suddenly I was in line for Scandinavian *smørbrod*—open-faced sandwiches decorated with single curls of cheese and parsley, or roast beef dotted with a semicolon of may-onnaise and shrimp. Danish money was required, and a new language. All around me were large families with blond, bored children, en route from Norway or Denmark to a holiday in Iceland. If they'd started from Denmark, they'd already been on board two days. There was a weary, competitive jostle in the cafeteria line, and a mingled smell of dark-roasted coffee and yogurt-scented vomit.

On deck the air was as fresh as a salty mountaintop though, with only sea in sight. I cheered up and strolled fore and aft, imagining myself one of those boldly adventurous women travelers of a hundred years ago, voyaging to the far North when it was considered one of the more remote and daring of destinations. Nowadays Scandinavia seems to many people synonymous with bland prosperity, and every self-respecting woman in search of risk is trekking across Australia, rafting the Boh in Borneo or finagling a flight to Antarctica. But in the eighteenth and nineteenth centuries, the North pulled voyagers like a magnet, visitors as well as polar explorers. Mary Wollstonecraft was one of the first literary figures to try her hand at describing the exotic North: her travel book in letters, *A Short Residence in Sweden, Norway and Denmark,* published in 1796, is often credited with starting the craze for icy adventures among the English (poet Robert Southey wrote to a friend: "She has made me in love with a cold climate, and frost and snow, with a northern moonlight"). Wollstonecraft made her journey with only a very young daughter for company; she used the trip (undertaken in reality for business reasons) as a way to reflect on nature, society and her own fragile existence. The terra incognita she explored was herself.

Most tourists these days like to be warm. But that was not always the case. Norah Gourlie, who wrote *A Winter with Finnish Lapps* (1939), begins her tale: "All my life the words 'Arctic Circle' have had a special thrill for me." She decides, on a particularly hot and stuffy day in September, to leave her boring life in London for a place she hardly knows except on the map. By December, when she embarks on a Finnish steamship for Helsinki, she's having second thoughts about the 2,000-mile journey before her (especially since she speaks no Finnish); nevertheless she completes her travels undaunted. Olive Murray Chapman also visited the far North, and describes one of her trips in *Across Lapland with Sledge and Reindeer*, and another in *Across Iceland*. Elizabeth Jane Oswald, from Edinburgh, made three visits to Iceland in the 1870s, and wrote about them in *By Fell and Fjord*. When Trollope voyaged by sea on the steamer *Mastiff* to Iceland in 1878, he was accompanied by a party of friends, one of whom, Jemima Blackburn, illustrated his book *How the Mastiffs Went to Iceland*, and later wrote her own account. Mrs. Alec Tweedie wrote of Norway and Iceland too, with self-importance and melodrama, in *A Girl's Ride in Iceland* and *A Winter Jaunt to Norway: With Accounts of Nansen, Ibsen, Bjørnsen, Brandes and Many Others.*

Many of these travelers to Iceland went through the Faroe Islands, but few left a record. Only American-born Elizabeth Taylor, who first visited in 1895 and spent almost ten years of her life here, seems to have made a specialty of this archipelago. Taylor was another one of those doughty lady travelers we find turning up in old photographs and on library shelves, their names appended to books with titles like *On Sledge and Horseback to Outcast Siberian Lepers*. They are clothed in long skirts, stout boots, traveling cloaks and Tyrolean hats, when they are not wearing bear furs or reindeer skins. Their arms are free: a retinue of natives is in the background, hauling portmanteaus and trunks. But they are far from weak. They can go without eating, and almost without sleep. They take for granted conditions we would find appalling. Their cheerfulness can be unnerving. After tramping her way through the Faroes, Taylor wrote: "The way up Stora Dimun is neither easy nor safe. In many places a fall means certain death, and no one subject to dizziness should attempt it. But the difficulties have been exaggerated. Anyone of ordinary activity, who is able to keep a cool head, can make the ascent if he wears Faroe footgear, has a good helper behind and takes thought for each footstep."

Like her cohorts in Africa and the Himalayas, Elizabeth Taylor was made of stern stuff. Long before she settled in the Faroes for an extended stay in her early forties, she'd traveled by horseback through much of Canada, been to Alaska and accompanied an expedition 2,300 miles along the Athabasca River and Great Slave Lake to the Mackenzie River before it poured into the Beaufort Sea. She had traveled by foot and horse cart over the remote Hardangervidda in Norway, and spent ten weeks in Iceland, where she studied the eider duck and visited lava fields and archeological remains. Like many of the women who traveled without male companionship or chaperone, but who had no real work to occupy them, she took notes constantly, gathered specimens, especially of plants, and sketched. Part of this was meant to be self-improvement; part was to look busy in a world that had no use for unmarried women without professions. Like many of the other ladies traveling in the North, Taylor meant to write a book and prove her knowledge and her worth; yet, though she published articles in publications from *The Atlantic* to *Field & Stream*, she never managed to pull her essays together into chapters. Recently, her letters and uncollected papers were gathered into a paperback with the irresistible title *The Far Islands and Other Cold Places*. It was this book that had first put the Faroes on the map for me.

Elizabeth Taylor's initial impression of the Faroes was so positive that I was chagrined to find that I felt almost immediately at a loss in the islands. Even though my room at the guesthouse had a splendid view of the sea, and the modern prints and blond furniture made a nice change from the frilly clutter of the average bed-and-breakfast in the Scottish Isles, my landlady, far from being a warm and chatty Shetlander, was gruff and cool. She spoke no English, only Faroese and Danish; we settled on Norwegian, but she was also practically deaf, so that any question I put to her was initially answered with a loud, cranky *"HVA?"* (WHAT?). She was elderly, thick-bodied, her face like a vanilla pudding with whiskers. Every step was obviously painful; she mostly sat in the foyer at a table with a telephone, papers and several full ashtrays under a sign that said No Smoking.

My first afternoon in Tórshavn foreshadowed the rest of my stay. I went to the post office first, eager to claim the package containing my Lonely Planet guide to Iceland and the Faroe Islands, which I'd cleverly sent to myself *post restante*. It wasn't there, there was no sign of it, and the woman at the counter made only the most cursory of searches before announcing, "I'm not surprised." Coming out of the post office, I looked down to see what time it was and found that my trusty Timex had popped off my wrist, leaving only a faint indentation on the skin. The young man at the tourist office thought the only place I might find a watch was the shopping center, a twenty-minute walk away. "But you'd better hurry—they close soon."

I took the opportunity to ask about a laundromat. He seemed bemused. "To wash your clothes yourself?" He engaged in a long conversation with a colleague while I perused the official Faroese tourist guide, which assured me, in exalted language, that the Faroe Islands were not about mass tourism, but about individual connections. *Each visitor is treated as an honored guest!* He passed me a slip of paper with an address on it. "This woman sometimes does laundry for tourists."

Sometimes? The watch shop was closed when I got there. I mooned around the supermarket and wondered at some of the food displayed. One refrigerated case had a shelf of a dairy product in cartons called CHEASY 0.1%, and a second shelf of Barbie yogurt in containers that displayed Barbie's pink and blond charms. I would not be disgruntled, I vowed. I would not sneer and get all curmudgeonly and Paul Therouxish. I would buck up and go to a concert at the Nordic House, which was said to be the most beautiful building in the Faroes. The man at the tourist office had told me that the Nordic House had a cafeteria. I'd have dinner there and write in my journal until the concert began.

As soon as I set off for the Nordic House, the overcast sky let loose and my walk, disappointingly along an unpicturesque highway with views of petrol stations, auto repair shops and a soccer stadium, was a wet, cold one. The cafeteria served only cake and coffee, as it turned out. I opened my journal and wrote chirpily, "The Nordic House is stunning. It combines the traditional farmhouse architecture of the turf roof that seems to blend into the hillside with the glass and polished wood expansiveness of modern Scandinavian design. Even though it's raining, it feels warm, light and spacious inside . . ."

And so on, down to the description and drawing of the cake on my plate. My heart wasn't in it. I was filling time as I filled pages. Thus does a writer struggle to shape her disappointment and loneliness.

"Well, it's beautiful of course. But I couldn't *live* here," said the Danish woman in a blue anorak, with frizzy blond hair like a ruff around her anxious face. "I can't imagine *living* in such an isolated place. Without . . . without . . ." she gestured in the direction of civilization: of Denmark, of Europe.

We were standing midway up a grassy slope whose arc was broken on the invisible side by what I knew to be a sheer cliff dropping down to the Atlantic breakers. I couldn't seem to proceed any further up the slope, even though it looked deceptively like the gently rising greensward of a fabulous golf course. Others from the tour bus had strolled up to what looked to me like the edge. From my vantage point below, they seemed to be chatting on the way to a fatal plunge. The soles of my feet, tender in hiking boots, quivered like fish.

"Could *you* live here? Could you?" she asked me. Behind us was the village of Gjógv (pronounced something like Jack). Around us the steep yet rounded hills were the softest green. A cleft in the cliff had made a natural narrow harbor for fishing boats, though the boats would have to be winched up hundreds of feet to the level of the village. The houses here were the color of bitter chocolate, with candy red doors and windows trimmed in white. Some roofs were grass, with bright yellow marsh marigolds and forget-me-nots; others were corrugated metal painted a silvery blue-green.

If Greek villages are defined by the dazzle of white against cobalt blue, Faroese villages empty the light of the world by their negative, dense black on leaf green. Originally the split timbers of the houses were tarred shiny-thick against the wind and rain coming straight over the cliffs; now it's paint that keeps them dark fudge. Ever since arriving in Tórshavn, I'd noticed postcards of paintings by Steffan Danielsen; his scenes of black houses with angled roofs of blue, orange and the floury verdigris of weathered copper, could have come straight from Gjógv.

The Danish woman was on the same tour I was, a day-long trip to the northern part of Eysturoy. There were two Germans on the tour; almost everyone else was Danish or Norwegian. Our guide spoke to us in a combination of English and what she called "Scandinavian." This seemed to be Norwegian with a few Danish words thrown in. It was symptomatic of the Faroes' odd relationship with Denmark that the Faroese preferred not to speak Danish, which they learned in school, with the Danes who visited, on the grounds that Danish is "difficult for other Scandinavians to understand." The Faroes were settled, like Orkney, Shetland and Iceland, by the seagoing Norse, and remained under the crown of Norway until the fifteenth century, when Norway itself fell under the control of Denmark for four hundred years. Since 1948 the Faroe Islands have been a self-governing, autonomous region of the Kingdom of Denmark. In the past the Faroese were exploited by the Danes, who controlled their economy through trade monopolies; now the Danes complain of losing money on the Faroes. The Danish government has contributed heavily to constructing the Faroese infrastructure of highways and tunnels, and to providing credit when fishing revenues have fallen. The Faroese proclaim their autonomy at every opportunity, however, and often show a great coolness towards Danish visitors, a fact that my companion acknowledged.

"I came for curiosity's sake," she said. "But I am having trouble liking it. In Denmark we were having a nice hot summer when I left last week. Here I've been cold every day, all the time. There's not very much to do. The people are not very friendly."

That was not Elizabeth Taylor's experience in the first extended period she lived here, from 1899 to 1905. Elizabeth Taylor liked the Faroese very much. Even on her brief pass-through visit she noticed the men, with their "ruddy blond thick half-curling hair and very thick soft beards." They put her in mind of the old Vikings in the sagas. Four years later, she was back to stay. "I am going up to the Faroes, & even to think of it gives me a feeling of strength and enthusiasm." She was thirty-nine then, a self-taught botanist, ornithologist, ethnologist. She planned to draw, to take notes, to gather specimens for the British Museum, for the Smithsonian, for collections at Harvard and Oxford. "In order to secure material, I must see different islands and have certain experiences . . . I must write about trout fishing, bird cliffs, whales, etc."

Elizabeth had grown up in St. Paul; her father was appointed the American consul to Winnipeg when she was thirteen. She was close to him and made visits over the years to Canada; he encouraged her explorations. Middle-class women didn't go to college in those days. The professions were closed to them. If they didn't immediately marry, their choices were few. They could be nurses or teachers. They could live with their families, helping out and finding protection. For many women, obviously, a life with such prospects was stultifying. Elizabeth Taylor first sought an identity as an artist. She studied at the Arts Students League in New York several summers; she went to Paris and took lessons at Colorossi and Academie Julien. She spent a winter in Venice. Like many Americans, she found that a small income went further in Europe. She did not feel she was particularly talented as an artist; she turned instead to writing, yet even though she published many articles, she felt undereducated. She did not want to be an amateur; she thought that if she settled in one place and thoroughly investigated it, the book that resulted would make a contribution to world knowledge. The Faroes appealed to her for their remoteness, and for the fact that no one else seemed to have written much about them.

She tramped, she painted, she botanized and collected specimens; she was rowed about by eight strong men. "So I climbed down and waited on the rocks for a lull, while the men kept the boat in a quiet spot under some cliffs across the inlet. 'Now!' cried a man who was watching the sea. The boat shot forward to where I stood, I tumbled in anyhow, waved a farewell to those on shore, and in an instant we were tossing high in a whirl of white water between the reefs, cutting through masses of foam, and reaching the open sea just before the next big wave broke. There we were safe; there was a little wind, and the great waves swept shoreward in unbroken lines. We could easily climb them and race down their outer slopes. It was a glorious day."

In spite of the effervescence in many of her descriptions, her time in the Faroes was not completely euphoric. Dependent on her writing for income, she was forced to be the guest of various Faroese. The winter she spent with the governor of Tórshavn was long and difficult. There were nine children, five of them babies; all of them suffered that winter from whooping cough, chicken pox and meningitis. The youngest baby died. The servants were "unruly." Another winter found her with a pastor's family on the northernmost island. Although she buoyed herself with thoughts that here were the essentials: salt-of-the-earth peasantry, pure air, good water ("As to society, who wants it? I don't."), her spirits understandably flagged. "The surf is so bad that in winter no visitors can come. . . . There are but two shops & all the people except one shopkeeper & school master are peasant fishermen." But soon she admonished herself: "Do not look melancholy about the cold & make folks regret you are in the house."

She made friends, but not many were women. Educated, Danish-speaking men—the schoolteachers, governors, consuls and pastors of the island—were her preferred companions. Hans Kristoffer, on the island of Vágar, was her special friend; she did not particularly like his wife, Katrina, whom she accused of interfering with the garden she was trying to cultivate next to Katrina's house. Taylor had wished to be a boy when growing up; all her life she envied male freedom. Like many Victorian women travelers she achieved a kind of genderless authority by coming to a less developed country from a more sophisticated culture. Her foreignness made freedom possible; her announced occupation, to gather as much material on the Faroes as possible in order to write a book, gave her a reason for living in a remote island archipelago in the Atlantic.

She found romance in wondering, "Am I or am I not a *Kalvakona?* That means a halibut woman, one who possesses mysterious powers that can charm a big halibut to the hook of a fisherman." She tells a charming story of fishermen who promise the *beita*—a choice bit cut from the fish between the forefins. "Last week, a man on the fishing bank promised me the beita, and a few minutes later he was having a sharp fight with a halibut that weighed almost two hundred pounds." In old photographs of the Faroes you will see dozens of women working in the fishing industry, as they worked all over the North Atlantic, particularly in Iceland and Norway, laying the split cod out to dry on the rocks and gathering them up if rain threatened. The women wear shawls and long dresses in the photographs; they stand next to great piles of dried cod, which were sold primarily in the Mediterranean for *baccalao*. But these women were invisible to Taylor; she does not describe them in her writing. She would rather be at a remove from everyday working life; she would rather be an outsider, a traveler, a halibut woman.

"What about you?" asked my Danish companion. She had just taken a photo of me (months later the photograph would be magneted to the refrigerator at home: I'm wearing the perpetual green rain jacket, my hair is flying. I look staunch and far-seeing rather than very cheerful), and we were strolling back through the little village. "Why would you come to the Faroes? Do you like it here?"

I wasn't sure what to answer. Back in Tórshavn, things were not going well. My landlady seemed to have taken a dislike to me. Two months earlier I'd faxed a request to stay three days; once here, I'd asked to change it to five, which she'd agreed to—I thought. Then, the night before (the evening of my third day), she'd knocked forcefully on my door and demanded to know how long I thought I was staying. "Two more nights," I said. "We agreed."

"HVA?!"

"TWO MORE DAYS."

"Impossible. I have other people coming. You must leave."

"I'm not leaving. We agreed."

"HVA?"

The morning before, I'd taken my clothes to the woman who was said to do laundry, and nearly had a tussle with her when she attempted to put them into a large bag full of other people's clothes. I said in both English and Norwegian, "How will you tell my clothes from anybody else's?" Finally her son came to the rescue and explained that his mother thought I was the same lady from England who had been by earlier and dropped off some clothes.

I bought a new watch, at a vastly inflated price. I went to the tourist office to arrange this trip to Eysturoy, and found my young friend in a puzzled mood. He had been an exchange student in America, he confided, and although he had asked his friends to come visit him, nobody would ever come to the Faroes. Why was that? I was American, could I tell him? I went to the post office several times looking for my Lonely Planet guide, to no avail. I collected quite a few stamps that showed an unfriendly sheep's head.

Back on the bus, leaving Gjógv for Ei i, another remote village in the north of Eysturoy, where Elizabeth Taylor had spent five years, our tour guide came back and sat by me to practice her English. She pointed out the "cheeps" on the hillside, and rehearsed what to say about the pilot-whale hunting, the famous *grindadráp*. She thought the two Germans might disapprove and wanted to explain that it was a long tradition in the Faroes. The people waited months for the pilot whales to blunder into shore. The resultant killing supplied the natives with necessary nourishment.

"What is the word for whale fat in English?"

"Blubber," I said.

"It's not *spekk?*"

"No, that's Norwegian."

"Blubber," she sounded it out. "Blubber, blubber, blubber. Are you in Greenpeace?"

I changed the subject. "Ei i," I said. "Isn't that where Elizabeth Taylor, the American traveler, had to live throughout the First World War?"

"I do not know her."

Elizabeth Taylor left the Faroes in 1906, after spending six years gathering information and specimens. She returned to the U.S. but did not progress with her book, though she managed to place a few articles and organize illustrated talks on the Faroes. She continued her restless ways, settling nowhere in America, visiting Europe again, living a time in Scotland. She made another appearance in the Faroes in 1913, and again, unluckily, in 1914. The First World War broke out and few ships came into or out of the Tórshavn harbor from abroad for five years. What was it like for her, without mail, on short rations, a perpetual guest? She was in her sixties by then; her vigorous cheerfulness must have been fading slightly. She discovered she did not like the cold, after all. Botanizing, painting, birding seemed less important. She pottered stoically in a borrowed garden, taught a local boy to paint. It would have been a good time to work on her book, perhaps to finish it. Instead, she brooded over her perfectionism, her procrastination. "Everyone seems to be dreadfully clever nowadays and the public wants things that are striking, a trifle sensational and picturesque, and I fear that is all beyond me." She published only two articles from this second long stay. One is called, wearily, "Five Years in a Faroe Attic."

I wouldn't have liked to be stuck in Ei i for five years. Taylor called it a "dirty, disagreeable little village." It was not as picturesque as Gjógv, though it was larger, ranged along two roads overlooking a beautiful wide bay, just the sort of bay an unlucky pod of pilot whales might mistakenly swim into. On a windy viewpoint where we stopped to use the toilets, our guide gave us an enthusiastic talk in English and Scandinavian about the *grindadráp*. The Germans, contrary to expectations, were not Green at all, but seemed very respectful about the need of the Faroese for all that blubber. The Norwegians, long-time whale hunters, also remained composed. Only the Danes seemed grossed out. The Danish woman asked me to take a picture of her. "I really don't want to hear what these people do to the poor whales," she said, gesturing me away from the group. She smiled into the camera, bravely, I thought. She'd said she was a schoolteacher. This wasn't her first trip away from Denmark, but it was the first time she'd traveled alone. "I return to Denmark tomorrow," she said. "I can hardly wait."

Back in Tórshavn, I sneaked into the guesthouse while the landlady was in the kitchen. I had half expected my room to have been cleaned out while I was gone, but everything was the same. In fact, she hadn't dusted a single day since I'd been here. What was I so desperately hanging on to? Some futile desire for control in a foreign place. My own things, arranged my own way; my own place, if even for a few nights.

But travel was about letting go, and there was no other way to experience it. I knew it was only when you let go that the best things happened. That was why I traveled, and why I found it so hard sometimes.

I was about seven when I first realized that a girl, a woman, could go off by herself to see the world. One day my mother and some friends took me along to say goodbye to someone at the Port of Los Angeles. From the dock we went up the gangplank of an ocean liner and down the corridor to a small stateroom. The voyager was a middle-aged lady whose name I don't remember, a teacher who had the summer off. She was going by ship around the whole world, and she took me on her knee and said, "I'll send you some postcards," which she later did, of Japan and India and Paris. Then there was a warning blast, and we all rushed off. We stood on the dock while colored streamers flew out and over the sides of the ship. The lady looked very small up there at the railing, wearing a hat and a corsage pinned to her jacket. "Goodbye!" she called. "Goodbye, goodbye," we called back. "Don't forget to write!"

The idea of her sea voyage was enormous to me, and all the way home in the car I thought about it, and laid my plans. My first trip around the world would have to be via the cardboard globe, which I spun and spun, letting my finger touch the countries under it. "I'm in Japan now," I announced to my brother. He spun the globe and ended in the Pacific. "I'm drowned," he said. I organized a game in the backyard of me on the picnic table throwing down some colored streamers to the mystified dog. I waved to my mother at the window: "Goodbye! Goodbye!"

"Goodbye!" she waved back from the kitchen. "Don't forget to write!"

I lay on my bed in Tórshavn and thought about women traveling, about all those ladies without proper professions who wrote books. I was hardly any different from them. I'd come to the Faroe Islands because they sounded adventurous, because they were wildly remote, because no one I knew had ever been here. I was a lady who had sailed off on a boat and had come to an island in the middle of nowhere precisely to write about it. And now, goddamn it, I had to write something interesting. Elizabeth Taylor and her failure to finish her book haunted me. Who is to say another person's life is futile? Yet I mourned for women of the past, whose wildest adventures, most passionate and courageous acts had been reduced to anecdotes about "intrepid Victorian lady travelers." Intrepid: well, that was one word I refused to use, about myself or any other unfortunate soul who found herself far away from home, having to depend on strangers.

I was so tired that I didn't eat dinner. I read a mystery and listened to a tape by Buddhist teacher Pema Chödrön on compassion, kept in my bag for just such self-pitying moods. I was waiting for the whiskery landlady to bang on my door and demand I leave instantly, but she didn't. Gradually I grew more peaceful; all the same, I fell asleep in my clothes, afraid of a nocturnal rousting.

In the morning I found I'd had a change of heart. Travel is the state of being homeless; we should welcome the opportunity it gives us to live nowhere. I wrote a note to the landlady in Norwegian, and said that I had thought about it, and that I would be leaving that morning.

She looked astonished and then grateful when I handed the slip of paper to her. She said, smiling somewhat ruefully, "I believe we had a misunderstanding. I am a little deaf, you know. Where will you go?"

"I don't know."

"I will call the Seaman's Hotel. They have reasonable rooms. I will drive you there."

Perhaps she just wanted to make sure I was really leaving. She called and there was a room at the Seaman's Hotel. I packed up quickly, suddenly lighthearted. I let her drive me the few short blocks; on the way we talked about the weather and whether or not it would rain. We parted cordially. She apologized again, and I marveled that I had ever been afraid of her.

Pretty Enough
to Be a Showgirl

by Chelsea Cain

The Sahara Hotel and Casino is one of the seediest, most garish tributes to low-ceilinged American architecture on the Vegas strip. The hallway carpets are orange, the attendants wear black polyester and the casino itself is so stuck in the late '70s, I half expected Dan Tana to strut through with his showgirl sidekick, Bea. Having said that, I should acknowledge that the hotel is currently undergoing major renovations and there are artists' pictorials of the finished product plastered throughout the building. The fanciful colored sketches look like stills from *Aladdin*, a sort of bright, Disney version of an Arab city where nothing ever explodes suddenly and you can still get a good cut of prime rib.

The hotel personnel talk about The Renovation as if it is the Rapture. They preface all talk of the future with "After The Renovation . . . "

"After The Renovation, we'll have a casino as large as some of the big resorts down the strip."

"After The Renovation, we'll have a whole new exterior."

"After The Renovation . . . "

Next door, the hulking abandoned frame of El Rancho squats

half-dismantled, awaiting demolition. Its once grand marquee announces "Coming Soon Country Land." For El Rancho, there will be no salvation, only a big new building with a big new theme and a lot of country music and roasted chicken.

The Sahara, built in 1952, is one of the "classic" casinos on the strip, which is why I decided to stay here. Call me nostalgic, but for me the attraction to Vegas lies not on the south side of the strip with the brand-new mega-resorts and theme-park façades, but on the north side—old Vegas: Frank, Elvis, Priscilla, martinis, girls in false eyelashes, men who wore ties. Back when you could watch an A-bomb mushroom from your hotel room balcony and still catch Dean Martin's set at the Copa Room.

I tried to get reservations at The Sands, but was reminded politely by my travel agent that it had been "blown to hell" just last year. So here I sit at the counter in the Caravan Room at the Sahara. It is your basic old-style diner, complete with a rotating cake display cabinet and a laminated menu that offers machine-dispensed juice. They have made small attempts at giving the place a North African flavor, but the end result is more Moroccan Denny's than anything else.

For the last half-hour I have been halfheartedly nibbling at a bowl of soupy oatmeal and watching an old man sitting at the other end of the Formica counter. He is wearing a red T-shirt, a black windbreaker and a black fedora with a jaunty small red feather stuck in the band. He's in his sixties, I think, though it's hard to tell as he has obviously done some hard living. His face is creased and gray, his hands thick. He sits, chain-smoking, a cigarette in one hand, a fork in the other, chatting gruffly with the wait staff, all of whom he apparently knows by name.

"Hey Edie," the man says. "Know how much a breakfast is down at the Holiday Inn?"

Edie is organizing condiments under the counter and doesn't look up. "How much?" she asks.

"Dollar forty-nine."

"Yeah?"

"Yep. Used to be you could get a breakfast for ninety-nine cents. Remember that? Ninety-nine cents." He shakes his head at the memory of it and draws a long thoughtful drag on his cigarette. Ah, the good old days, back when you could still get a cheap cheese omelet and no one blinked when you ordered a bloody mary.

I look more closely at his hands and notice that he is wearing a thick gold pinkie ring and has perfectly manicured square nails. A gangster? A pit boss? A stylish retiree? I smile happily. My first day and I have already come across a Vegas character.

This is actually my second trip to the city. My cousin Cecily and I drove through on our way from Iowa City to Los Angeles in the spring of 1995. We were nineteen and twenty-three respectively, and had both been reading a lot of Hunter S. Thompson. Cecily had never been to California and I had decided that I had to be more spontaneous (I think I had just rented *Annie Hall*), so one Sunday night while I was over at her house for dinner I mentioned the idea of a road trip.

Me: "So, I was thinking I'd drive to California the day after tomorrow. Want to come?"

Cecily: "Sure."

We left on Tuesday, with a tape of traveling music and a trunk full of summer clothes. Road trips, like marriages, are something that should require waiting periods before ensuing, as we had no idea what we were getting into. After being snowed-in in Denver for two days, we arrived in Vegas in the early evening of Day Three, a little stir-crazy and completely pooped.

We got a room at the Vagabond Inn on the strip, a cheap motel across from Treasure Island. It was the weekend of the big annual Grateful Dead show and the strip was full of deadheads on acid who had come to experience all the neon and flashing lights. It was a strange sight—dreadlocked teenagers in dancing-bear tie-dyed T-shirts, interspersed with thousands of plump Middle American women in jumpsuits and cigarette-clutching old people.

I made Cecily leave the room and walk the strip with me so that I could look around. It was early evening and the temperature was still in the 80s. The lights were just coming on. The sky was clear and pink with sunset. We headed south on the strip toward the big resorts. I was in awe of it, the grandiosity of it all.

I looked over at Cecily. Her lip was literally curled in disgust. We are both the children of ex-hippie, anti-capitalist, big-government liberals. I spent my early childhood on a farm in Iowa where my parents refused to buy me anything that was advertised on TV. Consumerism was greeted with the same hostility as polyester. Or Nixon. As for Cecily's parents, they still shop at the co-op and freeze a year's worth of homegrown-basil pesto every summer. When we told them that we were planning on spending a night in Vegas, they nodded carefully so as to appear completely supportive and not infringe on our personal exploration, but you could tell inside they were cringing.

Now we were on the strip and Cecily had confirmed every negative jibe she had ever heard about the city. "It's so vulgar," she growled.

But I loved it. I loved Las Vegas, even then. I was distraught. How could this be happening? This was against everything my parents had taught me. But I couldn't help it. It was wonderful. Beautiful. I wanted to stay forever.

Ahead of us a young hippie wearing a Phish T-shirt was clearly out of his mind on LSD. His motions were disjointed, as if his legs and arms were keeping different paces. He watched the scenery with an intensity that almost matched my own. Cecily was watching him too. She looked at me, then back at him. I could tell I was not the one she wished she were walking with.

We had been passing a huge hotel for what seemed like ages—I mean, this hotel had to have been four city blocks long—when the young man turned to Cecily and smiled.

"Man," he said, his pupils wide. "These hotels all look alike. I could've sworn we'd passed this same one seven or eight times already."

He stumbled on and Cecily insisted that we go back to the motel after that, where she spent the rest of the evening scribbling in her journal and periodically looking accusingly at me. I imagined the pages to be filled with mentions of my name, followed by negative adjectives and multiple exclamation points.

She was right. I was tainted. I had seen the Mecca of capitalism and I had not turned my head. I tried to explain my confusion to her. She just looked at me purposefully and underlined the sentence she had been writing.

I think Cecily knew even then that she would never—not even for a VW bus and a year's worth of patchouli—set foot in Vegas again. I, on the other hand, couldn't wait to come back. Only next time, I would come alone. I would shed the arched brows of my reproachful peers and embrace, unabashed, the casino culture with gusto. I would come alone and walk the strip as long as I wanted. See what I wanted. Talk to whom I wanted. I would see the place through my eyes and no one else's. No judgment. No guilt. Just me.

And 140,000 other tourists.

I have abandoned the Caravan Room and am now walking the north side of the strip.

It is February and in the mid-60s, cool enough that I have to wear a sweater but warm enough that I have left my big coat on the back of the chair in my room. On my side of the street, small gift shops promise "Souvenirs! Moccasins! Sunglasses! Cheap!" On the other side is a vast sandy lot, fenced off and filled with the early starts of construction. Propped up next to the trailer office, presumably left over from Christmas, are two life-size plastic Wise Men on camels.

A man slows down ahead of me. "A little chilly," he says to no one in particular.

"Not to me," I offer.

On the next block the man and I get to talking and he tells me that his name is Roland. He is a chubby Asian man, about thirty, with a Nike cap and a toothy grin. Though he lives in Honolulu, he comes to Vegas with his parents a few times a year. I ask him if he gambles. He says hardly ever and tells me that instead he spends his days walking the strip and riding the free hotel shuttles around the city.

Roland loves Las Vegas, and would like to move here, but his parents don't approve of the idea. "During the day it's dirty and all the cars bother me," he says. "But at night, when it's lit up, I think all the lights make it beautiful."

Not long after Roland and I part on the strip, I duck into the Desert Inn casino to look around. The casino is small and stately, if such a thing is possible. There are six huge columns, with a tall, dusty, faux palm tree between each. The ceiling is tall and painted with a star-and-moon theme reminiscent of those annoying afghans everyone bought a few years ago. The room has three domes, featuring three grand chandeliers. The game tables are made of wood. Even the waitresses in miniskirts are old.

On the far side of the room there is some excitement around a craps game and I wander over to investigate. A man named Lance is winning big. He is maybe forty, and is there with his pretty wife and ponytailed daughter. He looks like a political science professor: clean-shaven, glasses, casually dressed. My heart jumps when I see his bet. He has thousands of dollars on the table, which is only a fraction of the tens of thousands in chips that sit in front of him. His wife and daughter show no reaction at all when he wins or loses. They are either ambivalent or numb. But Lance is on a roll. He can't lose. He keeps throwing $500 chips out like jacks. He's so happy he's sweating.

"Wow," I say to an older man with dyed black hair who is betting exactly as Lance does. "He's doing pretty well."

"He lost twice that this morning," the man whispers, before laying a $10 chip on the number Lance just bet $1,000 on.

I leave before Lance can start to lose. Just as I am going he takes a $10,000 check from the casino and presses it, folded, into his twelve-year-old daughter's hand. "Take care of this for me, honey," he says.

At five o'clock my hotel room phone rings. It is Dori, my friend Brian's birthmother. They've only known each other a year, ever since Dori had him tracked down. Just by coincidence Dori is in town the same weekend I am and Brian has arranged for us to meet so she can show me the sights.

"Chelsea," she chirps on the car phone. "I'm coming to pick you up in the perfect Las Vegas touring vehicle—a Thunderbird with a sunroof." She wants to take me to Spago. Is there class in Vegas?

An hour later there is a knock at the door. I open it, and there is Dori. She is about forty-four and reminds me immediately of Kate Jackson, who was, incidentally, my favorite Charlie's Angel. Dori is wearing a black pantsuit, a white button-down blouse, a pale green vest and tasteful jewelry. She extends a hand. "I found you," she says.

We walk downstairs and join Dori's husband, John, whom she has left to mind the car in the parking lot. He is tall and friendly, like a high-school jock some twenty years later. Without being asked, John climbs into the back of the Thunderbird, and Dori sends me to the passenger seat. Then, with Dori at the wheel, we cruise up the strip.

It's dark now and, just as Roland said, the lights are beautiful. Dori, as if reading my thoughts, says, "I love this view at night." John grumbles something about hating Vegas from the back seat, but Dori and I ignore him. We are busy cruising.

The streets are full of people milling around from one casino to the next. Most of them are white; a few are Asian. Some carry plastic cups full of quarters with casino logos printed on the sides. Some walk with their hands in their pockets, faces up to take in the lights. Others are drunk, leaning on friends to keep from falling.

We pull into Caesars Palace, Dori's favorite casino, and park the Thunderbird in a lot behind the hotel. The casino at Caesars is mammoth, the biggest one I've been in so far. There are huge white pillars and gold gilding and casino employees in togas spraying women with Caesars Palace Perfume. I follow Dori, who is expertly weaving us through the casino into the mouth of a great big mall toward Spago.

After we have been seated and have ordered dinner, Dori turns to me, her eyes shining. "Did Brian tell you how we met?" she asks.

I tell her he has. He told me how the phone rang. How he picked it up. How he almost hung up when the person on the other end of the line asked for him by his full name, thinking it was a saleswoman. Then the woman told him she was calling on behalf of his birthmother and that he had three choices: he could choose no contact in which case he would never be bothered again, limited contacted through an intermediary, or full, open contact. "C," Brian said. "I want the last one."

They talked on the phone, exchanged photos and then Dori flew out to see him. They have been close ever since. It's funny, even though I know Brian and he is my age, it is Dori's experience that I relate to—the pain she must have felt giving up a baby and the courage it took to look for him so many years later.

"It must have been amazing for you," I say to Dori, "to see him all grown up like that. Did he look like what you had imagined?"

"Well, of course I had imagined him getting older every year," she says. "Every birthday I would adjust the image. Then, when he was seventeen, I just sort of stopped aging him in my mind. He remained seventeen. Then, when I met him, he was this man, all grown up." She laughs. "Of course, I'm probably not what Brian imagined either. I think he had the classic male adoptee trailer-trash mom fantasy."

Instead, she is Dream Mom. Young, hip, stylish, beautiful, smart, funny. The envy of Little League. I try to conceive of what it must have been like to wonder where you're from your whole life, to run through all the horrible Manson-clan-baby scenarios, and then have Dori appear like Kelly LeBrock in *Weird Science*, a manifestation of all your adolescent fantasies.

While we have been talking, the sky painted on the ceiling of the mall has been getting darker. It apparently goes through a cycle each hour, from dawn to midnight. By the time we get up to go it has gone from dawn to dusk to dawn and it is nearing midafternoon again.

Our body clocks probably permanently traumatized, we leave the restaurant and the mall, climb back into the Thunderbird and head to the Hilton where we drop John off before heading downtown to see the Fremont Street Experience. It is an Experience, rather than just a street, because the downtown casinos got together and had a roof built over it, and every night on the hour they play really loud music and colorful, dizzying images light up overhead. Dori and I watch the show and are not impressed, so we soon leave to find rhinestone sunglasses, which we have decided we must wear while we are in Vegas.

While we are shopping, Dori tells me about the first times she came to Vegas. With her boyfriend the racecar driver. With her boyfriend the big-band player. She was seventeen when Brian was born.

I remember the poem she once put together from one of those magnetic poetry sets on Brian's refrigerator: "I may have to ask the music goddess to play a less frantic song."

Eventually, unable to find sunglasses to our liking and both fading fast, Dori whisks me back to The Sahara.

"Good night, Miss Chelsea," she says. My mother is the only one to have ever called me that before. She died last summer of cancer, and for a moment Dori's words freeze me. It is like a small gift, a memory.

"Thank you," I say, before getting out of the car.

❄

I am completely naked and a strange woman is slathering my body with mud.

Let me explain. I woke up late this morning, Vegas style, and went down to get some Yuban at the Caravan Room, where I am now a regular. The old man in the black fedora was sitting exactly where I left him, wearing the same clothes. He nodded affably in my direction. I nodded back. Then, after soupy oatmeal, I walked over to the Desert Inn to look around again, hoping to see Lance at the craps table. He wasn't around so I decided to explore the hotel and found a sign that said Spa with an arrow after it, which I followed obediently until I found myself in a whole other building where a woman in a jump suit convinced me I needed a French clay wrap and she was just the woman to do it. I changed into a white robe and white plastic slippers and then she escorted me to a small room where I took off the robe and lay back on a table.

Now she is covering me in camel-colored mud "from France." It's slippery and slimy and I am freezing. She's telling me that she came here nine years ago to visit her sister. She ended up staying because she got a job in what she'd "gone to school for," which makes me wonder what, exactly, she majored in.

Done with the mud, she folds up the plastic sheet I am lying on, wrapping it tightly around my body. She continues folding up layers, two sheets and three blankets, until I am like a giant, human joint. Then she turns out the lights and leaves.

Wait.

I am trying not to panic. My entire body feels like it is cementing together. I concentrate on breathing. I am alone in a dark room completely immobile. If there is a fire, I realize, I am totally fucked.

I slowly wiggle my foot until, centimeter by centimeter, I am able to work it over next to my other foot. I rub one big toe against the other. It gives me an inordinate amount of comfort.

After what seems like years, she returns. I practically weep, I am so happy to see her. She peels me like a banana and props me up, then she pulls the plastic sheet off my mud-caked body and sends me to the shower where I spend fifteen minutes trying to get the clay off with a loofah sponge.

When I have rubbed the top layer of skin clean off, she lays me back on the table and covers me with moisturizer because the mud has sucked out all the water in my body and if I don't get it back I'll die. Finally, I am allowed back into the locker room where I change into my clothes. I pay my $45 and leave.

I see Lance again, as I am coming out of the spa. He is standing on a hotel room balcony three floors above me. He's half inside the room, half out, wearing a pair of purple swimming shorts. He doesn't notice me. He just stands, arms at his sides, staring out into the clear early evening. I stop and turn around to see what he sees. It is perfectly quiet. There's no one else around. The mountains are cool shadows against the pale pink light. And it's just me and Lance—sharing this peaceful, contemplative moment.

When I go inside, he is still standing there, his arms slack. He hasn't looked down. He hasn't moved. One of two things, I decide. He is either basking in the glory of his winnings, or he is thinking about jumping.

From the Desert Inn I get a cab down the strip to the MGM Grand where I have a ticket to ride the Skyscreamer. It is part of the theme park set up behind the hotel. In a nutshell: They haul you up 250 feet backwards and then drop you at an angle that propels you down and forward at speeds approaching seventy miles per hour. The painting on the brochure shows a cartoon man slamming straight out of the picture, his face contorted in ecstatic terror.

They can hook three people to a "flight," however I have decided to fly solo, which costs a little more, but, I assure myself, puts less stress on the wires.

First, I am dressed in a lead apron, resembling the type x-ray technicians wear. It is pulled up over my clothes and fastened tightly behind me and around each leg. On the back of the apron is a bevy of thick black cords that will all attach to the two wires that will decide whether I live or die today.

Then I am walking out onto the field. There are no mats, only a huge bed of pansies, which, though pretty, wouldn't do much to break a fall. Two technicians direct me to climb aboard a crane lift, which they raise up to the level where the wires fall. Then, after a brief inspection of my gear (I'm hoping these teenagers make more than minimum wage) they snap something behind my back and suddenly, with a jerk, I am being lifted above their heads.

I reach for my side to feel the ripcord, which I have been instructed to pull when I get to the top of the crane and hear "three-two-one-Fly." It is still there. So I fold my arms across my chest, as I have been told to do, and keep my legs stiff and straight behind me, my feet in the foot bar attached with cords to my apron.

The earth is falling away. Heads tilt backwards to watch me disappear skyward. It's terrifying. I am a human without gravity.

I remember standing on the high dive at City Park pool in Iowa City, Iowa. I am five. My dad, his hair and beard still long, is standing on the pool edge below me.

"Jump," he's saying. "Don't look down, just jump."

I lift my head, forcing myself to keep it up, toward the horizon. Beyond the expansive colored lights of the city the mountains sit solidly at the base of the sky. So much desert, just beyond so much chaos.

Three-two-one-Fly. Three-two-one-Fly. I keep repeating it like a mantra. I am afraid, once I get to the top, I'll freeze, and I won't be able to pull the cord.

Up in the sky, Vegas is quiet and beautiful, like when you fly into the city at night. It's like a long, pregnant pause. There is no past, no future, only this one moment. It's what Vegas is all about—the roll of the dice, the flip of a card, the pull of a slot machine. Nothing matters but that one second that will determine whether you win or lose.

I wanted to come to Vegas again to hate it. I wanted to be able to tell my friends horrible, funny stories of grotesque casinos and desperate gamblers. I wanted to be able to disparage the insane optimism of the millions of Middle Americans who spend hard-earned vacations at a roulette wheel losing their children's college education money. I wanted to draw huge social metaphors about Who We Are and what will happen if, as the intellectuals fear, some future civilization digs up Las Vegas and draws conclusions about our culture based on old slot machines and sequined panties.

But my plan failed because I am having a fabulous time. I am done apologizing. I love Las Vegas. I am an American and I love big gaudy casinos and fake façades and free drinks and people on the make. I love being told, as I have been by three Vegas cab drivers, that I am "pretty enough to be a showgirl." Even tomorrow when I will lose $107 at blackjack I will be having the time of my life. Vegas is the ultimate tease. It is the promise of all that can be yours—after your number comes up, after that single quarter makes you a million, after The Renovation.

I am reeled nearly to the top of the crane now, face down, 250 feet above the ground. It is a breathtaking view, a perfect, exhilarating moment. I am fabulous and alone. I am a goddess. I am Venus de Milo. But just before I can let out a breath to enjoy it I hear the call:

"Three-two-one-Fly."

I pull the ripcord and fall.

Every cell in my body recognizes immediately that something has gone very wrong. I am free-falling. I am slamming straight down. My body immediately sends out a rush of endorphins, so at least when I die, I'll feel good. Then the wire catches and swings me forward. I open my eyes and I am flying in the night sky. I stretch my arms straight out on either side as I seem to hang there in the air for a moment, suspended in space, before the wire swings me back pendulum-style, to and fro, until I lose all momentum and am lowered slowly back to the ground.

But I am not yet ready to be an earth dweller. I want to ride my high.

I want to fly again. I want to feel my blood throbbing through my head as my extremities go numb. I want to be in the sky.

So, like a true Vegas gambler, I pull another wad of crumpled bills from my pocket. It's only money.

"Again," I say to the teenagers. "Take me up again."

Passing Through Bandit Country

by Faith Adiele

I am on a train in southern Thailand headed north up the Malay Peninsula. The train, windows shut tight against the black night air, rattles from side to side. Outside, thick vegetation crowds against a landscape so different from the mountains of the north where I have spent two years. If I squint hard, I can make out rubber trees, dark tendrils reaching to the ground, bright red flowers like flecks of blood on a shadowy body, shuttered houses on stilts. Each stop looks ominously static, like the set of *Swiss Family Robinson* might look once movie production has shut down.

Southern Thais say two things to me. The first is phrased as query, after a sharp glance at my sarong and locally tooled sandals: "Are you Malay?"

"No, American," I usually admit, reluctantly owning up to all that it implies, unless I'm negotiating for budget accommodations, in which case I give myself leeway to claim my father's nationality: "Nigerian."

"You could be Malay," they insist, eager to explain that there is an indigenous group on the peninsula with Negroid features. Light brown skin and curly hair just like mine. With my smooth Thai, they assure me, I could almost "pass."

These earnest ethnic Chinese and Thais and Laos encouraging me, a Nigerian-Scandinavian-American girl, to pass for Malay make me smile. The idea of passing has long intrigued me, my child's fancy piqued by accounts of light-skinned blacks who left home and became white, trading all ties to self and family for freedom, something I could understand, or wealth, something I could not. The only biracial member of my family, I devoured tales of Tragic Mulattas who married white men then waited in horror to see how dark their children would turn out.

For me, with my brown skin and dark curls and round nose, passing in its most commonly used sense—for white—was out of the question. As if to underscore the point, I'd been born to a Scandinavian-American mother whose family of tall blonds embodies American ideals more than most Americans do. While it didn't bother me not to look like them, it was frustrating not even to be able to pass for what I actually was—biracial. I was fascinated by those mixed-race children with golden skin and wild sheaves of hair like straw. Delicate, exotic birds, they clung to their white mothers in public, as if their blue and green and hazel eyes that passed through and over me, refusing to see the world staring at them, were indeed transparent. Unlike them, I looked like every other brown girl, my split heritage hidden from the naked eye.

I worried. How, then, would my tribespeople, the other Nigerian-Scandinavian Americans, recognize and come to claim me?

I wanted most to be recognized as Nigerian, a foreign identity I imagined might account for my perpetual feelings of misplacement in the U.S. In college, I studied other African students—their dark skin firm as tree trunks, their bodies so strong they nearly burst out of their flimsy European clothes—and gave up. There was no imitating the deliberate roll of the girls' hips, the way the boys threw back their heads and laughed, white teeth flashing. They were too confident to have come from any country I knew. And so I passed for African American, a dynamic which, carrying no privilege, was not even considered passing. I was just another insecure brown girl on the shores of America.

The second thing locals on the Malay Peninsula say to me is: "Be careful of armed bandits."

Southern Thailand is notorious for its gun-toting robbers and smugglers who roam in bold bands, sometimes posing as shaven, saffron-clad monks, oftentimes murdering their victims. The Bangkok papers are filled with sensational reports of gangs attacking long-distance buses, then slinking into jungle lairs or melting over the border to Malaysia. It is whispered that some villages are virtually owned by bandit leaders, who conscript young men into service much like the drug warlords of the north. Popular books and movies, on the other hand, claim that bandits find willing followers easily, due to their Robin Hood–like tendencies to steal from rich landowners and give to poor villagers.

So far I've been lucky. A woman—and *farang* (foreigner) at that—traveling solo with all her wealth in a single bag is almost too easy a mark. When queried about the existence and location of my Protective Male, I reply that I am a serious student on *thudong* (pilgrimage) and have only recently stopped being a Buddhist nun.

"Buad maechi?" the Thai exclaim in disbelief, and I nod, yes, I did indeed ordain. My close cap of curls, just now recovering from the razor, supports this claim. All interest in my recalcitrant Protective Male now lost to the desire to make merit to improve their karma, they tell me which guesthouses are not in league with bandits, which towns to avoid. And except for once hearing gunshots in the road during dinner near the Malaysian border and having to shutter the kerosene lamps and lie with my face pressed to the floorboards for the rest of the evening, nothing untoward has happened.

Staring out the train window at the murky, abandoned streets, I decide that good karma and luck may not be enough this time. It occurs to me that the Thais' two discussion points are somehow enmeshed to my advantage, that I can best *be careful* of armed robbers by *passing* as Malay.

Many of the bandits are rumored to be ethnic Malays who practice Islam, members in fact of the Muslim separatist movement fighting against the domination of the Thai Buddhist government. The less foreign I am, I try to reassure myself, the greater the likelihood that I will be passed over when choices are made to rape, rob and kill.

I get up and stagger through the rocking train, keeping my movements muted and tight, resolving to be less forthcoming in my conversations. In the north, no matter how Thai I acted, I was always too big, too brown, my body movements too unrestrained. There was never any possibility of melting into the scenery. Now, if viewed at a distance, my very brownness might save me.

In the dining car, three men in the snowy shirtsleeves and dress slacks of Thai businessmen blow my cover. First they send the waiter to my table to ask if I speak English, then they insist on buying me dinner. They look to be in their mid-twenties, which means thirty-something, and are on a slow, steady path to drunkenness, having chosen pricey Singha beer rather than cheap Mekong whiskey. Everything about them, from their pinkening faces and expansive gestures to their courtly invitations of "Please to join us," seems more intent on impressing one another than me. I accept.

Their questions, phrased in excellent English, are the usual suspects: Where do you come from? How do you like Thailand? Where is your husband? Can you eat Thai food?

I reply in English, with a few Thai words dropped in, pretending to speak far less than I actually do. This is Plan B: if unable to pass as Malay, always make sure your opponent underestimates you.

They crow with delight to hear my simple Thai, and when I cover my rice with tiny green heaps of chilies, there is much giggling and nudging. Look, look, they tell each other with delight: the farang eats Thai chilies!

Their obvious lack of familiarity with foreigners lessens the likelihood of their being hustlers. Still, I shake my head when they ask if I drink Singha and keep to tiny, chilled bottles of orange Fanta.

They order another round and tick off a list of beautiful beach islands near the gulf, places like Phuket, Hat Yai, Ko Samui, the so-called James Bond Island, all of which will later be immortalized in big budget movies, blond starlets spilling onto the sand like oil slicks.

I explain that I'm not on vacation. I'm on a pilgrimage in search of famous nuns.

In my pocket is my most valuable possession, next to my passport: a list of nuns and temples. Next to each woman or temple my teacher has scribbled the name of the province in which she or it is located or, if I'm lucky, the town. Nothing more. Imagining myself a black female Paul Theroux, I will traverse Southeast Asia from Malaysia all the way up to Burma, throwing myself off the train wherever I hear of someone or some-place I should see. The words "I've heard of some nuns living near . . ." are enough to start me fumbling for my bag, heading for the exit.

"Let me see," the youngest and best-dressed businessman insists, hold-ing out his hand. It occurs to me that this might be his promotion celebra-tion or that he could be the CEO's son who has just landed his first big deal. He studies the list, his eyes tiny slits of slate in a lobster-red face. I feel drunk just looking at him.

"Wait a minute," he says, miraculously acquiring a backbone and jabbing a manicured finger at the very next stop on my list. "You can't go there! Phetchaburi is owned by bandits!"

The train jolts around a corner, throwing my heart against my rib cage. I am scheduled to disembark in Phetchaburi tonight. The town is crucial to my pilgrimage; one of the only centers for nuns is rumored to be nearby.

I shrug, feigning indifference. *"Mai pen rai,"* I say, invoking Thailand's most commonly used phrase. *Never mind. It's okay. No problem.*

"No, no," he insists, his eyes sharpening with increasing sobriety. "The train gets in at three in the morning. They know who arrives, where they stay!"

He whips around to his friends and blurts a flurry of southern dialect.

Though most of the words are familiar, I assume a blank expression, heart still racing.

"What should she do?" one of the men asks. *"Mai dii leuy."* *It's not good.*

"She shouldn't go alone," he replies. "They kidnap visitors and plantation workers to extort money."

"Why doesn't she get off at your stop?" the third suggests.

"Yes," my would-be savior agrees, turning his palms to face upward, a gesture I think might be safe to interpret as sincere. "My town is larger and more secure. I can make sure she gets to a guesthouse. In the morning I can come with my car to drive her to *samnak maechi* (the nun center)."

"Dii lao," the second man counsels. *Good enough.*

It is indeed a good plan. I decide to accept. I know that to ask a Thai for help, even directions, is to embark on an extended relationship in which his responsibility will not end until I have achieved my goal or safely reached my destination.

The first businessman, face red above his pristine white linen shirt, turns back to me and proposes his solution, speaking careful, clear English. "You should not get off at Phetchaburi, which is the next stop," he cautions. "You should get off at Ratchaburi, the following stop, where I live." He explains why.

I look skeptical for a few minutes before making a show of allowing myself to be convinced.

The bill is then settled, a ritual involving a race to unzip their clutch wallets of Italian leather and shouted claims and counter-claims of being the eldest and thus responsible for paying. Each tosses red and tan bills onto a mound on the table.

I thank all three, placing my hands together in a steeple and bringing them to my forehead in a traditional *wai*. This delights them immensely, though their drunken attempts to return the gesture look more Three Stooge–like than Thai. Afterwards, I head back toward second class, while they exit out the front of the dining car, to first class, fresh bottles of Singha clinking in their hands.

"See you in a few hours," the first businessman says. "Remember not to get off at Phetchaburi—wait for Ratchaburi!" We agree to meet on the platform.

Back at my seat, I find that a family, a tiny mother with three children, has joined me. Trying to keep my head respectfully below the mother's, I duck into my window seat, diagonally across from hers. Once seated, I nod and smile. The broad planes of her face twitch a moment, as if processing the information that she has inadvertently installed her family next to someone strange, be it Malay or farang, then smooth into determined pleasantness. The two younger children freeze in mid-gesture, saucer-eyed and speechless.

The eldest child, a boy of about ten, has ended up in the seat next to mine. Spine rigid as a dancer's, he perches at the absolute edge; one more inch forward, and he would be levitating in air. He makes a fluttering gesture with his hand, an unspoken plea. His mother snaps a single syllable in southern dialect, its meaning unmistakable: *Stay!*

Keeping his head perfectly still, the boy monitors me out of the corners of his eyes, pupils rotating in their sockets as if he were performing *khon*, a Thai masked dance based on the Ramayana. He is Hanuman, the Monkey General, terrifying the demon army with his jerky movements and wildly spinning eyeballs.

Grinning to myself, I fall into that half-waking state of train travel. My limbs loosen and follow the jarring rhythm. Outside an epic battle rages, blue-faced demons pitted against Lord Rama and the monkey soldiers, little Hanuman poker-straight at my side.

When the conductor comes through the car, calling Phetchaburi, my original destination, I consider jumping up and dashing for the exit. Why have you allowed your plan to be modified? I reprimand myself. What if the businessman, now drunk, has forgotten our agreement? Or what if he was just talking? What if there are no armed robbers?

I press my nose to the cold glass and peer out. The platform looks empty, though it's too dark to be sure. What does a bandit-owned town look like? I wonder. I imagine clusters of men with machine guns on every corner. Will they be dressed in dark blue farmers' shirts with red headbands and sashes like the opium smugglers of the north? Or in snug polyester pants with flared legs and mirrored sunglasses, like the blood vendetta gangsters in Bollywood movies? I imagine a banner strung across the train station: Welcome to Bandit Territory! spelled out in six-inch letters.

I decide to get off the train. Stick to my original plan. Rely on myself. I lean forward to grab my knapsack from under my seat.

Just then Hanuman nods off, his head dropping face-first into the crook of my elbow. He is warm as a furnace, his soft cheeks like sun-ripened peaches against my skin.

Startled, I bolt upright and jerk my arm away. The stubble of his shaven head scrapes along the tender flesh of my inner arm. He squirms into fetal position, his small, round head falling in my lap like a gift.

Across the aisle, his family dozes, piled atop one another, the younger children's mouths half-open like tiny, budding flowers. I rest my hand lightly on the shoulder of the sleeping boy. The train hurtles through bandit territory.

An hour later we reach Ratchaburi, my new destination. Reluctantly, I lift the boy from my lap. His eyes flutter open for a split second, momentarily wild, then close, the lids settling into smiling gold crescents. I drape him over both seats, then grab my knapsack and sprint to the end of the car.

The conductor watches as I disembark and scour the length of the train in both directions. *"Khon urn?"* he asks. *Someone else?*

I nod.

A minute later he jerks his chin at me—"Malay?"

I nod.

We wait some more. The station is locked and dark. No banner, which is good. Except for a *samloh* driver asleep in the back of his three-wheeled richsha, the platform is empty.

Finally, the train conductor shrugs. "Sure this is the right stop?"

I wonder if I got them mixed up and was supposed to have gotten off at Phetchaburi, the first stop. "Did a man get off at the last stop?" I ask.

He shakes his head, the gold braid on his cap glinting in the light from the train doorway. "No one likes to get off at these stops at night."

This is why he has kept the train waiting. I stare open-mouthed, just now beginning to comprehend the size of his concern, of my stupidity. I know nothing about this town, other than that it is an hour north of my original destination, closer to Bangkok, and therefore supposedly larger and safer. For all I know, this is the heart of bandit territory, and the businessman gets a commission on all farang women he lures here.

The train begins to snort and strain, like an animal in restraint, and the conductor hops onto the metal step. *"Glaap maa?"* he offers. *Do you want to get back on?*

I shake my head. In the temple they taught us to confront the very things that terrify us. Or perhaps I am simply paralyzed with indecision.

With a great squeal, the train pulls away. "Good luck," the conductor calls. "Be careful!"

I hoist my knapsack to my shoulder and turn to find the samloh driver sitting up, regarding me.

"Samloh?" he inquires.

I nod briskly and scramble into the back. "Take me to the Chinese hotel," I bark. "I'm late."

As the driver begins to pilot the samloh through the abandoned streets in that slow, standing pedal that resembles slow-motion running, I pray that the stereotype about samloh drivers being drug pushers, pimps or bandit informants is greatly exaggerated. I also pray that there *is* a Chinese hotel.

Though the town doesn't seem as large as promised, the center resembles any other Thai town at night—dark and shuttered, with metal gates pulled down over shop entrances, crushed glass atop stucco gates and decorative grilles covering the windows of upstairs apartments. These are standard security measures, as common as the high sidewalks to protect against flooding, so I tell myself there is no reason to read them as ominous.

I think about Maechi Roongduan, the head nun at my temple. It was she who inspired me to make this pilgrimage. When she was in her late twenties, not much older than I, she spent three months walking from one end of Thailand to the other with only an umbrella, a mosquito net, an alms-bowl and the robes on her back. She reached the Malay Peninsula during rubber season, which meant that the villagers worked at night, stripping trees by candlelight, and slept during the day, when alms-rounds happen. As a result, she went for days without food and had to meditate frequently to overcome hunger pangs. Often, alone in empty fields, the stench of rubber heavy in the dark air, she came out of meditation to find cobras with their heads in her lap.

"Perhaps drawn by my body heat," she'd marveled to me, and I had instead marveled at her and her fierce determination to love all creatures, no matter the cost.

To my amazement, the samloh driver deposits me at what is indeed a Chinese hotel, a modest gray stone building in the center of town. I pay him, tipping just enough to suggest gratitude but not wealth, before thrusting my hand through the iron gate and ringing the bell.

The ubiquitous old Chinese watchman in white undershirt, drawstring pajama bottoms and slippers shuffles across the courtyard with a lantern and a heavy ring of keys. Without question, he shows me to a room, clean and spartan, and points out the shower room.

Once inside the stone room, I ladle cool water from a giant jar over my body, shaking a bit in the chill air, allowing myself a few tears of relief under the camouflage of water. For a short time in this tiny, gray space, I am me. Not moving. Not negotiating. Not passing into any particular shape.

I have just returned to my room when the watchman knocks on the door and announces that someone has come for me.

My heart thuds. This is it. The samloh driver has sold me out!

"No visitors," I cry, eyeing the flimsy bolt. "It's too late, and I'm a respectable girl."

"No, no, it's me," a familiar voice protests, and I crack the door to find the businessman from the train standing in the hallway. He is red as ever, his boyish face sheepish. "May I come in?"

"Only for a minute," I say, "I must sleep."

He enters the room and plops heavily on the bed.

Alarmed, I leave the door open wide and stand between it and him. "What happened to you?"

"I fell asleep," he says, rubbing his puffy eyes, "and missed our stop. I had to get off at the next town and find a taxi to bring me back to Ratchaburi. It was difficult at this hour. Then I had to get to this hotel."

"How did you know where I was?"

He chuckles. "How many farang get off the train in the middle of the night? I went to the train station and asked the samloh driver. He brought me here."

I join his laughter, though it occurs to me that my initial assumption was correct and the driver did indeed sell me out, albeit to this bumbling businessman instead of a bandit king.

"How did you know about this place?" he asks.

I grin. "I didn't! I knew this wasn't a tourist town, so if there was a hotel at all, it would be a 'traveler's hotel' for traders. I just guessed that it would be owned by ethnic Chinese. I said, 'Take me to the Chinese hotel' and it worked."

He roars. "That's very clever. You're quite resourceful!" He shakes his head. "Here I was supposed to protect you, but you did fine without me."

I duck my head modestly.

When he expresses some interest in more drink, I tell him it's time to go. He stands up, shoulders slumping in exhaustion, his fine linen wilting like a warm carnation, and says he'll be back with his car at eleven to take me to the nun center.

"I will make it up to you," he vows. "Eleven it is!"

At half past noon the following afternoon I consider my options. Who knows how far the nun center is and how long it will take me to find it? I need to budget time to travel back to Phetchaburi, time to find the center, time to meet the nuns and see the place, time to return here to Ratchaburi. I want to be back on the train this evening and get the hell out of bandit territory before dark.

The Chinese hotel owner confirms that there is indeed an evening train and tells me where the marketplace is. He's never heard of a nun center in this town or the next, however.

"If a man comes," I tell him, "please explain that I had to go but will be back for the evening train."

The walk through town feels odd. I am used to two extremes, either tourist metropolises like Chiang Mai and Bangkok that teem with expatriates and English-language signs or small, traditional villages, where everyone turns out on the dirt path to greet the farang. I have never before negotiated a mid-sized city filled with ethnic Chinese, Thais, Laos, Indians and Malays. I feel like an extra who didn't get the script.

At the market I wait beneath the sign for *tuk-tuk* going to Phetchaburi. Several Nissan pickups pass by, the narrow, padded benches in back already crowded with passengers. Finally a newer Nissan pulls up and parks. The driver gets out and heads into the market. A pretty young woman remains behind in the passenger's seat.

I approach and lean in through the open driver's window. "Are you going to Phetchaburi?" I ask. "I'm looking for this center—" I proffer the piece of paper. "I think it's on the road between here and Phetchaburi, somewhere in the country."

She squints at the paper, frowning. "I'm not sure," she says, "I'll have to ask him."

The driver returns with a giant burlap bag of rice draped over his shoulder. He staggers to the back and tosses it in, then joins us, slapping his palms together. He has the same face as the girl and looks a bit older, in his early twenties. *"Arai na?"* he asks us. *What is it?*

"Can we take her to this place?" the girl asks. "It's a temple."

He gives me a quick once-over. "A temple?"

"Well, a nun center, really," I explain.

The three of us study my teacher's list of names and provinces. I know what they must be thinking. Thai temples are cursed with long, flowery names that no one uses. In common parlance, they are known by descriptive nicknames: Marble Temple, Cave Temple, Temple of the Emerald Buddha, Temple of the Reclining Buddha, Temple of the Ceylonese Buddha. Without knowing its nickname or address, a temple is nearly impossible to locate.

"Get in." The driver motions for the girl to slide over.

"Oh no," I protest, "I can get in the back."

No, no, both insist, and so I squeeze into the front. We start off immediately, without waiting to load more passengers.

Worried that I've allowed my fat farang itinerary to supersede everyone else's, I glance back to check on the others through the small window in the cab. The pickup bed is empty, save for the bag of rice. There are no vinyl benches, no intricate grillwork on the canopy, no passengers. This is not a tuk-tuk.

I whip around to regard my companions. The young man drives hunched over, conferring softly with the girl. It dawns on me. They are brother and sister, come to market to do shopping, not pick up fares. I have just commandeered the private car of some family out doing errands.

"Khaw thod!" I cry. *Excuse me!* "I thought you were a tuk-tuk! I am

so ashamed! Please," I beg, fumbling for the door handle, "you don't have to take me."

"No, no," they assure me. *Mai pen rai. Never mind. No problem.*

For the next hour I cringe against the door of the cab, trying to make myself as small as possible, as if the size of my gall could somehow shrink with my body, while my shy hosts motor around town, silently intent on their task, asking none of the usual, eager questions of me.

At each bend in the muddy, rutted roads, the brother disembarks and asks for directions from befuddled monks and laypeople. At each wrong temple, we are directed to another, equally wrong.

Finally an old woman sends us to the long-distance bus park, where a driver in a silky disco shirt and wraparound sunglasses assures us that yes, he passes by the road to the nun center.

As they hand me over, my hosts apologize for abandoning me before my destination has been reached. They would like to take me to the center themselves, the sister explains, a crease appearing between her perfect brows, but their mother expected them home an hour ago. Can I possibly forgive them? They lean forward, twin faces rosy with sudden boldness and affection, looking for all the world as if we have spent a lovely afternoon together.

"Are you Malay?" the brother blurts out, finally daring to ask something of me, of this interaction.

"No, American," I say, for once happy to be so, eager to give them a story for their mother that's a fair exchange for their generosity. "I used to be a nun in the north, and now I'm on pilgrimage. You've helped so much."

Their eyes widen, and we all grin. I entered their truck under misapprehension and they invited me under a misapprehension of their own, and all this time we've been sitting side by side, mistaking one another for someone easier to imagine. Passing.

"Goodbye!" the sister calls out the window. "Good luck!" her brother adds. Both wave. "We'll miss you."

※

When I return to the Chinese hotel that evening, after the bus ride into the countryside and the three-kilometer hike down a dirt road, after my tour of the nun center and my afternoon spent talking with the head nun, after catching a ride back to Ratchaburi with some local farmers, I find the businessman from the train waiting in the lobby.

He looks forlorn yet dapper in fresh linen and glossy leather sandals.

"I overslept again," he wails, standing at my approach. "It took me forever to get home last night—the samloh driver didn't wait outside—so I was completely exhausted." He blushes and hangs his head. "I got here at one."

I make a flowery apology for not waiting and explain that everything worked out. Ten kilometers outside of town, the long-distance bus had stopped alongside a lonely stretch of rice paddies, hectares and hectares of emerald and gold fields broken only by the occasional, morose-looking water buffalo. The afternoon sun beat down, hotter than I was used to in the north.

"Here?" I'd asked the driver. "This is the nun center?"

He'd shrugged, eyes camouflaged behind the sunglasses gripping his face, and pointed to a dirt path bisecting the road. "There are nuns down there," he'd said. "I hear."

Fair enough. I'd thanked him. *"Khob khun kha."*

The bus had lumbered away, and I'd started down the path, trying not to think about how I'd get back to town. After all, I'd made it the entire length of Southeast Asia with no plan.

After reporting on the success of my visit to the nun center, I collect my bag from the old Chinese watchman, who startles me by flashing a row of betel-stained teeth, and ask the businessman to do me the great favor of seeing me to the train.

Perking up a bit, he ushers me to a sparkling cream Mercedes. As he holds open the door, he shakes his head. "You're a woman alone," he marvels, "a poor student, a farang." He pauses, as if pondering this triple source of my supposed isolation, before concluding, "but you don't need any help."

And though it isn't quite true, I smile modestly, once again accepting the compliment, momentarily relishing what it is to be Malay.

Prufrock in Paradise

by E. J. Levy

*D*estino

The word for destiny and destination are one and the same in Portuguese: destino. So one might say that I arrived at my destino on the fourth of January, halfway through my junior year at Yale, when I landed in Salvador, Bahia, Brazil, to spend a year studying the environmental consequences of economic development projects in the Brazilian Amazon.

As a sophomore, I'd applied for and been awarded a generous fellowship by Rotary Foundation International, which offered grants to students, scholars and journalists to fund international research. I had been lucky to get the money and I knew it. I wanted to make good use of my time. In my application, I'd proposed to work at the National Institute for Amazonian Research in Manaus, Amazonas, one of the premier institutions for the study of tropical moist forests. I wanted to be a part of the team of researchers whose work and names I had come to know from reading journals. I wanted to be among the biologists and zoologists who seemed to me heroic in their efforts to halt the devastation of the vast tracts of forest and rivers and communities known as the Amazon. I was eager to save part of the disappearing world.

But something had gone wrong. The fellowship office's command of geography was sadly lacking, and someone in the Foundation's headquarters in Chicago had succeeded in sending me to Salvador, Bahia, a coastal tourist capital some 3,400 miles southeast of the Amazon I had come to study. I'd booked a hotel in Salvador and figured I'd spend maybe a week there, maybe less, to get my bearings, practice my Portuguese and obtain my money from the Rotarians, before heading northwest to the Amazon.

My second morning in Salvador, I wake fortified by a good night's sleep, with the courage to go down to breakfast. Like Eliot's ambivalent hero transposed to the Tropics, I dare to eat a mango. But first I will have to get out of bed.

The day begins well. I rise a little after seven and pull open the curtains, letting in a watery white light. At this hour, the air outside in the street is still cool. The sun is a soft angled glow, not the hard brightness it will gain as it rises in the sky toward noon. Above the buildings that face my hotel, the sky is robin's-egg blue, delicate, almost friendly.

I shower quickly and dress in khaki midthigh-length shorts and a gauzy shirt of rainbow patchwork fabric. I put on my tennis shoes and cinch around my hips a money belt, in which I tuck my passport, my driver's license and $150 cash (the remainder of my money, $250 in cash and traveler's checks, I stow at the very bottom of my suitcase). I plan to carry this pouch of cash and documents with me whenever I go out, in case someone should break into my room. I carry my camera too, just to be safe.

Mine is not a private paranoia. The travel guides I have skimmed warn of the danger of theft, and just before I flew down here there was a much-publicized murder in Rio in which a German tourist was killed when he was found to have no money to give the thieves who held him up at gunpoint. They were children, if I recall. In their fury, they had shot the man out of spite.

I take the stairs down to the lobby, where the café is separated from the main lobby by folding screens. There are eight or ten small tables there, covered in white linen. Only one is occupied, by a couple speaking a language I cannot make out. Breakfast comes with my room, and I'm glad to take advantage of it, but I am embarrassed to eat alone. I stand at the entrance a little uncertainly until a waiter comes over and extends his arm toward the room in a gesture that suggests I can choose my place. I take a table by the window, far from the entrance and the lobby.

As I take my seat, the waiter gives my chair a little shove toward the table, which, though meant to be a courtesy, feels like what it is—a shove from behind.

Quer café? he asks, when I am seated.

I nod, pleased to understand the offer of coffee.

Por favor, I say. Please.

Americano ou com leite? he asks.

I am not sure what he means by *americano,* so I opt for *com leite* (with milk) to be able to answer.

Tem também escolha de suco, he says. *Suco de laranja, abacaxi, manga, maracujá e de tomate. O que quer?*

I am stumped by his flurry of words. Escolha sounds like school, laranja is orange. I cannot make out the rest.

Repete, por favor, I say, embarrassed to have to ask him to repeat himself.

Pois não, he says. Of course. *Temos sucos . . .* He speaks slowly and loudly and I feel ashamed to be subject to this speech, but I listen, watching his lips as if that will help me comprehend the list: laranja, abacaxi, maracujá, manga, goiaba, tomate. I am pretty sure the first word is orange, the last tomato. I hazard a guess, like a game show contestant.

Quero laranja, I say.

Suco de laranja, 'ta certa?

Suco de laranja. I nod, unsure what I am agreeing to. The waiter, apparently satisfied, turns and leaves me there.

I think I have secured coffee with milk and orange juice and I wait, braced to weather egg options, when, to my relief, the waiter returns with a lovely cup of milky coffee, fresh-squeezed orange juice, a basket of warm fragrant rolls and a plate of sliced fruit—pineapple, mango, bananas, slices of pale green melon.

Obrigada, I say, thanking him.

Número de quarto? he asks.

I look at him, confused. Clearly this is not an egg option. *Número* is number. *Quarto,* room. But why would the guy want my room number? Who does he think I am?

Número, he repeats, loudly, as if I were deaf. The people at the other table look over as if I were causing a commotion. He points to the ceiling, poking at it. *Quarto,* he says, louder still. *Pra pagar,* he is shouting now. He pulls out the check, shows me the place on it where he must write the room number.

Preciso. Número. De. Quarto, he says again, slowly, loudly.

I nod. I know now what he is asking, but I do not know how to say it in Portuguese, or rather, I do, but I have temporarily forgotten how to count. Me, the student of economics. Me, the girl in love with numbers.

Entendo, I manage. *Mais, não sei como dizer.* I point to the pen in his pocket. *Por favor.* I can't remember the word for pen.

He hands it to me. I write on my napkin, 217. My room number.

'Brigado, he says, sighing, with an almost imperceptible wag of his head. And then he goes to gather the dishes from the table of the other guests, who have left their chairs and me alone here.

I open my cloth napkin and lay it across my lap, conscious of each move I make and how it might look to others were they to observe me. Alone, I feel observed even if I am not, even though there is no one here to observe me but me.

I try to focus on the things before me: the shiny, heavy stainless steel cutlery, the white tablecloth, the thick plain china, the pads of iced butter set out on a plate, the basket of rolls. I reach across the table, careful not to drag my sleeve in my coffee or fruit plate. I clasp a small hard roll. I put it on my bread plate, stab a pad of butter with my fork and scrape that onto my plate too. I crack the shell of the crusty roll as if it were an enormous yellow egg. I set half of the roll on the plate; half, I hold in my left hand. I lift my butter knife, cut half a pat of butter, lather it on the soft white interior of the roll in my hand. I proceed slowly, carefully, unhurried, as if I were conducting a public service demonstration on how to butter a roll.

I don't want to appear needy, too hungry, desperate or nuts.

I chew slowly, conscious of each clench of my jaw, each swallow, each tumbling crumb. I eat, conscious of the waiter in the corner loitering by the coffee pot. I eat, self-conscious to the point of anguish. Each bite, a drag. I cut a tiny square of fruit with the side of my fork, fearful of cutting inexpertly and sending a slice of mango or melon onto the floor. I cut and chew, cut and chew, cut and chew, cut and chew.

After two rolls and a glass of juice, a cup of coffee and maybe thirteen bites of fruit, I am exhausted. I am relieved to push back my chair and leave. I consider pocketing a few rolls to eat in private, but I'm afraid that the waiter, who has temporarily abandoned his post by the coffee pot, will catch me and think I'm a pig.

Praia do Sol
When I get back to my room, I put on my bathing suit, over which I pull a T-shirt and khaki shorts. My skin prickles with the unfamiliar feel of skin against air.

Today, I will be brave; I will go to the beach.

As a rule, I do not like beaches. Or rather, I like to walk along them but I have never gotten the hang of sunbathing, which seems to me at twenty-one an inordinately dull form of recreation (recreation itself being a category I find inordinately dull). Sunbathing—like sex (it seems to me at twenty-one)—is hot, sweaty and boring, an uncomfortable stint on one's back, a waste of precious time which might better be spent in more fruitful pursuits, but I reason that in no time at all I will be in the Amazon, where there will be no coastal beaches, some 1,000 miles inland from the Atlantic coast; I should take advantage of this opportunity.

Taking advantage of one's opportunities is a watchword of my clan and the American middle class from which I come. It is among the principal tenets of our secular faith, along with the edifying aspects of painful experience. We believe in making the most of what we're given; we believe in learning from our mistakes (this last at odds with the tenet that says we shouldn't make any: Education, solid reading and forethought should obviate these).

I lace my feet into tennis shoes and cinch my money belt once more onto my waist. Then it occurs to me that perhaps I shouldn't take all my money with me. For a moment I debate the options: If I hide my money in my suitcase, it could be stolen while I'm out. If I carry it with me, I could be held up and lose it all.

I decide to outwit my prospective assailants by settling on a compromise. I will carry a beach bag, stuffed with a towel and suntan oil and a plastic bag with a comb, my passport, my student ID (in case I should need two forms of ID to cash, say, a traveler's check) and my room key—nothing of interest to thieves. In the front pocket of my money belt, I'll place only enough *cruzeiros* to pay bus fare and pay off any muggers. The rest of my cash and traveler's checks I'll hide in the sole of my tennis shoe. Should I be mugged, I can hand over my cruzeiros without anyone suspecting that I'm carrying $400 in my shoe. I leave my camera hidden among my socks in a drawer.

And I'm ready for my day at the beach.

At the hotel front desk, I lean my elbows on the black marble counter and ask where the nearest beach is. The clerk tells me that Barra has a nice beach and is nearby, just a few miles from here, down Avenida Sete de Setembro.

I remember the name as one my driver mentioned as he drove me here.

I ask if I can catch a bus to Barra, though I say this wrong—using the verb *tomar* instead of *pegar*—and it comes out sounding as if I'm asking if I can drink or seize the bus. I try again, more simply.

The bus goes there? I ask.

He nods. *Vai,* he says, his voice gaining volume, like the waiter's. *Mais tem pegar no outro lado.*

He comes out from behind his desk and walks to the doors; he points across the street where a small crowd is gathered.

Lá, he says. There. *Pôde pegar o ônibus lá.* You can get the bus over there.

I thank him and push out through the doors and cross the street.

At the stop, I ask a woman next to me whether I can catch the bus to Barra here, just to make sure I'm in the right place and because I know now how to ask: *Posso pegar o ônibus pra Barra aqui?*

The woman is short, the crown of her head on level with my small breasts. When she looks up at me, I see she has tiny eyes.

Pôde, she says. The word, in her mouth, sounds jointed, two-syllabled: it sounds like pawgee, drawn out, like a hen squawking. I wonder whether she is from the interior, one of the numerous poor who come from the countryside—the vast *sertão*—to the coastal cities to find work but often don't. She has the slightly vacant expression of people who have spent a long time looking out across empty spaces, as if it were hard to focus the eyes on nearby things.

The skin of her face is lined and tanned. Her dark hair is pulled back in a loose bun, threaded with gray. Perhaps thirty-five, she looks already old. Her face has the softness of age, like apple flesh. A basket hangs from her arm, and she wears a thin cotton dress printed with blue flowers, gray from wear. The shelf of her bosom sags over her sash to meet the soft shelf of her belly.

Obrigada, I say.

Nada, she returns, and squints once more into the street.

As the bus pulls up, streaming a plume of black diesel smoke, the matron sets her palm on my forearm.

Isto, she says, looking up into my face. *Isto vai pra Barra, entendeu?* Understand? she asks, and I do: This bus goes to Barra.

The others at the stop form an orderly line when the bus pulls up, and unhurriedly we board at the back. At the turnstile, the cashier asks me for my fare, but I don't know how much it is, unaccustomed as yet to the unfamiliar currency.

Me deixa, the matron says, Allow me. She opens my palm and picks among the change and then we push into the crush of bodies already crowding the seats and aisle. I clasp the metal handrail overhead and hang on. A man stands to offer the woman his seat.

I feel almost heroic as we ride along the wide avenue. Each small exchange, a victory: discovering which bus runs to Barra (only later will I learn that all buses bound west from here go through Barra), getting on, fishing out coins for fare, riding.

Over the heads of the other passengers, I can see out the windows. I watch the buildings go past, the low stucco structures and the unpromising cement; grim young girls in uniforms file out to play ball or study behind the bars that enclose the cobblestone courtyard of an ornate white stucco building that bears the words *escola* and *convento;* palm trees, the flat blue sky.

And then we drop down a hill, winding through a narrowed street. An elegant new high-rise apartment building fills the view on the left; an old three-story cement building, worn out and lined with cracks, is visible on the right. The driver has to honk, taking each turn, to clear the road in case someone should happen to be coming from the other direction, and I hold on, trying to keep my balance, swinging lightly into the passengers beside me, falling against them with a dull doughy weight.

And then the view breaks to the right and there is open water, the whole lovely lapis lazuli of the Atlantic, and I think, it will all work out all right. I will get to the Amazon, I will do something that counts here, help save that fragile forest. There is this, after all, this ocean and beauty, and, call it what you will, it is the same thing I love at home—the blue magnificent Atlantic, glistening with sunlight. And out there an island. *Ilha,* I say the word in my head. Ilha de Itaparica.

The bus shudders and smokes down the curving avenue past a long white cement balustrade with vase-shaped posts. To the left, the land rises steeply into hilly neighborhoods; to the right, it falls away sharply to the sea. I can see waves breaking on black rocks. Below is a club, boats moored at a dock and a glistening aqua pool. There is a smell of salt and the sea and diesel.

Abruptly, the bus swings toward the curb, then stops to let people off across from what I can see—by the street sign posted on the other side of the avenue—is Avenida John F. Kennedy.

The matron taps me on the arm, urgently. *Próximo,* she says. *Barra é o próximo.*

Aqui? I say. There is no beach in sight, but I grab my bag, ready to get off.

Aqui não, the matron grabs my wrist and shakes her head vigorously. *O próximo.*

I stay on the bus, uncertain and afraid of missing my stop.

The bus rumbles on down the hill, swaying around each turn, until we take the last S-curve—past a *farmácia* on the right, a few shops on the left—and make a final sharp turn to the right around a small mosaic *praça* of black and white marble, a near 180-degree turn that sends those of us in the aisle gently arcing.

The matron seated in front of me places her hand on my forearm and says, loudly, *Aqui aw. Barra é aqui.*

I nod and thank her and then push anxiously to the front of the bus, trying not to get trapped inside with the others.

When I step down into the street, the smells change. To the scent of diesel is added coconut suntan oil, fish, salt, shit and the seductive scent of boiling palm oil, which is really the smell of onions left to boil in the clear flame-orange *dendê*, a staple of Bahian cuisine.

As the bus pulls away, I stand on the sidewalk facing the street, the beach at my back, surveying for a moment this place. There is a laundry, with a window at which one can deliver clothing to have it washed; there is a farmácia, and a juice and snack bar, with small round metal tables and chairs overlooking the street and ocean.

In front of the *lavanderia*, a large corrugated refrigerator box lies flattened on its side, a pair of bare human feet sticking out. Directly across from me, an old woman sits beside a boiling pot of oil in which little pale fleshy balls, like matzo, float and hiss. Her face is the color of bittersweet chocolate, gaunt and shiny with sweat, her body hidden under layers of white lace, her head wrapped in a white turban. She calls out in a nasal singsong, *acarajé, vatapá,* hawking her wares.

To my left is the praça. There, young kids with Rasta hair sit on blankets on which they've spread jewelry made of bent wire, beads and shells. A small wooden hut houses a magazine vendor, his offerings clipped by clothespins to a strand of wire alongside bunches of red bananas. A clothesline strung with tie-dyed shirts and cotton dresses sways in the breeze.

On either side of me, people loiter, watching the street, watching the waves, leaning on the balustrade above the beach that runs the length of the promenade for three miles in either direction. I lean my elbows on the railing, and for a moment I am happy here.

But the beach is a disappointment, small and semicircular and smelly, enclosed on the right by rocks, on the left by a fort. There are skiffs beached at one end; bodies are everywhere. The waves slop in, like bath water. There are no palm trees. It is less a beach than an enormous ashtray.

Nevertheless, when I see stairs leading down to the sand to my right, I take them. Bottle tops and cigarette butts litter the beach, but these grow fewer as I walk closer to the water. I choose a place halfway down, modestly distant from others. I flap my towel out and take a seat, slide off my clothes and fold them on top of my shoes to form a pillow. I rub suntan oil on my arms and where I can reach on my back.

Vendors of fruit and *sucos,* no more than kids, scuff through the sand carrying styrofoam coolers of sodas on ice, the coolers larger than the children and borne on straps around their slender necks. I lie back, and close my eyes.

When I feel someone near me I look up and find some women laying out towels a few feet away. A few minutes later, I open my eyes and see a man—in shorts, sandals, three-day stubble and a ratty shirt—seated on his heels two feet from my head. I worry that he is some sort of creep, but the others ignore him so I ignore him, too.

When I feel sand flicked at me a few moments later, I turn and see the man digging what seems to be a reverse sand castle, a sand pit. He looks uninterested in me, and so after a moment I close my eyes. Either because he stops digging or because I am inured, I stop noticing the sand and doze.

After maybe an hour, I wake with the tender raw puffiness that signals a burn. I sit up and press a thumb into the flesh of my thigh and watch the skin go white. A bad sign. When I reach for the plastic bag, I find it is gone. I pat the sand; I stand and look around.

Você falta alguma coisa? One of the women seated behind me asks if I've lost something.

Minha bolsa, I say. My purse. I left it here.

The woman stands up to help me look, but the woman next to her says, *Já foi embora.* It's already gone. She has large Jackie O sunglasses and thick curling chestnut hair.

She tells me that she saw the whole thing happen. She saw the man with the three-day stubble slowly bury my beach bag under sand until he could slip his hand inside and remove the contents without notice.

I want to ask the woman in the sunglasses why the hell she didn't wake me, but her friend beats me to it.

Why didn't you do something? she asks the other.

He could've had a knife, Jackie O responds. Who knows what he might've done?

She's right. Money is not worth dying for. Still it's rough to lose my key, to be locked out of the only place that's mine.

The first woman tells me that I must go immediately to *o centro*. Have you been to the lower city, the city center?

I shake my head no.

Well, you must go there, she says, immediately. You must go to the police station and file a report. You can take a taxi.

She rests a hand on my back. Do you have money? Do you need some? She offers me cab fare, but I remember that I have my money in my shoe.

Thanks, I say. I tell them that he got my key, passport and ID, but no money.

He can sell the passport, the kind woman says. You'll have to report it.

I sit on the sand, the beach blurry now through my tears, the two women crouched beside me. My mouth tastes salty with snot.

He could be dangerous, Jackie O observes. If he has your hotel key, he could come back for more. He knows where you're staying, who you are.

I do not want to have to hail a cab and spend money I cannot afford in order to tell a cop in broken Portuguese that my passport is gone. I am tired, I am hot, I am exhausted, I am scared.

You have to go to the police, they say.

So, tired, hot, exhausted, scared, I thank them, and I do.

The Clerk

The clerk at the front desk of the Praia do Sol is pissed.

How could my key be stolen at the beach? Didn't I know that I was to return my key to the desk before leaving?

I hadn't known that, I say.

I wonder, should I have? What One Should Know is a source of great anxiety for me, a source of acute pain and confusion. I often feel that I do not know what others seem to: how to pick a hotel, how to eat alone, how to enjoy a day at the beach, what to do in a foreign country on a $22,000 fellowship until the Rotarians hand over the money they promised to give you before you agreed to come to this place, which is 3427 miles southeast of the place you want to be.

You will have to change rooms, the clerk says, frowning. The thief may come back, he says. He explains that the key tag bears not just the hotel name but my room number as well. He sighs, tells me they'll have to have the lock changed.

I have caused them trouble. He lets me know it.

The Cop

The police station in Salvador is small and white and stucco, a single-story building in a forgotten section of the lower city, and the cop I speak to does not seem optimistic about the chances of recovering my passport. Like the hotel clerk, he is incredulous that I would bring my passport and key to the beach.

Why did you have them with you? he asks.

I was trying to protect them, I say.

He laughs.

I do not tell him that I thought I was supposed to carry identification on me at all times, that I had read this somewhere.

He tells me that is nuts.

Leave those things in your hotel safe, he says. Carry only a little money on you, in case you are robbed.

He tells me to go to the American embassy and get a new passport, gives me the address, wishes me luck.

I tell him I need it.

The Ambassador

The American embassy, unlike the police station, is located in a posh part of town. West of the city center, it is nestled among the houses of the rich on a wide, quiet, well-maintained street in an affluent residential neighborhood, one of several white stucco homes with iron gates enclosing private gardens.

I stand on the sidewalk in front of the embassy and speak to a clerk through an intercom before the clerk agrees to let me in. A buzzer sounds; the lock on the gate releases; I push my way in.

Inside the cubicle-sized lobby (red carpet, white walls, blue chairs), I explain to the clerk through a tiny bulletproof window that I have lost my passport and need to get a new one today.

She explains that I cannot get a passport today, it will take weeks. I can fill out an application here but they will have to send it on to Dallas. But first, she says, you must bring the following items.

She pushes a Xeroxed sheet of paper toward me through a hole at the bottom of the bulletproof window. On it is a checklist of items required for a passport application: two recent black and white photos, a valid ID, $45 cash or traveler's checks or cashier's check.

But you cannot apply today, she says. She looks at the clock above me. You're too late. We accept passport applications only until two o'clock each day. You'll have to come back tomorrow.

I ask if I might simply fill out the paperwork while I am here today, to expedite the process, and since I have come a long way.

She asks if I have brought my photos.

What photos, I ask.

The photos you need for your passport application, she says. You cannot get a passport without photos or proper identification.

But my identification was stolen, I tell her. That's the problem. That's why I am here. I was robbed.

You need identification, she tells me, in order for us to issue a passport. Or how do we know you are who you say you are?

But my identification was stolen, I say. With my passport.

And you need two photos, she says, as if closing the subject. Two, two by three inches.

I have no photos of myself and no idea where to get them. I have had a hell of a time simply getting here. I am near tears when I ask to speak to someone else, someone in the embassy itself. The clerk says that everyone is gone for lunch; they won't be back for a while.

You might as well come back tomorrow, she says.

May I wait, I ask.

You can do what you want, she says.

I take a seat in a blue chair, and stare at the limp flag in the corner, the smiling face of an aging B-movie actor framed on the wall, a U.S. president. I am still in the chair twenty minutes later when a woman—short-haired, with a square blocky face and the build of a sumo wrestler—comes through the front door with a paper bag.

Do you work here, Madame? I say, in Portuguese.

She looks at me.

Yes, she says, in English. May I help you?

I need a passport; mine has been stolen. Please, can you let me fill out the forms?

I told her she is too late, the clerk says.

I'm afraid that's not my area, the woman says.

Please, I say. I must look desperate, near tears. I am.

One moment, she says. I'll see what I can do.

She disappears behind a heavy fireproof door, beyond which I glimpse stairs going up.

I wait. After a few minutes, the phone rings and then the clerk says, You may go up now.

I ascend the staircase and find among the empty offices plump Gertrude Stein, seated in a leather chair behind an impressive mahogany desk, eating her lunch from a bag. The walls of her office are covered with photos of dance troupes and framed posters of traveling exhibitions, the tasteful, neutral decor of a doctor's office. I take the seat she offers.

Gertrude Stein, it turns out, is in charge of USIA in Salvador, the branch of the Foreign Service responsible for cultural and artistic exchanges. She asks me what she can do for me and I tell her.

Midway through my story, because she is being nice and because her office is comfortable and because the chair I am in smells expensive and of leather, I cry.

She asks if I speak Portuguese and when I say I understand better than I speak it, she speaks in a Portuguese slow and simple enough that I can understand and converse. She assures me that it will be no problem to get a new passport, though it will take time. She gets me the forms I need and tells me where I can get photos and suggests I come tomorrow with these and it will be done right away, she'll see to it.

Then she leans back and asks me what I am doing here.

I tell her I'm down from Yale and on my way to the Amazon, to study the ecological consequences of development projects.

She tells me there is another student here from Yale, and asks if I know her, a Fulbright scholar. She gives a name I do not recognize.

I tell her that I don't know her.

She leans across the desk and tells me that she likes me better. The other girl is very stuck up, she says. She doesn't talk. She is very arrogant. But you, she says, talk. You don't know the language very well, but you try.

I am grateful that someone sees my failings as a strong suit. She writes down a name and number on a small square sheet of paper and pushes it across the desk.

You should call her, she says.

I smile and thank her. I tell her I will call, knowing that I won't.

Outside the embassy, the heat of the day has cooled and there's a breeze that smells of salt water and tar, and because the sky is blue and beautiful and the palm fronds overhead are clattering like beaks striking, an obscurely exciting sound, a reminder that I am far from home, in the Tropics, and because I have nothing better to do and have time on my hands and no one waiting for me back at the hotel or anywhere really, I decide to walk to Barra, which I figure is a few miles from the embassy, a clear shot along the winding cobblestone promenade. Truth is, I am afraid of getting on a bus, afraid it will take me somewhere I do not want to go. That I'll get lost. A five-mile walk seems easier than asking directions in a foreign language.

It is a beautiful afternoon and the walk, I tell myself, will do me good.

By the time I get to Barra, almost two hours later, the sun is setting and my calves are cramping and I am lightheaded with hunger. I have not eaten since breakfast. I think about stopping in the café I saw earlier, but I'd have to sit alone at a table; I think about buying a candy bar from a magazine vendor in the port, but I am sick of candy, craving food more substantial than that; then I see the old Bahiana dressed in lace and seated by her pot of boiling oil and decide on that.

I cross the street and ask the woman in the turban how much. I don't ask her what it is because I wouldn't understand the answer and I don't really need to know. The smell is intoxicating. The scent of onion and salt and cashews and cilantro and palm oil fills my nostrils and my mouth waters. She names her price and I pay it.

I watch her scoop a hot bean ball from the pot, its surface crisp and orange from frying. She holds it in a wax paper napkin. She asks me if I like it spicy, and I say yes and watch her slit the bean ball's belly with a knife and spread on red palm oil laced with red pepper seeds. Over this, she spreads a thick layer of cashew paste flecked with shrimp and spices, over which she sprinkles dried shrimp, their pink heads and eyes still attached, observing me, as I receive the acarajé she hands up.

This is my first taste of acarajé and vatapá, which I will later learn to make at a cooking school in the old section of town, foods that bear the traces still of their West African origins, as so much of Bahian culture does. Acarajé is a fried bean ball made of black-eyed-pea paste ground with garlic and spices then fried in palm oil, a staple of the cuisine for which Bahia is famous. Vatapá is the thick salty cashew paste blended of garlic, onions, dried shrimp, tomato, coriander and palm oil. Both are supremely good. Eating them, with the horizon going pink, I am happy, even hopeful, as I wait to catch the bus to my hotel.

Dog Master

by Ayun Halliday

Ubud, Bali, is renowned almost as much for its foul-tempered home-less dogs as it is for those cute wooden carvings of frogs and monkeys and striped cats holding fishing poles. The crafts attract droves of Western tourists to Ubud's many guesthouses and luxury hideaways. The dogs are the wild force keeping the tourists' needs and desires from overrunning the place entirely.

Many Western tourists have a take-charge attitude toward the bald-ing, growling curs that slink around the edges of Ubud's central market. It's clear that the dogs belong to no one, but you'll be hard-pressed to find one with Benji's hobo charm. Since they're not pets, argue the tourists, they should be rounded up and euthanized en masse, before they become more of a public health hazard than they already are. "It's kinder than letting them suffer any more in these miserable conditions," the tourists add, guiltily thinking of beloved, healthy Rover back home, picking at his pricey Eukanuba kibble in a kennel whose rates rival those of a first-class Balinese guesthouse.

The citizens of Ubud are in no rush to do away with the dog population.

Instead, they teach the tourists their trick of pretending to hurl a rock at a threatening dog. The dogs usually fall for it. It's not that different from that old standby "Who's Got the Ball? Who's Got the Ball? Where did the ball go, boy?" The guesthouse owners and the guys who make their living selling wooden frog sculptures cluck their tongues in sympathy when a tourist comes to them with a dog story. They know that the dogs are potentially bad for business. I, on the other hand, would argue that the dogs are potentially good for business. Ubud, once a sleepy inland town surrounded by rice paddies, has become so heavily touristed that it feels only slightly more "authentic" than Kuta Beach, that sexy, surfin' destination most visitors to Bali hit first, to work on their tans. You can get M&Ms and Diet Coke in Ubud. You can receive faxes and check email and arrange for your cratefuls of flying frogs to be Fed Exed anywhere in the world. Abbreviated performances of traditional dances are staged nightly. They're beautiful, but the experience is not much different than taking in a live show at Disneyland and the number of camera-flashes-per-minute is enough to convince you that you're at an 'N Sync concert. Sure, Mick Jagger and Jerri Hall got married in Ubud, but as a tourist destination, it's lost its edge. Now that Western-style toilets are widely available, there's nothing to stop your grandmother from loving the place.

Except for the dogs. The dogs, feral and threatening, are like nothing you'd run into back home.

Balinese women spend a part of every morning placing beautifully constructed offerings of fruit, flowers and incense to the gods in various locations around their homes and businesses. Bali's indigenous religion is a unique spin on Hinduism, with numerous deities, demons and characters who seem to exist purely for comic relief. As boggling as the pantheon is to most Western visitors, it's a cinch to even the smallest Balinese child because everyone on the island shares the same faith. Temples are everywhere, festivals are frequent and ritual observance is embedded in the fabric of daily life. I remember how long it took me to weave a single one of those palm frond crosses we wore pinned to the front of our blouses on the Palm Sundays of my childhood. In the time it takes a Dutch tourist to roll a cigarette, a Balinese woman and her kids can knock out a half-dozen delicate palm baskets to contain their offerings to the gods. The demons get presents too, nothing fancy, just a few spoonfuls of cooked rice on scraps of banana leaf left on the ground. The dogs are always ready to pounce on the offerings intended for the demons. As reported in that most venerable of guidebooks, Lonely Planet's *South-East Asia on a Shoestring,* this is just another part of Balinese theology. The dogs, being minions of the demons, are welcome, and indeed expected, to gobble the rice from the ground. No problem. This is the sort of easy-to-comprehend detail that tourists love to repeat to their less well-traveled friends, and since every Westerner in Ubud is packing a copy of *Lonely Planet,* it's not uncommon to overhear someone who's been there a week explaining the dog-demon relationship to someone who's only just arrived.

A tourist doesn't have to wander too far afield to score her own personal Ubud dog story. The miserable beasts are omnipresent and will obligingly raise their hackles and growl at anyone who smells like sunscreen. If the tourist has yet to be briefed on the imaginary-rock-throwing ruse, a local is sure to hear the barking and come to the rescue before the dog can attack. A story about a tense standoff with a mangy, potentially rabid mongrel is a good story. A story about the fourteen shots you had to get in the stomach after the sucker bit you is not—which is why there are many "If the monkey grab your camera let him have your camera" signs in Ubud's fabled Monkey Forest. The monkeys are pretty irresistible, particularly the baby ones who sit in your lap and have yet to grow the huge yellowed fangs of their parents. There's a reason there is no Dog Forest in Ubud.

The peanut vendors of Ubud congregate near the tourist entrance to the Monkey Forest. Accordingly, the monkeys also congregate near the entrance. The tourists congregate near the monkeys and if monkeys are what you've come to see there's little reason to plunge deeper into the forest. On the other hand, there's little reason not to plunge deeper into the forest. Few tourists have anything more pressing than another banana shake and several thousand flying frogs requiring their immediate return to town. One afternoon I wandered to the back of the Monkey Forest and out into the rice paddies. At a crossroads, I met a local man who was on his way to Ubud with a couple of baskets of souvenirs slung milkmaid-style on a pole across his shoulders. He told me that if I walked another mile or so I would come to a small village where a wedding was about to take place.

Now, every visitor to Bali, well, maybe not the Australian college students whooping it up on spring break, but every other visitor to Bali wants to stumble onto a funeral. An enormous funeral pyre shaped like a bull that cost the bereaved an entire year's wages? Now that's something to tell the folks back home! Don't forget your camera! If you can't score a funeral, a wedding's a not-too-shabby second. I sped off, thrilled at the possibility of an authentic experience. I came to a gorge spanned by a fallen tree. The locals were zipping across it in rubber flip-flops, balancing bundles on their heads, their arms swinging at their sides. I froze, overcome by memories of third-grade gym period humiliations involving the balance beam. Finally, a local guy offered me his hand and crossed the log backwards, cooing encouragingly as I inched along behind him. There was no charge for this service, though he no doubt went his way pleased that he had a good story to regale his family with at dinner, how he helped a doughy, whimpering tourist across the bridge.

There was nothing shaking in the alleged wedding village, a few dogs skulking around the perimeter, some young men drinking Cokes. There were a couple of other Western tourists acting on the same hot tip. I waited around on what I hoped were the sidelines for an hour or so, trying to exude a sort of Peace Corpsy nonchalance, lest I be mistaken for a mere tourist. Eventually I attracted a man eager to practice his English. After answering the by-now-familiar battery of questions concerning my age, hometown and marital status, I asked him about the wedding. He told me to come back around midnight, when things should be in full swing. "Yes, yes, wedding," he promised, and if I liked, a puppet show. Puppet show! All right! A wedding and a puppet show in a dusty settlement reachable only by fallen log: if that didn't constitute authenticity, nothing did. I couldn't be any more in the swim if I were a field reporter for *Lonely Planet*. I recrossed the rudimentary "bridge" on my hands and knees, flush with excitement, determined to rest up for the all-night party ahead of me.

Eight hours later, I entered the dark Monkey Forest with my flashlight and camera, dressed in a backpacker's facsimile of wedding finery. The forest was kind of creepy. The monkeys were off-duty, apparently sleeping off the daily peanut binge. I padded past the tumbledown temple and a small cemetery and then out into the rice fields where I walked on a narrow track, banked on either side with piled earth that must have been serving some irrigation purpose. A full moon rose high in the sky. Elsewhere in Southeast Asia, Western tourists were getting blind drunk on rice wine and shaking their shamefully clad booties at Full Moon parties staged on beaches that still resembled paradise. What would they take home with them? I was on my way to an authentic experience, I reassured myself, trying not to let the deathly quiet get the best of my imagination. The walk seemed longer than it had that afternoon. Suddenly, I heard a low rumbling coming from one of the dark banks. A one-eared silhouette rose into view like the Great Pumpkin arriving at last. It was a dog, his short fur bristling, his single ear a hard-won souvenir of past battle. He was growling, but they all growled. He would probably growl until I passed by his particular rice paddy, as a matter of dog principle. Pretending that I hadn't noticed him, I marched a little further along the path.

The dog trotted along the bank, growling louder. I hesitated. Should I try the old invisible rock trick? What if he could tell I was faking and lunged for my throat? That damn dog. Couldn't he see I was no ordinary tourist? I was there because I wanted to learn more about his culture! I wasn't the type to claim I'd been to Bali just because I'd seen some regularly scheduled dance performances and had a backpack stuffed with wooden frogs! I was after the authentic experience!

Suddenly the growling rang in both ears. I looked to the opposite bank. The first dog had summoned one of his confederates, a muscular piebald number with half a tail. When he growled his lips rode up over his gums. I thought about shouting for help, sheepishly wondering if the souvenir salesman I'd met earlier in the day would be the one to rescue me from two local dogs he knew to be no more dangerous than a couple of tough-talking second-grade boys. I was prepared to eat a big helping of humble pie at the gorge, where I'd have to waylay a local to lead me across the log in the dark. I didn't like the idea of playing the cowardly helpless American twice in one night. Neither did I like the idea of disease-carrying fangs ripping into my soft unprotected belly.

What I really didn't like was the idea of me, alone in the middle of nowhere, surrounded, as I now was, by half a dozen snarling, unloved dogs who didn't speak my language. I turned my head slowly, pleading silently with them not to hurt me. I remembered that time in Amsterdam when I was attacked by an angry prostitute who thought I'd taken her picture. I'd been surrounded then, too, not by dogs but by glassy-eyed men, titillated by the prospect of two women ripping each other to shreds.

One of the dogs bounded down the bank. I squeezed my eyes shut and gripped my flashlight, knowing that they would probably get the best of me even if I'd had a machine gun. I braced myself to be knocked down, but when I opened my eyes, the dog was standing about five feet in front of me, blocking the path. He barked and the others took up his cry. I had no idea what this meant. I knew what to do if my stepfather's well-trained Labrador retriever made the moves on a plate of toast and I knew that you were supposed to clap your hands if you met a bear in the woods, but I didn't know what to do about a gang of dogs who, from all appearances, were on the verge of Clockwork Orange-ing me. At any moment the horseshoe could close into a ring and that's when the fangs and fur would really start to fly.

I chose the bear-in-the-woods route, without the clapping. I backed up. Very slowly, I backed down the path, toward Ubud, away from the wedding and the authentic Balinese experience. The dogs stood their ground, growling, ready should I attempt a fast one. As if I'd back up only to plunge into their midst like some cocky invisible rock! The dogs receded in the distance, their warning sounds drowned out by a chorus of frogs, genuine amphibious ones. I kept walking backwards. The dogs had been very clear about that. When I got to the edge of the Monkey Forest, I turned around and hurried as quickly as I could without running to the entrance. Surely the monkeys would not bother to teach me the same lesson the dogs had hammered home with such eloquence.

While Balinese faith is a form of Hinduism, the lesson learned here is closer to the famous Zen koan that exhorts: "If you meet the Buddha on the road, kill him!"

If Dog meets Traveler on the road, he is inclined to mistake Traveler for Buddha. Dog's nature, demonic though it may be, is also very pure, very Zen. Dog will not hesitate to kill Buddha. Better for Traveler to back up slowly, thanking Doggy for sharing his wisdom. The only authentic experience is the one Traveler is experiencing. Weddings are not feathers for a cap, even if they involve crossing a fallen log by moonlight. Monkeys are not on call round-the-clock. Invisible rocks are only good weapons when nothing more than dignity is at stake. Traveler cannot return home with any stories if Traveler's throat has been ripped open on journey. The folks who fly home with backpacks full of flying frogs have been to Bali just as much as Traveler has. Perhaps Traveler should start leaving rice on the sidewalks of Brooklyn.

The Pleasures of the Unobserved Life

by Joan Chatfield-Taylor

It was the sixth column on the right side of the cathedral at Vezelay that made me realize there is more to solo travel than frissons of fear on dark streets, awkward moments in restaurants and the cursed single supplement.

I found myself in Burgundy, staying with friends whose days are filled with growing grapes and making wine. After breakfast, as my hostess set off to charm a covey of Dutch wine buyers, I stepped into my rented Renault and set off in search of Romanesque churches.

I am no expert on twelfth-century ecclesiastical architecture, but I have been deeply moved by the Romanesque churches and cathedrals that punctuate the landscape of provincial France. The solidity of ancient stones, the rays of dust-sparkled sunlight coming through the windows, the sound of my own footsteps in the echoing dimness and the smell of candle wax are all part of the experience. I love the vigorous carvings, especially the scenes of familiar Bible stories around the capitals of the columns. The rough-featured, individualistic faces suggest that the sculptor was inspired more by his local baker than by a distant saint, and the depictions of local plants and animals speak of the agricultural society of medieval France.

Burgundy is rich in Romanesque churches, and I had planned a day's tour that would encompass the great cathedrals of Autun and Vezelay. Part of the drill in visiting these churches is to examine each and every capital, identifying each sculpted scene with the help of a guidebook. I did this slowly and carefully at Autun, but at Vezelay, I stopped at the sixth capital on the right, shut my book, turned on my heel and went out into the breezy spring day.

If I had been traveling with someone, I would have had to explain what I was doing. If I had been with my learned brother, a hard-core sightseer who reads ten guidebooks beforehand and drives fifty miles out of his way to see an isolated chapel in a field, I would have felt guilty at abandoning the stone saints, and, worse, embarrassed at my lack of intellectual discipline. If I had been with my then-husband, whose stern French education skipped any mention of art history, I would have felt that I had to stay, dutifully inspecting every last capital, if only to show off how much more cultivated I was than he.

But I was alone on the cold paving stones in Vezelay, and I had reached that moment of visual overload that makes it pointless to keep trudging through churches or museums. I had had it with carvings for that day, and I could do exactly what I wanted.

Suddenly, I realized, I had the luxury of the unobserved life.

To some, this might sound like loneliness, or, at least, nothing worth seeking. To me, at an age when I was coming to regret how much of my life I had wasted worrying about what other people thought, it was a revelation. It wasn't simply being able to skip the boring parts without explaining myself. Traveling alone, as invisible as a ghost, was also a method of self-discovery. What, in fact, did I do when no one was watching? Was I really an art lover, or was I a serious shopper? A systematic sightseer, or a casual stroller? Shy and standoffish, or easy to talk to?

After that epiphany in Burgundy I went home to San Francisco and a life filled with schedules and responsibilities. Every day was a juggling act, as I dealt with work and teenage children and the wrenching sight of my vibrant mother struggling against the incoherence of Alzheimer's. I felt confined, partly because there weren't enough hours in the day to allow for purely personal activities. I also felt constricted because I had lived in San Francisco most of my life, and I was entwined in a web of friends and acquaintances and vaguely familiar faces, some from as far back as grade school.

I lived in a city, but it might as well have been a village. When I went into the market to pick up dinner, I was apt to run into one of my mother's former bridge partners or a fellow room mother at my son's school. I felt molded by relationships and by other people's eyes and expectations and assumptions. I conformed to myriad roles—wife, mother, fashion editor, daughter—until I began to wonder who I really was. And then the web began to loosen. My mother died, my children went away to college, I was divorced. The chance to try out a new life suddenly seemed possible, and I bought a one-way ticket to Paris.

When I rented out my apartment in San Francisco for six months, I committed myself to a situation in which I would be more alone than I had ever been. But as I rode into Paris on a rainy fall afternoon, peering out the bus window as the raindrops flattened autumn leaves on the sidewalks, I had another revelation. What, I thought, if I never did anything in Paris but lie around on the sofa and read trashy novels? Or sleep every day until two in the afternoon? Or hang around in a neighborhood café flirting with men and drinking *vin rouge* at eleven in the morning? See how many movies I could go to in a month? Ride around in circles on the Metro all day? Ridiculous notions, every one, but the point of my musings was: Who would know? For the first time in my life, I could be almost as crazy as I wanted, with the assurance that no one would be watching. Compared to my life at home, I would be living in a vacuum, free to turn myself in any direction, like an astronaut floating free outside the confines of the spaceship.

I didn't choose my neighborhood in Paris. It was thrust upon me by the kindness of my wine-making friends in Burgundy, so busy with their vineyards that they rarely have time to use their apartment in the ninth arrondissement. In that unpretentious neighborhood they had the vision to turn a former garment factory into a thoroughly modern living space, an airy white rectangle lit by a sixty-foot-long wall of metal-framed windows that once illuminated the work of dozens of seamstresses.

This spare and modern box, filled with books and paintings that expressed nothing of me, was the perfect setting to redefine myself. Moving in involved nothing more than unpacking a couple of suitcases, propping up a photograph of my children next to the bed and heading out to explore my new *quartier.*

The heart and soul of the neighborhood was the Rue des Martyrs, an authentic and unchanged market street that has so far avoided the encroachments of the ubiquitous chain stores that have erased the differences between neighborhoods elsewhere in Paris. Here the *petit commerçant,* the fiercely independent shopkeeper, thrives. In the space of a few hundred yards, nine fruit and vegetable stores, six bakeries and pastry shops, ten delicatessens, four cheese shops, two fish vendors, six butchers and two wine shops vied for my business—and that was just for food.

I spent weeks choosing which bakery had the best baguette and where to buy my salads. French shopkeepers are lords of their little domains, and, since self-service is still more the exception than the rule, they're the ones who get to pick out the reddest strawberries and the perfect cheese for you. Only when they know that you will be coming back do they go into the back of the store for the fresher bunch of tarragon.

One Sunday morning I walked into the Fromagerie Molard. Monsieur Molard, round and solid as a well-made Camembert, took his work seriously, to the point of grimness.

"I want three cheeses," I said. "First, a Pont l'Eveque." Monsieur came from behind his counter to the marble slab along the opposite wall, where cheeses were displayed in a way—some unwrapped, without a wall of glass between them and the customer—that would have horrified an American health inspector. Of course, everyone in Paris knows that only the proprietor is allowed to select and touch the merchandise. I murmured, "For tonight," as he began to press each golden Pont l'Eveque gently with his thumb. Then I said, "And I want a chèvre." He moved down the marble slab to the goat cheeses, round or pyramidal, oval or square, white as snow or gray with ash. He asked me whether I preferred my goat cheese young or old, and I opted for middle-aged.

Then I said, "And I want the third cheese to be something I've never tasted." For the first time, I saw a twinkle in his eye and a sliver of a smile. That day we settled on an unctuous blue cheese from the Loire. It was the beginning of a beautiful relationship. Every two weeks I allowed myself a cheese orgy, and I always chose two cheeses and let him pick the third. He took pleasure in introducing me to new things.

In the same spirit, I made a resolution about my stay in France: Whatever someone suggested, I would say yes. Whatever I was curious about, I would explore. Whatever new idea popped into my head, I would consider.

It wasn't long before I got to test my resolve.

"Would you like to go to the *hammam* with me next Saturday?" asked my young friend Susan.

"Of course," I answered blithely. I had read about hammams in the Middle East and knew that they were an exotic form of public bath, with scrubbing and massage as part of the package. I had seen the word on signs around Paris, usually on seedy-looking establishments tucked away in shadowy corners. I had never been tempted, and I certainly never would have crossed the threshold on my own. This time, however, I had a companion, and we were planning to go to the hammam that is part of Paris's largest mosque.

The following Saturday we took the Metro to the Place Monge, and walked a couple of blocks to the mosque, a walled complex of buildings built of white stucco and green tile in Hispanic-Moorish style, as exotic and unexpected a creature in gray-hued Paris as a peacock amidst a flock of wrens. The mosque is a center of Islamic culture, offering classes in Arabic, religious services and traditional businesses, including a restaurant, café, gift shop and the hammam. We found the sign for the hammam, opened the door and were transported into a scene from an Orientalist painting. Just beyond the high desk where a white-clad woman collected our three hundred francs was a large square room. The walls, painted in intricate stripes of color and pattern, rose to a windowed dome that cast beams of soft light on dozens of nude women reclining on cushions, drinking tea, chatting and having massages.

As lovely as the scene was, the sight of all those naked women suddenly reminded me of something I had apparently forgotten when I enthusiastically agreed to come along on this expedition. I am excessively modest. I've had my share of massages and beauty treatments, but they were all back in the puritanical United States, where private rooms, voluminous terry cloth robes and low lights eliminate the possibility of being seen unclothed.

At that point, however, there was no turning back. We paid our money and received locker keys, a couple of receipts and two paper cups of a mysterious brown slime.

"What are we supposed to do with this stuff?" Susan asked, sniffing cautiously at the mysterious jelly. The woman at the desk muttered something about "*le gommage*" but refused to elaborate further. We stripped off our clothes in the locker room, rented a couple of skimpy towels and headed into the labyrinth. In the next room we found communal showers and a woman armed with a rough-textured mitt, who waved us on to the steam room, a high-ceilinged space faced in pale gray marble. Skylights cast a soft illumination on a dozen or so women sitting in alcoves. I found a corner for myself, covered a bit of my skin with my sodden towel and let the steam open every pore as I watched the scene around me.

The hammam's customers were youngish Parisians, the kind of brisk women who sell airline tickets or work for public relations firms. Saturday morning at the baths was clearly a social event for many of them. Groups of two or three clustered together, chatting and scrubbing themselves or each other with loofahs and soaps they carried in plastic baskets. I kept an eye out for anyone using the mysterious brown slime, but no one seemed to have it. I considered asking, but it was intimidating to break into the intimacy of the conversations around me. Even stark naked, Parisians have a certain formality.

After an hour of steamy heat, we went back to the showers, still clutching our paper cups. I tried rubbing the slime on me while I was in the shower, but the stuff just slipped off in little globs, without apparent effect. The woman wielding the rough mitt didn't seem to care about it either. In long, sweeping strokes, she stripped off layers of dirt and skin, leaving us clean and polished.

Now it was our turn to lounge like houris in the gorgeous massage room. After half an hour of mint tea and gossip, the masseuses snatched our soggy receipts and pointed us towards tables. My masseuse was a small but solid middle-aged woman who spoke only Arabic and gave a no-nonsense massage enhanced by generous quantities of scented oil. The firm kneading, the soft light and the murmur of female voices were relaxing until I suddenly heard a male voice a couple of feet from my head. I opened my eyes to find a boy, about ten or eleven years old, discussing some small domestic crisis with another masseuse who was apparently his mother. As he talked, he gave a helping hand, clearing away tea glasses and trays and our abandoned cups of slime.

He seemed unruffled, but his presence jolted me back to reality. Almost three hours after our arrival, we got dressed and went to the adjacent restaurant to eat heaps of vegetable couscous. On the way home, in the familiar rubbery fumes of the Metro, the smell of frankincense lingered on my skin.

Not every day was so exotic, but the morning at the hammam gave me courage to try other unfamiliar experiences. My week began officially on Wednesday, because that is the day that *Pariscope,* the fat little weekly magazine that lists everything that's going on in Paris, appears on every newsstand in town. At lunchtime on Wednesday, whether I was at home eating soup and leftover Camembert or in whatever café I happened upon around one o'clock, I took a yellow marker and circled everything that interested me. For the first time in a lifetime of visiting Paris, I had time to do almost all of it.

There were the big art exhibitions at the Louvre and the Grand Palais, of course, but I also had time to indulge my interest in photography by wandering around galleries on the Left Bank and in the Marais. I went to classical concerts at the Châtelet and operas at the Bastille, but I also went to movies, including gritty Russian pastorals and Moroccan thrillers unlikely to come to America.

Being alone was rarely a problem. I've heard that Paris is a city where more than a third of the population lives alone, and I never felt self-conscious or unsafe, even late at night when I walked home from the movies along the raffish Boulevard du Faubourg Montmartre. La Coupole, the historic brasserie on the Boulevard du Montparnasse, is one of hundreds of restaurants where single people flock, armed with a book, to eat a proper three-course meal and drink a decent wine in unrushed solitude.

One dank February morning, a headline caught my eye. "Le Gout du Noir," it announced—the taste of black. A fashion show? A meal of caviar, truffles, squid ink and licorice? No, Le Gout du Noir is the name of a series of dinners held in complete darkness, designed to let sighted people know what it's like to be blind.

The idea struck a chord with me. All my life I have been curious about the experience of blindness. I knew several vision-impaired people in Paris, who impressed me with their effortless dexterity in handling course after course at dinner parties and restaurants. I called to reserve a place and was startled to discover that there were only three places left for the entire month. A few days later, I hurried through the brightly lit corridors of the Forum des Halles, a cavernous underground shopping center that replaced the picturesque wholesale food markets in the center of Paris. I walked into a space that is usually an art gallery. The windows were masked with paper, but the door was open and a line of people was forming. By eight o'clock, almost fifty people of all ages were drinking sangria in a dimly lit reception area.

A young man appeared from behind a heavy velvet curtain to explain the procedure.

"You will be divided into groups of eight. You will put your hand on the shoulder of the person in front of you, and each group will be led into the dining room. When you get to your table, you will find that the first course is already there. The main course will be brought to the table, but you will have to get up and serve yourself dessert from a buffet."

Our group, mostly young people who had come alone, was the last one to file behind the curtain. In seconds, we were in complete blackness. I was suddenly intensely aware of the smell of stew.

As I felt around for my fork and knife, a warm voice cut into our nervous chatter. Jean-Claude, the blind person in charge of our table, explained, "In front of you is wine, in a pitcher with a handle, and water, in a container without a handle. There is also bread in a basket."

We began to eat. I got off to a messy start, plunging my thumb directly in the sauce. I cut what I thought was a small piece and then discovered that I had a slab of fish mousse flapping on my fork. I poured wine cautiously, measuring my progress with a finger inside the glass. I was rather proud of myself for not spilling a drop until Jean-Claude commented that sticking your finger is not considered the best way to measure the wine.

"If you put your finger in the glass, it draws attention to the fact that you're blind," he said. "It's much more discreet to listen to the sound of the wine—*gloog, gloog, gloog*—as it goes into the glass."

As we proceeded, course by course, the French began to argue about exactly what we were eating. The conversation became livelier, and we asked Jean-Claude about his life. He described his work, assisted by a talking computer, his participation in a chorus and the challenge of using a subway system where the stations are not announced. He told us why he preferred not to have a guide dog—"everyone speaks to the dog and not the owner!"—and how he would rather be blind than deaf because "you're much more isolated if you're deaf."

Two hours later, we filed out of the room. In a few steps, we were walking into the light and saw Jean-Claude for the first time. Jocelyne, the young woman who sat to my right, looked at him with an astonished smile and said joyfully, "You are black, and so am I!" Finally, almost reluctantly, we retrieved our coats and emerged into the crowded street outside. I closed my eyes and tried to imagine myself walking sightless through the clutter of signs and potted plants and café furniture on the sidewalk. I was terrified at the thought.

The more I tried new things, the more courageous I found myself. I made a friend who was even more of a student of *Pariscope* than I. She loved avant-garde performances, and she was always suggesting oddball excursions, like a play featuring two men and sixteen cardboard boxes, an opera that combined live singers and video, a wine-bar lunch of pig's ears and snails to celebrate the Nouveau Beaujolais—usually in distant, unfamiliar parts of the city.

A few days before my return to the United States, she said sadly, "I'm really sorry that you're leaving, because you're the only person I know who never says no." After a lifetime of caution, it was the greatest compliment I could have received. I went to Paris to try out a new life, and I discovered a braver self in the process. Did it last once I went back home? Yes, in astonishing ways—but that's another story.

In the Mist

by Ingrid Emerick

I met the nun that day on a narrow dirt path that wound through a tiny forest. I was pedaling a dilapidated old rental through the misty Irish countryside and had pulled over to what I thought was an abandoned convent, home to a Celtic ogham stone. I desperately had to pee and the secluded woods around the old buildings seemed like an unobtrusive spot for a quick stop. Of course, I didn't know it was sacrosanct ground I had chosen.

I had been traveling across Ireland for nearly two weeks by then. I was on this trip alone, but certainly not lacking in company. Ireland is not the place to come if you seek strict solitude. After two weeks of nearly constant companionship from one new friend or another, I was actually craving some solitary time. After spending the night in Dingle, a picturesque port town in the southwest of the country, I turned down several invitations for various excursions from my fellow hostelers and told my new German acquaintance that I wanted to take our planned bike trip alone. I wanted to see Slea Head, the westernmost tip of Ireland, and I wanted to see it on my own.

I "hired" a bike, as the Irish say, and headed off that morning on what the Germans in my hostel had assured me was a leisurely little jaunt. Bloody Germans. I cursed them for much of the next fifteen miles. Fifteen miles is not much of a bike ride, true, but there was not a single flat stretch and the old crappy rental made it seem like thirty. Of course, turning back was not an option—I couldn't bear facing the smug Germans—so on I went.

Despite its rigors, it was an incredibly lovely ride. The area just west of Dingle has the largest concentration of ancient sites in all of County Kerry, if not in all of Ireland. So there were lots of good reasons to stop and catch my breath along the way. Around nearly every bend were ring forts, round houses (typical dwellings for the Iron-Age Celts) and ogham stones, the ancient markers left by the Druids ("ogham" refers to the twenty-five-character Druid alphabet inspired by Ogma, God of Eloquence). Best of all, though, were the lambs. In my opinion spring is the best time to visit Ireland: fewer tourists, mild weather, and everywhere lambs. The road I was traveling on hugged the rugged coastline with lush green fields roll-ing into the raucous ocean below. Dotted all over these green, green fields were little lambs, wobbly on their new legs, curious about me yet mightily protected by some mean-looking rams.

I pushed up the long hill and was rewarded by a breathtaking view of the wild Atlantic and the lonely Blasket Islands. Just four miles off the mainland, the seven small islands that comprise the Blaskets peacefully slumber in the cold Atlantic. The last inhabitants abandoned the islands in 1953. Life there was just too hard even for those tenacious folks. Perched on the side of the road, the boggy land beneath my feet tumbling down to the ocean, I gazed out on the little lonely islands and tried to imagine a life of such isolation and hardship.

They say that on the Aran Islands, due north of here in Galway Bay, life was so hard that the people couldn't even afford musical instruments to entertain themselves in the long evenings (as was common on the main-land). They had only their stories. Aran is famous in Ireland and elsewhere as the land of ghost stories, including many about the infamous banshees. When goosebumps began to appear on my legs from the constant wind, its occasional eerie wail sounding like that of the legendary banshees, I knew it was time to head back to Dingle and the warmth of a pub.

After a few miles of pedaling, I came upon the deserted convent I had passed on the way out. I wandered into the woods and then, walking back to my bike a few moments later, still zipping up my jeans, I spied her. A little old woman was coming down the path toward me. It took me a moment to realize, to my horror, that this was no ordinary old woman but a nun, her head bent in quiet prayer, her fingers moving nimbly over her rosary beads. Oh, my God, had she seen me zipping up my pants? Did she know I'd just peed on her convent grounds? I tried to think of a plausible reason I would be in the woods. Nothing came to mind. Lying to a nun after peeing on consecrated ground seemed like the wrong direction to go in, so I braced myself for the inevitable inquiry.

"A bit muddy in there, isn't it?" she remarked cheerfully, her voice rising in the Irish way of phrasing a half-question/half-statement.

"Yes, it is!" I replied, wholly relieved by her friendly tone.

"Oh, you're a Yank, are you?" This was a constant refrain I had come to hear throughout my travels in Ireland. I guess I look Irish enough to surprise people with my American accent.

"Yeah, I am."

"And are you traveling alone?" she asked, with a hint of surprise in her voice.

"Yes, I am," I answered again. She must have been about eighty years old and no taller than five feet. She had quick eyes that sparkled when she talked and obviously missed very little.

"Ay, it is so good that you girls these days can travel on your own. It wasn't so much like that back when I was your age. I am glad that has changed. It is good to get out and see the world for yourself."

I was a little surprised by how progressive she seemed. Not having been raised Catholic, I had always imagined nuns to be rather conservative and narrow-minded. Clergy, in general, like police officers, have always made me a bit nervous. I'm certain I'll say something that will land me in trouble, or, at the very least, reveal me for the heathen or troublemaker I surely am.

"And how are you findin' Ireland, may I ask?"

"Oh, I like it very much. I've been having an amazing time."

"And may I ask what you like so much about it?"

My mind flooded with all the things I had come to love—the green fields; the ancient, crumbling buildings; the smell of burning peat in the crisp night air; the warm glow of a pub fire. Oh, and the lovely music one could hear nearly everywhere at night when musicians brought their instruments to the pubs and played in a relaxed way around a table, pints of Guinness in front of them, starting and stopping as they pleased, as friends talked or danced or just listened, their feet tapping.

"Oh, the countryside, all the history and, of course, the people. The people are so warm and welcoming," I said, thinking of how much more I could say on this topic.

"And where are you from?"

"The States," I replied, forgetting for a moment that we had already covered this.

"Well, I know that, lass, but where are you from in America specifically?"

"Oh, of course. Seattle, in Washington State," I said, thinking she might not know where Seattle was. It was 1995 and Kurt Cobain had tragically killed himself less than a year before, so thanks to grunge and this sad news, Seattle was on the map, at least in the consciousness of young Europeans. I wasn't sure, though, how much Irish nuns knew about Nirvana—the band at least.

"Ay, weather a bit like ours, I imagine."

"Yes, definitely, very green as well," I said.

"And are you here visiting family?"

I paused a moment before answering. So many of the Americans who visit Ireland are looking for family, or at least some understanding of what their Irish roots mean. Over a quarter of the Irish population left the country during the potato famine of the mid-1800s and an estimated 1.5 million found their way to the shores of America. Young Irish people are still leaving, although in smaller numbers as the home economy improves. Ireland is such a romantic place to Americans, especially Irish-Americans, because of what can be found here that simply does not exist in America—the long history, the traditions and a seemingly simpler way of life. It is still one of Europe's most rural countries. Especially in the west of the country, outside of the few cities and larger towns, many of the roads are unpaved, there are no malls, no billboards, few street lamps, shops or even cars. It gives one the feeling of traveling back in time.

"No," I replied, "just visiting."

"Well, you must be Irish, are you not?"

"I don't know," I replied a little uncomfortably. "I was adopted, so I don't know exactly where my roots are."

"Well, you look like a nice Irish girl to me," she said firmly, as if that settled it.

I was curious about my roots, and Ireland had intrigued me partly for that reason. I had known I was adopted for as long as I could remember and figured that one day I might try and find my birthmother. Beyond that I didn't dwell on it too much, but I hated not knowing where my ancestors came from. I felt somehow unattached to the world. More than knowing my medical history or even what my real mother looked like, I longed to know where I came from, where my ancestors had lived. My parents had only sketchy information on my heritage. Definitely European and probably from the British Isles, judging from my reddish-brown curly hair and freckled complexion. I knew nothing more specific than that. I had hoped I was Irish, as Ireland, with its pantheon of writers, musicians and wild revolutionaries, seemed far more interesting to me than England or Wales. On this trip, my first solo one and my first to Europe, I had come to Ireland in part to find my ancestral home, as if I would somehow feel a connection by simply being here. Faced with the possibility of never knowing anything more about my identity, that elusive, potential connection seemed like enough. It seemed like everything.

"Now, may I ask you, dear, were your parents good to you?"

"Oh, yes," I replied, a bit taken back by the question. I had never gotten that response to the revelation that I was adopted.

"And if you don't mind me asking, were you raised a Catholic?" she inquired.

Oh, great, I thought, here comes the religious inquisition. This is why I hate talking to spiritual people; the conversation inevitably leads to this. "No, actually, I was raised a Protestant," I replied. I had never thought there was much difference between Protestants and Catholics, but being in Ireland and knowing full well the bitter history of a people divided, at least primarily, on this distinction, made me hesitant to admit that I was raised Protestant, since I sided with the Catholics, like most liberal Americans, on the whole Irish issue.

This didn't seem to matter much to her, though, as she followed right up with, "And do you have a religion now?" as if she could sense that I was not a practicing Protestant.

"No," I hesitated. "Jury is still out on that one," I quipped.

"Ay, you're in the mist," she replied with a pleasant finality that ended our brief conversation and set me thinking as I followed her directions to the resident ogham stone.

That was it. I was in the mist.

The Irish have some really fabulous phrases. Like the gray, misty days that we get way too much of in Seattle, they call "soft days." I first heard that from a farmer as I passed his field. I waved hello and he waved back and exclaimed, "Ay, 'tis a soft day." What optimism there is in that comment. I'd always thought of days like that as depressing and dreary, but no, they were soft days and there was beauty in that. Not too cold, not too warm, just some nice mist and a temperate clime. I decided then and there that if I was going to survive in Seattle, or anywhere, I'd have to adopt the Irish attitude toward weather. Soft days for me from now on.

And now, "in the mist." That pretty much summed up my spiritual life as well as my life in general. I left the nun on the darkening forest path and roamed the quiet convent grounds thinking about why I had come on this trip in the first place. I knew I needed to find something. Stuck in a dead-end relationship, bored with my job, my life, marooned in the dead center of my twenties, I was not sure what I wanted next. Intuitively, though, I knew I needed some time alone. I would make a pilgrimage. But what was I searching for? I wasn't really sure. Was I looking to find my roots, people who looked like me, some feeling of commonality, the sense of a homeland? Or was I looking to run away from my life, from the mess that it was? To find an excuse to get away from a relationship that was dying a slow death? To regain my lost confidence so I could face some hard choices upon my return? I must have come for all these reasons, and yet none was apparent. In the mist I was, about both what I was looking for and where I was headed.

As I trudged back to the road, the day was no longer soft but turning rather hard, with the rain now pouring down and the wind kicking up. While I was mustering the courage to start pedaling back, thinking of the hearty Blasket Islanders and all the rain and wind they must have endured, a car stopped and a lovely Irish couple asked if I could use a lift to town. Admittedly less sturdy than those island folk, how could I turn down that invitation? I climbed into the back of their car after securing my bike in the trunk and settled back, grateful for the warmth of the car.

That evening, warm and snug at the hostel, I thought about how uncanny it is that people seem to find us when we most need them, whether a nun in the woods who offers new insight when the path is unclear or friendly strangers in a car who offer a lift when it is cold and dark. Here, on my own in Ireland, I was reminded that the universe is there for us, ready to lend a hand, reveal a mystery, offer shelter from the storm and, perhaps most important, to teach a lesson. We rarely know what it is we are seeking when we set out, and even if we do, it is not often what we end up finding.

And so I found an unexpected lesson in Ireland: days can be soft and people are often in the mist. Understanding and accepting our utter inability to change this, and maybe even enjoying it a bit, is the key; that, and trusting that when we are ready a path will be revealed in a dark wood. If we're lucky, a sage might be sent our direction to offer the truth we didn't even know we were seeking. All we can do is know when to listen.

Barefoot Bliss
in Belize

by Marianne Ilaw

There's a small enchanted island in the middle of the Caribbean Sea, thirty-five miles off the coast of Belize. It's like a storybook land, where locals and tourists alike putter around in eco-friendly golf carts, the streets are paved with sand, and a big night out might mean strolling through the town plaza, gazing at the stars and slurping on a fresh-churned coconut ice-cream cone.

A mere half-mile away from the shore is the longest barrier reef in the Western Hemisphere, attracting divers, snorkelers, fishermen and nature lovers. For years, Ambergris Caye has been a well-kept secret, familiar only to the Caribbean cognoscenti. Although it is the largest and most developed of Belize's two hundred offshore cays—offering such amenities as air-conditioned hotels, safe drinking water, satellite TV and even a cyber café where you can communicate with friends and family back home at the click of a mouse—it is still light-years away from such Caribbean tourist magnets as St. Martin, the Bahamas and Aruba. Overrun with duty-free shops, high-rise hotels and lobster-faced tourists sporting Bahama Mama T-shirts, these vacation spots are small-scale versions of Miami

Beach. And that will never happen to Ambergris Caye—not only because it lacks the infrastructure, terrain and resources to support mass tourism, but because its citizens wouldn't permit it.

However, it is no longer unknown, thanks to the 2001 shock-reality show *Temptation Island*. Filmed on the isolated north end of the island, this show brought a group of nubile, hormonally charged singles together for the express purpose of tearing apart the committed twosomes in the group. Travel agents reported a deluge of inquiries about Ambergris after the series aired, but its relative inaccessibility (three connecting flights from New York) and its lack of glitzy, all-inclusive resorts probably will deter the average package-tour traveler—thank heavens.

For years I had dreamed of visiting Ambergris Caye. Why, even the name sounds magical. Legend has it that the island was once a whaling center, and clumps of ambergris (a waxy substance produced by whales, used commonly in perfume) would float on the surface of the sea.

I have been traipsing around the Caribbean for nearly twenty years, fulfilling a post-college vow to visit as much of the region as possible. I've danced barefoot in St. Lucia, hiked the rainforest in Dominica, chatted with boat builders in Bequia, munched conch in Abaco—all alone. But Ambergris Caye was going to be different. Remote and romantic, I was sure that I would visit it one day with a lover or husband in tow. I carried brochures on Belize in my tote bag, and would gaze at them dreamily during my morning commute on the grubby New York City subway.

"A fine place for a honeymoon," I would murmur as I flipped through the colorful catalog filled with alluring photos of sunsets, foamy surf and thatched-roof beach bars. I had even selected the hotel I would book—the pastel pink, beachfront Mayan Princess, smack dab in the middle of town, central to all the action.

In my fantasy, my husband and I would laugh and joke as we navigated the coastal roads in our rented golf cart. We would pore over cases filled with colorful handicrafts in the shops that stayed open until 9:00 and 10:00 P.M., and then enjoy a late dinner at Elvi's Kitchen, known worldwide for its fresh seafood and funky tropical ambience.

But guess what? Mr. Wonderful never materialized. Oh, sure, I've had plenty of suitors, but most of them cowardly crawled away once they realized that I would never suppress my intellect or curiosity about the world, and that I fully intended to indulge my passion for foreign travel and cultural exploration. And while I am certainly capable of compromising in a relationship—sitting through mindless shoot-'em-up films, dining at wretched all-you-can-eat buffet restaurants—it seemed that compromising was a one-way street: "But Marianne, why do we have to go where there are *bugs* and no cable TV? Can't we just go to Vegas?"

I think not.

I decided that I was not going to wait for a partner to visit the island of my dreams. When I told friends about my plans, they were impressed. "So you're finally gonna do it, huh, girl?" "You've been talking about it for years; good for you!" "Belize—how exotic. I know *I* couldn't pick up and go there alone." My travel agent just chuckled when I sat before her and said, "Belize . . . Ambergris Caye . . . Eight days, seven nights." She shook her head. "You always know what you want. You make my job easier!"

My American Airlines flights from New York to Miami and on to Belize City were comfortable and uneventful. I arrived at the Belize International Airport ready for an adventure. When I walked out onto the sticky tarmac to board the plane for the cay, I realized that I was getting a little more than I had bargained for. A tiny, battered, eight-seat propeller plane stood forlornly at the gate. It looked like somebody's science-class project! A wave of panic spread over me. I've traveled in small planes before, but never one this fragile-looking.

At that moment, I fervently wished that I had a big strong man to hold my hand, hug me and tell me not to worry, but that was not to be. I immediately regressed and whimpered for my deceased mother. I desperately craved her comforting arms. But then something clicked: My mother had *never, ever* coddled me—she always pushed me into deep water. And so with her in mind, I walked toward the aircraft on wobbly legs. I fished around in my shoulder bag until I found what I was looking for: my beloved mother's crystal rosary beads. I clutched them and implored her to watch over me. For good measure, I dug in my purse for my medallions of Chango, the powerful African deity, and Santo Niño, given to me by an aunt in the Philippines.

With a fistful of talismans, I was ready. I climbed aboard, only blanching momentarily when a fellow passenger leaned toward me, snapped on her seatbelt and said cheerfully, "In case of emergency—Goodbye!"

I relaxed once we were up in the air, and pressed my face against the smudged windowpane, marveling at the shimmering turquoise sea that flowed over the breathtaking barrier reef. "I did it, Mom, I did it," I whispered to the downy clouds above us.

As the taxi driver drove me the few blocks from the airstrip to the Mayan Princess, I took in the sights and sounds of San Pedro. It looked just as it did in the brochures: sandy streets, golf carts whirring around, children laughing and playing in the surf.

After being warmly welcomed at the hotel's front desk, I eagerly followed the clerk up to my room, which was comfortably furnished with a kitchen, a sitting area, two ceiling fans, a large color TV and a firm queen-size bed. I gasped at the postcard-perfect view—the magnificent French doors were thrown open to the breeze, and the fluttering gossamer curtains framed the shimmering cerulean sea just yards away. A woven pink hammock stretched across the balcony, beckoning me.

San Pedro is the main town on Ambergris Caye, named for Saint Peter, the patron saint of fishermen. Tourist officials have dubbed it "La Isla Bonita" after Madonna's hit song about a mythical island named San Pedro—

which I played endlessly on my portable cassette player. The town is extremely laid-back and unpretentious, drawing backpackers, serious divers and travelers who want something more than an all-inclusive, tour bus- and casino-filled vacation destination.

I grinned as I trudged around barefoot, eavesdropping on conversations—one of my favorite pastimes. On tourist-packed islands, I'd overheard such mundane comments as, "Wow! Rolexes are cheap down here," and "Let's check out the all-you-can-eat buffet at the Tropicana!" But San Pedro drew a different breed of visitor. I chuckled one morning as I heard a young backpacker sigh and earnestly caution his companion, "You would *never* recognize Managua today!" A few paces later, a college student shrieked, "Josh saw a scorpion on the ceiling this morning!" Definitely not the duty-free crowd.

Truly, it's the Caribbean the way it used to be, perhaps twenty or thirty years ago, but it's unlike any other place in the region. Belize's exotic culture represents a unique fusion of Latin America and the British West Indies (formerly British Honduras, Belize received its independence in 1981). Sort of like a blend between, oh, Antigua and the Dominican Republic. Olive-skinned, straight-haired mestizos greet each other with, "Mon, where yuh been, bwoy?" Coffee-colored, dreadlocked fishermen chat away in fluent Spanish.

And I fit right in. Tawny beige, with thick dark wavy hair and a vaguely Latino/Polynesian appearance, I am a proud blend of Black, Indian and Filipino heritage (Tiger Woods would probably dub me a "Blindipino"). In the United States, I'm considered exotic and unique, and perfect strangers feel at ease asking intrusive questions about my ethnic background— "Isn't it weird being mixed like you?" "Oh, so you're a mutt!" "Are you a war baby?" In Belize, I was routinely greeted in Spanish or the local Creole patois. "You're an American?" people would ask, puzzled. "You look like one of us!" But it was more than just looks. On my first night on the island, I learned why I was viewed as "different" from other Americans.

As I was returning from a quick dinner, the hotel's night clerk, Russ, started peppering me with questions about New York. "Teenagers drive BMWs, right? Everyone needs a gun and even bus drivers can buy a big house, yes?" I laughed and tried to deconstruct the stereotypes. Soon, we were joined by a group of teenage boys, who peered at me shyly until I urged them to speak their minds. They interrogated me about American youth, cell phones, rap music, Nikes, celebrities and sports. "Okay, I'll answer your questions if you promise to teach me how to dance punta," I offered. Edgar, Victor and "Ninja" looked at me, delighted and surprised. "You know about punta?" they demanded. Yes, I replied, explaining that I had dated a Honduran who introduced me to the throbbing, percussive Garifuna rhythms. I could move easily to the music, but I wanted to coordinate the frantic hip shimmies with the fancy footwork. They were impressed. I ran to my room to get my mini-stereo, some sodas for them and some Belizean ginger wine for me.

Their eyes lit up when I slipped in my tape and turned up the volume to "Sopa de Caracol," a punta classic. They clapped and spoke at once. "We never met an American like you before!" "Most of them don't speak to us, they don't know about our music, and they are not nice like you." "And you look just like us!" "Marianne, when you go home, can you please send us some rap music with cursing in it?"

Even though I didn't understand the Garifuna language (Garifuna are descendants of escaped Africans and Carib Indians who fled the Eastern Caribbean in the eighteenth century for the Central American coast), I knew the chorus by heart, and sang along phonetically: "*Watanegi Konsu, nula rami wanaga.*" They laughed and corrected my pronunciation, then jumped up and demanded that I follow their motions.

I spent many happy evenings in the breezy lobby, joking, dancing and slurping on juicy mangoes with the young men who insisted on being my "bodyguards." Russ somberly informed me that he was a trained government sniper and suggested that he was available for hire, if I wanted to bring him to New York. Throughout the week, the young men followed me around town. They brought me fresh orange juice from the plant where one of them worked, surprised me with pretty seashells, and carried my packages. Even when they weren't in sight, they knew my whereabouts— "We saw you swimming at 3:00 P.M." "You really know how to handle that golf cart." "We watched you using the computer in the cyber café. We never knew anyone personally who knows how to use a computer."

They were all handsome young men and they each admitted to having a crush on me, but I nipped that in the bud. "Call me *tía* (auntie) if you like," I said firmly, "but I don't do young boys. You could all be my sons!" These teens were struggling to earn a living, unlike the spoiled, materialistic, college-bound youngsters I knew back home. They did odd jobs, like raking sand at a resort, delivering fresh produce, repairing fishing boats. They often went hungry. I occasionally slipped them some greenbacks so that they could eat a decent meal, treated them to ice cream and snacks, and shared my kitchen's larder with them. On the day I departed, they presented me with a little basket filled with a sampler of local rums and a handful of scenic postcards. It was precious to me, all the more so because I knew that they could barely afford to feed themselves.

I thought about this often as I sat down to sumptuous meals and solicitous service. My "gringo guilt" was more poignant since the men and women who served and cleaned up were brown, just like me. Frequently, I'd fight back tears as I watched people who resembled my successful, well-educated relatives sweeping floors and scrubbing tables. "There but for the grace of God go I," whizzed through my mind as I slipped them generous tips.

The prospect of eating every meal alone probably serves as a serious deterrent to traveling solo. Many women I know who travel for business prefer to order room service or wolf down a burger in front of the television. Not this queen. I want a prime table—preferably ocean-view—attentive service, and the opportunity to savor an appetizing meal without being pitied by other diners or patronized by condescending waiters.

I remember once, in St. Lucia, I waltzed into a charming seaside restaurant and waited to be seated. Although more than half of the dining room was empty, the maitre d' led me to a small table tucked behind the serving station. I swept my hand dramatically around the room and exclaimed, "With all of these tables, you're going to put me in the corner?" He bowed his head deferentially. "But Madame, I thought that since you are dining alone, you would be, um, more comfortable in the corner." Flabbergasted, I pointed haughtily to a table in the center of the room, elegantly set with flickering candles and tropical blossoms, and boasting an enviable view of the sea. "That is where I want to sit," I informed him. "Just because I am alone does not mean that I can't enjoy the same experience as all these couples. And no, I am not uncomfortable dining alone. I came to this island by myself, didn't I?" I heard chuckles from the other side of the room and a thick German accent called out, "American, aren't you? And I bet you are from New York!" I gave a triumphant "thumbs up" and glided toward my table. And I had a thoroughly enjoyable meal.

Solo diners are often self-conscious and embarrassed. They feel that everyone else in the restaurant is looking at them with pity. But that's not necessarily the case. Often, other diners are intrigued at the sight of a confident woman savoring her dinner, completely at ease. I have met women who tell me they admire my "courage" to eat alone at a fancy restaurant. I never take a book, or papers to review. And I don't hurry the meal, either. Some men seem to feel intimidated by it—I've noticed them stealing glances at me occasionally, to see how I order, taste wine, pay the bill. I guess that's always been a man's province. But just because these tasks have been traditionally handled by men, it doesn't mean that a woman without a partner has to spend her vacations eating fast food or room-service meals.

There was one restaurant on Ambergris Caye that I was anxious to visit. Very pricey, very chic, Mambo was located in the oh-so-hip, upscale

Mata Chica resort at the north end of the island. When I inquired about it, locals told me it was "very special, very romantic." "Go there with someone you love," my hotel's pretty receptionist suggested. I smiled at her and said, "Well, I love *me,* so I guess I am going."

I quickly made a reservation and was told that a water taxi would pick me up that evening at the pier near my hotel. I would be lying if I told you that I didn't feel wistful about going to Mambo alone. But I also would have kicked myself had I let this trip pass without experiencing the Mata Chica magic I had been hearing about.

I dressed carefully, pleased that I looked like the New York City writer that I am. I donned a flowing tangerine gauze-and-chiffon dress I'd snapped up for $20 at an Indian boutique, big gold gypsy hoops and black, sequined thong sandals that set off my tanned, pedicured feet adorned with silver toe rings and beaded anklets. My mane of dark curls cascaded from my brand-new Mexican leather headband embroidered with a Mayan design. I topped off my multiethnic ensemble with a colorfully woven Guatemalan shoulder pouch. With a quick spritz of my Jamaican Khus-Khus perfume, I was off.

I waited at the pier with two couples. They looked at me curiously, but offered friendly smiles. Shortly, we climbed aboard a launch for the quick ride to Mambo. We made a few stops at other hotel piers along the way to pick up other guests. It soon became apparent that I was the only "singleton."

We docked and climbed down to the lush resort grounds. The owner, a dapper Frenchman, greeted us at the pier. I felt as if I were clambering down from the *Fantasy Island* water taxi, fully expecting Tattoo to pop out from the shrubs and shout, "Enjoy yourself!"

We were given a tour of the property and I watched as the couples all nodded appreciatively at the exotic, earthy accommodations. "We'll have to stay here next time," some of them murmured. I had no one to murmur to, so I just asked for a brochure.

We entered the dining area, which looked more like an artist's home than a restaurant. Art from Africa, Latin America and Asia adorned the walls. Candles gave the cavernous room a soft, sultry glow. Worldbeat music—much of it familiar—throbbed from the expensive stereo system. After ordering drinks, the guests—about twenty in all—sank into comfortable sofas and love seats and made pleasant small talk. I sipped my potent rum punch, sang along to the Susana Baca soundtrack, and chatted with others about living in New York, working as a writer and traveling alone.

A smiling waiter informed us that we would be seated for dinner soon. I scanned the room, looking for a small table where I would be comfortable. But it was not to be. The owner took my elbow and led me along to a communal table where five honeymooning couples were seated. "Oh, no," I protested, "You're all honeymooners—you want to be alone." "No, no," they insisted. "Please join us—we want to hear stories about New York." One tipsy Texan laughed and drawled, "Sit here honey, you're more interesting than my husband."

This was not going to be easy. I suddenly despised my commitment-phobic ex-boyfriend who bailed out on our third anniversary after repeatedly asking me to marry him. He should have been by my side, on *our* honeymoon. But I held my head high and graciously took a seat.

The dinner, featuring grilled lobster and heavenly chocolate mousse, was delectable. The table full of Southerners laughed uproariously as I regaled them with stories of daily life in the Big Apple. And when the checks came, I pulled out my wallet along with the five husbands. At first I felt somewhat envious of the wives, who sat passively as their mates scrutinized the bills. But I rallied when I realized that I probably earned as much as, if not more than, some of the men. And did that cheer me up? You bet it did, because I would rather pay my own way in this world than be saddled with someone who offers treats and luxuries if I promise to "behave," as some of my ex-boyfriends have done.

As we ambled contentedly back to the boat, the couples instinctively reached for their partners' hands. Everyone was quiet as the launch zipped over the waves, the moon casting a silver shadow on the inky sea. The couples hugged and caressed each other as they snuggled close. Brave as I may be, I am only human, and I was grateful for the cloak of velvety darkness that hid the wistful longing evident on my face.

Once again, I mentally cursed my ex-boyfriend, but then I realized that he probably never would have come to Belize with me, anyway. After all, he spent his first honeymoon in a chain hotel in Aruba, and was frightened by the wild goats that roamed the streets when we visited Nevis. Yes, it was painful not to have someone to share this experience with, but I knew that I wouldn't be alone forever. I lifted my chin and assured myself that one day, I would find a man who would truly relish a trip like this. "I will come back here with someone special," I whispered to the stars.

As the boat docked near my hotel, I bid a cheery goodnight to the couples. One of the women clasped my hand warmly and said, "You are such a fascinating woman. You came to Belize alone, you're wearing a cool Indian dress, speaking French to the owner, Spanish to the waiter, and singing along to that rainforest music—you knew all the words! I admire you."

And that was my hug for the night.

I felt very comfortable at Elvi's Kitchen, a San Pedro institution. Elvi's began in 1974 as a small burger shack. Later, the owner set up picnic tables under the shade of an enormous flamboyant tree. She built the restaurant around the tree, and today it grows right through the roof of the restaurant, whose floors are covered in sand. The picnic-style tables, the friendly staff and the alluring background music (ranging from Mayan flute to Caribbean calypso) create a convivial atmosphere.

I ate at Elvi's several times, once with a group of divers from Iowa I had met on the beach. But even when I was alone, I felt like a welcome guest at a lively party. I enjoyed coconut shrimp, fish in black bean sauce, chicken with tropical fruit glaze and frosty drinks. Once I became a "regular," the staff would greet me warmly and tease me. One handsome waiter claimed that he was only thirty, but had sired twenty-eight children—by different mothers. "Would you like a Belizean boyfriend?" he asked slyly. I demurred, and as I wrapped my shawl around my shoulders to leave, he whispered, "Meet me at the disco tonight!" I was mildly flattered, but, as a veteran Caribbean traveler, I've heard every line imaginable from horny men eager to hook up with a single American tourist. And although I'm in my forties, I'm not undergoing a midlife crisis where I'm compelled to "get my groove back" with a hot island stud like my sistah Stella did. Yet I will be the first to admit that the real-life men on *Temptation Island* were tempting indeed. As a woman of color who adores her melanin-infused brothers, I was in heaven! The wonderful hybrid of cultures— Afro-Caribbean, Mexican, Mestizo, Indian, European—has produced some stunningly attractive men in every hue—chocolate, bronze, olive-toned. It was a feast for the eyes to watch handsome hunks hopping down from fishing boats, deftly wielding trays of tropical libations, raking seaweed from the water's edge. Still, even if I so desired, I would not have been able to hook up with a suitor—my little band of bodyguards would never have allowed it.

So I passed on the "local charm" and simply enjoyed the sights and sounds of San Pedro. The days folded lazily into each other. I rented a golf cart, swam, shopped barefoot in the charming shops on Barrier Reef Drive, boned up on local history in the one-room library, and met friendly folks wherever I turned. One afternoon, I popped into the offices of Tropic Air, one of the two local airlines, to say hi to the owner, the brother of a colleague. He promptly invited me into his office where he regaled me with island tales for two full hours. Can you imagine that kind of hospitality if you showed up unannounced to meet the president of, say, United Airlines?

As the week wore on, I felt more and more like a Belizean. I'd set out early on the sandy streets and stroll barefooted over to the bakery to pick up fresh tropical-fruit tarts or warm banana bread, then pop into the fruit stand to select an armful of plump, juicy mangoes. Locals greeted me warmly and I felt as if I belonged. Settling on my private balcony, I would enjoy my breakfast and watch the beach come alive. I planned my day as I sipped steamy cups of fresh-brewed tea, fragrant with coarse brown sugar and tropical lime.

The biggest benefit of traveling alone, of course, is the luxury of being absolutely selfish. You don't have to coordinate schedules, share bathrooms or put up with cranky traveling companions. One evening, I chuckled at how my friends might disapprove if they saw me lighting up a Cuban cigar. Although I had quit smoking years before, the lure of the forbidden (in America) stogy was too strong.

So I curled up in the hammock, threw back a tumbler of fiery coconut rum and blew smoke rings toward the sky as I blasted Celia Cruz's Cuban classic, "Santa Barbara." As the throbbing congas, the warmth of the rum and the thick, humid air ignited my senses, I felt strong and empowered.

Unencumbered, I was as free as the frigate birds that wheeled overhead. I did what I pleased, when I pleased. One afternoon, I decided to explore the isolated north end of the island. I was curious about the hand-pulled ferry I had read so much about, so I got into my golf cart and trundled off. A line of tourists' golf carts snaked from the riverbank, waiting to cross the channel. When I saw the "ferry," I had the same reaction I'd had to the teeny plane: panic. The ferry was simply a weather-beaten wooden raft about thirty feet long, attached to a rope that was pulled manually to the other side. When it was my turn to cross, the two drivers flanking me pulled back. The ferry accommodated three or four golf carts, but no one wanted to go first—one wrong move and you'd sail over the edge and into the drink.

"Oh, come on, guys, you're gonna make me lead?" I groaned. Now, let me be frank. I have driving issues. Simply put, I am a bad driver. How bad? Well, let's just say that my license should *only* be used as a form of identification.

The ferryman grinned and waved me forward. He threw down two beat-up planks to guide me and steadied the rope as the ferry swayed from side to side. I scratched my arms anxiously and gulped. "Come on, New York, you can do it!" the other drivers roared. To calm my nerves, I cranked up the volume on the cassette player, blasted "La Isla Bonita" and tapped the accelerator gently. As Madonna trilled on about the wonders of San Pedro, I eased the vehicle up the makeshift ramp, slid carefully along the length of the ferry and braked securely a mere three inches from the edge of the plank. Yessss! La Isla Bonita! The other drivers clapped and followed me onto the ferry, singing along merrily to the chorus.

"Mom, I did it again," I whispered to the sky.

Once we reached the other side, I was emboldened by my actions. I felt powerful and brave, capable of anything. And as long as I live, this image will be etched into my brain: I'm driving barefoot along the deserted north coast, blasting my music and watching the foamy surf slap against the shoreline. The wind is whipping through my hair and the setting sun glints off my brand-new Mexican silver bracelets. I pull into a dense coconut grove just yards away from the sea, take a swig of chilled mango nectar and sigh: "It doesn't get any better than this."

Too soon, it was time to leave the enchanted island. My last full day in San Pedro was bittersweet. I made my final purchases of art, jewelry and punta tapes, dined at Elvi's one more time, strolled the beach at sunset and bought a lovely charcoal sketch of the tropics from an artist known as Island Dog. I dropped by the quaint wooden Catholic church to pray for safe passage, then watched the children frolic in the waterfront park, with its looming Maya statues and pyramid. I bid farewell to the terrific Iowan couple I had befriended, popped into Big Daddy's disco to shake my booty a bit and sadly exchanged addresses with my young "bodyguards." We talked and laughed as they pushed me on the playground swings under the moonlight.

That night, I slept fitfully and awoke before dawn. I threw open the French doors and gazed at the velvety gray sky streaked with arcs of raspberry and blue. Fishermen were sleepily loading nets onto their vessels, as young beach boys carefully raked the tangles of seaweed that had washed ashore overnight. I watched quietly as the sun rose high in the sky, took a deep gulp of the salty air and then padded back to the bed, where I stretched and yawned like a kitten underneath the whirling ceiling fan.

I was melancholy when I reached the tiny San Pedro airport a few hours later. I sat on the porch of the shack that served as the "terminal" and pouted like a spoiled child. This time, I wasn't afraid of the plane. I petulantly shoved my carry-on under the seat, buckled myself in and waved farewell to the palm trees. As we began our ascent and climbed higher and higher above the sparkling sea, I glanced at the pilot fiddling with the controls in the cockpit. I did a double take. Tattooed on his forearm was a huge, menacing cobra. Fearless and proud, the creature seemed to challenge anyone to take him on. I could relate to *that*. I had arrived in Belize meekly, unsure of what awaited me. Would I feel lonely, so far off the beaten track? Would I get bored without the usual Caribbean distractions of duty-free shopping, museums and colonial plantations? Now, after more than a week on Ambergris Caye, I had learned about my capabilities and courage. I had no one to lean on but myself, and I realized I had done a damn good job: I felt as brave and bold as the cobra. I chuckled to myself and knew instantly that I would return to Belize one day.

"This is my kind of place," I whispered to the clouds.

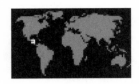

Be Kind
to the Muchachos

by Ginny NiCarthy

My favorite mode of travel is whichever one I'm experiencing at the moment: with friends, on a tour—or alone. Travel with others is always a challenge, a risky road on which many a romance, and some friendships, have foundered. But a trip fraught with disasters or swarms of mosquitoes can also create trench buddies. Years later, the drop of an ordinary phrase like "bargain tour" or "leaky roof" sends reminiscing travel companions into spasms of laughter that only those who were there can appreciate.

When you wander alone, you don't get that bonus of an increased intimate connection with friends. But you just might find another kind of treasure. On the road, alone, I often discover aspects of myself that surprise me, usually triggered by someone unexpectedly met, someone I'd never have paused long enough to truly see had I been with a friend or group. In real time, those encounters might last only as long as a butterfly's life. Yet the warmth of them, or the insight gained, or the irksome snag in my image of myself, lingers for years. On my first trip to Guatemala, that kind of gift came to me from Jorge.

An unruly array of exhaust-spewing, gear-grinding, parking, turning buses jockeyed for position. My bus had just pulled into some northern Guatemalan town, but the question was, which one? I hadn't heard an announcement, but I knew approximately how long it took to reach Huehue (short for Huehuetenango). I checked my watch, and figured this must be it. I left the bus, and I hadn't yet gathered my luggage or my wits when a stocky, dark-skinned man shouted from the top of another bus, his staccato voice charged with frenetic energy.

"México, sí? México? México?"

Idly curious, I looked around to see whom he bellowed at, then slowly realized his words were aimed at me. His beefy arm was in the act of tossing one of my bags, retrieved from the roof of my bus, onto the top of another bus, apparently headed for Mexico City.

"No!" I shouted up to him.

Again he bellowed, *"México, sí?"*

"No!" I had been in Guatemala only a couple of weeks, had come from Mexico, and was nowhere near ready to go back yet. I pointed to the ground. *"Aquí! Ahora! Por favor!"* Paltry though my Spanish vocabulary was, it felt good to snap out those words—Here! Now! Please!—which resounded in my ear like the three magic words in a fairy tale. The message registered. In a flash my prince of the moment reloaded the bags on his back and zoomed down the ladder.

Relieved, I waited to retrieve them, and planned to ask the young man for the name of a good cheap hotel. But my momentary serenity was ruptured as, stupefied, I watched him snatch two smaller bags from me, add them to his already formidable burden and, without a word, jog down the street, weaving in and out of curb-to-curb people. Now and then, he glanced back and waved me forward. I followed, panting, too intent on keeping track of him to be properly annoyed.

I'd spent nearly all my time in Guatemala in the city of Quetzaltenango, where my home-stay family showed me everything I needed to know to get around the town. That family connection had been a benefit of the language school I attended. Now I would spend the night in Huehue before I continued on to the sister school in a tiny village high in the *altiplano*.

A few months earlier, my friend Ruth had watched me get organized for a year-long stay in Mexico and Central America, and entreated me to change my doggedly independent ways: "I know you'd rather find your own way; I understand that you prefer to carry your own bags. But please. This time let the muchachos help." Muchachos, she explained, are young men or boys, especially the ones who hover around buses and tourist havens, hoping to earn money by showing tourists to hotels or other sites. "They need the tips," Ruth reminded me, "and it won't hurt to let somebody show you the way, for once."

Forty years of friendship, and she still couldn't accept my habit of bumbling through life, often incompetently, but insistently on my own. Better to be a damned fool, even at the occasional cost of wasted time and squandered money, than to ask for help. "You're a guy," another friend used to say, as if affectionately joking.

But it isn't that "guy" type of pride that deters me from asking directions—or so I like to think. On most trips, I eventually do ask, but I prefer to find my own way if I can. That can lead to all manner of (sometimes idiotic) deviations. It ups the suspense, the very stuff of adventure. I have good reasons for preferring my own mistakes to the security of sound advice from a hired expert. I hate to think of how many times I've been guided away from intriguing neighborhoods, restaurants or hotels because they aren't safe for ladies. And, I prefer to schlep my own luggage so I don't have to wait at carousels or fret about whether some stranger I've entrusted with my gear has collected it all. If I lose it, I have only myself to blame.

So it was not at all like me to let some stranger race away with my bags without protest. When I finally caught up with this bundle of steaming vigor, he told me his name was Jorge and that he would take me to the

Hotel Mary. My Spanish still hovered at the level of a cocker spaniel—I could understand a lot of words, so long as they were accompanied by hand signals—and I knew nothing about this town, so I told myself it wouldn't hurt to look at the hotel. Besides, a glance at Jorge's bedraggled jacket told me my friend Ruth was right about the need for tip money. I asked Jorge to slow down, but, as I would later discover, he operated at only two tempos. He gyrated with enthusiastic bursts of animation or collapsed into a hungover stupor of despair.

The Hotel Mary suited me fine, which was remarkable, since most self-appointed guides imagined I was a proper American lady who would want to stay in a safe area in a pricey hotel. Surely it wasn't upmarket attire that gave that impression. It must have been my age: At sixty-two, some measure of caution and decorum was expected. But clearly, Jorge had a more practiced eye than most. He correctly pegged me as imprudent about safety, and a bargain hunter to boot. The neighborhood was fine, and the price just right—somewhere between budget and sleaze. My room looked reasonably clean, and heavy, flowered curtains covered what appeared to be generous windows. What more could I want? As I fished for a tip, Jorge rattled off information and advice about the next leg of my trip. I must buy my ticket for Todos Santos early in the morning, he said. I succumbed to the luxury of his guidance and told him he could come for me and my baggage the next day.

As he shut the door behind him, I pulled the curtain open. Bang. It crashed to the floor, taking the bracket with it. A large hole in the plaster gaped at me. I always did like a street view, and now I had it in spades. This was one of those times I was glad I didn't have a sensible, refined or modest roommate, who might want to complain to management or traipse about the city looking for something better.

In the morning Jorge arrived at nine. Like a burro on speed, he again darted through crowded streets while I trailed behind, barely able to spot his bulky form a half-block ahead. I caught up at the bus ticket office, which was hardly more than a window in a building so tiny I'd surely have missed it without my guide to point it out. With my ticket secured and certain I was early, I began to mosey toward the bus. But it was not Jorge's plan for me to mosey anywhere. He scrambled up the ladder and tossed the rest of my luggage onto the roof, giving me only seconds to retrieve the bag I wanted to carry on.

Half prepared to stand, I boarded the crowded bus. But before I could settle on a place in the aisle, Jorge stormed in and began to direct a small indigenous woman to move. She and her four children had appropriated my designated seat. She passively resisted removal, while I stood wondering about the ethics of displacing her, even if she was in my seat. She had arrived first, and she and her family no doubt needed to sit far more than I. But Jorge was wrapped up in his drama of removal, and I didn't see how I could convey my reservations without wounding his professional pride. So I let him alone to do his job. The woman soon gave up the seat and took the one next to me. That worked out well, since before the bus had even taken off, her one-year-old perched on my hip-bone, the three-year-old slept in my arms and the mother lolled her head onto my shoulder, softly snoring.

A week later, on my way back from Todos Santos, I hitched a ride on a truck. As we pulled into Huehue again, I poked my head out from under the tarp, and scanned the crowd for Jorge, even as I asked myself why in the world I expected him. But there he was, standing by the side of the truck. His grin welcomed me like an old friend—as if I'd sent a telegram asking him to meet me. Again he carried my bags to the Hotel Mary, and I began to wonder whether this could get to be a habit. Depending on him, I mean. I almost believed I could learn to like it.

I explored the market, buying gifts for friends, but later that night I realized that a textile I'd bought wasn't at all right for the person I planned to give it to. I hoped I could return it or make a trade. The next morning, weaving in and out of stalls, I searched in vain for the woman who had sold it to me. Entering a market building from one street, I traipsed up and down aisles of woven cloth, crafts, fruit and meat, invariably exiting, thoroughly disoriented, onto a different street. Back I would go, but all the stalls began to look alike, and I always managed to get stuck in a huge butchers' section, nearly overpowered by the odor of slaughtered animals soon to be someone's dinner. Not a comfort to my vegetarian sensibilities. For a while I couldn't find a way out to any street at all. The nightmarish maze seemed to close in on me.

Eventually, I maneuvered my way toward light and air and stood on the sidewalk, grateful to breathe deeply once again. As I gazed around, bewildered, and tried to determine the direction of my hotel, a voice from across the street startled me. I turned to see what was being hawked so loudly. Jorge. Calling to me. He hurried toward me, and when he asked, *"Cómo está?"* I spilled out my frustration over not finding the woman I'd looked for. Jorge moved instantly into rescue mode. What did she look like, he demanded, what was her stall like, what did she sell?

"I can find her," he said. "I know her."

"Please don't bother, Jorge. I'm tired, and it's impossible."

But he sank his teeth into my problem, and yanked it away from me. Refusing to let me snatch it back, he was determined to wrestle with it in his own way. Or else he hadn't understood my protestations in bungled Spanish at all. He kept saying he knew exactly where to find my woman. Then he led me up and down rows of vendors, in and out of market buildings, asking people if they knew the woman. By that time, the return of my purchase had ceased to seem important, but how could I not cooperate with this man who was working so hard to make my life easier? To one person after another, I wearily described the small woman in the tiny stall near a door at the corner of a building who kept her baby with her in a buggy. Eyes would light up and we'd be sent this way, then that. It would turn out to be another woman who had a ten-year-old, or no child at all.

"Jorge, that's enough. It isn't that important," I implored. But he wouldn't give up. I was about to insist he stop the search, when suddenly there it was, the stall where I had bought the cloth. At last, I was able to make a trade. My next problem was what to pay Jorge. I had asked him, as well as other Guatemalans, how much they charged for their services, but they typically said, "Pay what you want."

Now, for a brief moment, I longed for my own country, where people announced—flatly, rudely, greedily or seductively—the price of their services. I made a wild guess at what might be a reasonable hourly wage for a guide, and paid Jorge accordingly. I couldn't tell from his response whether it was too much or too little. Then I asked him if he'd consider speaking Spanish with me for the equivalent of a dollar and a half an hour. He could make some money and I could practice the language. At least I knew the going rate for that service, since I'd inquired about it at my school. Jorge agreed to meet me at my hotel at seven that evening.

When the time arrived, I waited for him at the front door. No Jorge. An hour later, disappointed and trying not to give in to anger, I gave up. The next morning I meandered toward the *zócalo*. I hadn't gone far before I encountered Jorge, settled on a curbstone, head in hands. If I hadn't known him, I would have assumed he was a beggar, though he looked too wrapped in despair even to put a hand out. My previous night's irritation slid into concern.

"What happened to you last night?" I asked. "I thought we were going to speak Spanish."

"Ooooh," he said. "I couldn't come. I was at a funeral." He looked up at me through red-rimmed eyes.

"Oh, come on, Jorge. You look hungover. Like you must have been drinking all night."

"I was. My best friend died."

I sat on the step with him, commiserating as well as I could and listened as he poured out his woes. He had no wife, no children and little money. Now he'd lost his only good friend. And yes, of course he'd been drunk, he said. He was sad, sad, sad. In fact, he was a mess: doughy pockmarked face, small red eyes, dirty clothes and tangled hair. A dispirited lump of sorrow. Such a young man, to experience so much sorrow. But rather suddenly, he roused himself to offer unsolicited advice about nearby places I should visit, and I was touched by his concern for me.

On a bus again, following his advice to visit the town of Aguacatan, I mused about my feelings for Jorge. Picturing him, I realized that he hadn't looked much worse than usual that day. His nails were always dirt-filled, his hair greasy, his suit spotted. I had never noticed all that before, and I was surprised to realize how fond I'd become of him. Still, I was puzzled about my willingness to let him take over whenever he found me in apparent need. I had started out persuading myself he needed my money, that it was the least I could do in this impoverished country, which my country had robbed of its one chance for democracy fifty years earlier. But now I wondered who was leaning on whom.

I prepared to leave Huehue the next morning. I wanted Jorge to carry my bags, so I searched for him at the bus stop, but he was nowhere to be found. Carlos, another muchacho, led me through a maze of streets, conferring with friends and colleagues along the way about where his friend might be, until we reached a packing and shipping office where Jorge sometimes worked.

"*A la frontera*," the manager said, when we asked if he knew where Jorge might be.

"What frontier?"

"*Frontera de México.*"

Of course. I had arrived by way of Guatemala City, and had forgotten that the border was only an hour away by bus. I felt curiously let down, and when Carlos offered to take my bags in the morning, I reluctantly agreed to let him.

But in the morning he didn't show up. After waiting fifteen minutes I loaded one bag on my back, and picked up the other two. The men at the hotel were impressed, and, laughing, made a great to-do about how strong I was. I had never seen a muchacho offer to help out a local woman, and I asked if they hadn't noticed Guatemalan women half my size carrying twice the weight. Their response was to laugh louder.

I had almost reached the ticket office when suddenly, like an apparition, Jorge appeared, bright-eyed and cheerful. He grabbed my extra bags and hurtled down the street. A bus had just rounded the corner on the way out of town and Jorge yelled at the driver to stop. Traffic halted while I struggled out of the straps holding my backpack. My hero whisked it up to the roof, and carefully secured it to the railing. Next he was in the bus commandeering a window seat for me.

As I plunked myself down, he berated me. "Why didn't you ask me to carry your luggage?" But his voice sounded more disappointed than angry.

"I looked for you," I said defensively, "but they said you'd gone to the frontier."

"I did. Last night. But I came back this morning." As if I should have known. As if he had come back just for me.

He seemed hurt. Rejected, even. I told myself I exaggerated, that living on the edge as he did, he simply felt the loss of that bit of money. But I couldn't persuade myself it was true. And even if that were so, what did it have to do with the hollow in the pit of my stomach? As I searched for the answer, Jorge clasped my hands and, with a sorrowful smile, said goodbye.

That was not quite the end of our relationship. The following year when I once more came through Huehue I looked around for Jorge as I left the bus, and again felt foolishly dejected not to see him. I hefted my bags, which felt heavier than they ought to have, and started toward a loading dock where I'd heard I might get a truck ride to Todos Santos. The city felt empty.

Then I saw him, trudging along, empty-handed for once. I started toward him. When he saw me, he picked up speed. He reached in my direction—for my bag, I thought. But, as he came closer, he stretched both arms out, welcoming me. Surprising myself, I fell into his open arms. We smiled at each other, and then smiled some more—across a couple of generations; across cultures.

Later, I thought it odd that I stood on that dusty road hugging this man I didn't even know, really. At the time it seemed the most natural thing in the world to do, though I doubt it was what Ruth had in mind when she exhorted me, "Be kind to the muchachos."

I have not been back to Huehue since, but sometimes when I'm traveling alone in some other country, I rather resent the need to carry my own bags. Once in a while when I'm lost or confused or tired, I long for the sight of a grubby man with a loud voice and a speedy body and a big heart to help me find my way.

For Your Kind Information and Necessary Action, Please

by Jamie Zeppa

Editor's Note: At age twenty-three, Jamie Zeppa traveled alone to Bhutan, where she spent her first of two years there teaching in a remote mountain village. The following excerpt is taken from her memoir, Beyond the Sky and the Earth.

I am in a drugstore. The aisles seem unusually long, it is some kind of superstore, and everything gleams under the overhead lights. I push my cart slowly, studying the shelves carefully. What do I need? Look, here's this bath gel new and improved with a flip-top lid. The drugstore leads into a grocery store. I stand in the cereal section, considering deeply: Shreddies or Fruit Loops? The store will close soon, I have to hurry. "Shoppers," a glad voice says, "visit our ladies' department for unbelievable savings." I wake up, blinking: I am in Pema Gatshel. I must push back against the dark disorientation this realization causes if I am to get out of bed, and it seems I must get out of bed: someone is knocking on the door.

On the doorstep are two of my students. Karma Dorji, who rescued me on the way to Tsebar, is short and sturdy, with a round, cherubic face, nut-brown skin, and a distinctive cowlick. Norbu is taller, with a crooked little grin and a perpetually runny nose. Their *ghos* are faded, and on their feet they wear rubber sandals. Silently they offer their presents: a bundle of spinach, a cloth bag of potatoes, a handful of spring onions. Karma Dorji reaches inside his gho and removes a small brown egg. "Thank you!" I say. "Thank you very much!" They look embarrassed at my effusive thanks.

"My mother is giving," Norbu says.

"Please tell your mother thank you," I say, wondering if I should be paying for these things.

"Yes, miss." They leap down the ladder-like stairs and bound across the playing field.

Back inside, I hear water sputtering from a tap. This means I must fill every bucket, basin, pot, pan, bottle, kettle, jug, mug and cup right now, before the water disappears. In the kitchen, I pump up the kerosene stove until it is hissing steadily, throw a lit match at it and run into the bedroom, waiting for the explosion. When none comes, I creep back to the kitchen and put a pot of water on the blue flame. It immediately dies, and I have to repeat the process.

In the bathroom, the water has stopped. I have one full bucket. I can either bathe or wash my clothes. The drain is partially blocked, and although I have stuck a variety of implements down there—thick branches, thin willow wands, a piece of barbed wire—there is always a swamp in the middle of the bathroom. Gritting my teeth, I squat next to the bucket, and begin to pour the cold water over myself with a plastic jug. By the time I have finished, I am shivering violently and have to climb back into bed for several minutes before I can begin my daily *kira* ritual, a series of physical and mental contortions as I swathe and pin and belt the length of cloth around me. Sometimes, I stop, exasperated, holding some unexplained end, trying to figure out how it got free and where I should put it, and I wonder if I shouldn't just give up and wear a skirt and sweater. No, I will not give Mrs. Joy the satisfaction. Yesterday in the bazaar, an old woman stopped me and began to tuck in various parts of my kira, pulling the skirt down as she yanked the top up. Stepping back, she studied her adjustments critically. *"Dikpé?"* I asked. Okay? She shook her head and waved me on: it was still wrong, but it was the best she could do with me.

With the egg Norbu has brought me, I make a pancake, which I eat with Bhutan's own Mixed Fruit Jam, and then I leave for school, descending the steep staircase slowly, backwards, clutching the rails.

At school, I sit in the staff room with the other teachers, watching the students in the playing field. Many of them did not start school until they were eight or nine, which means that most of the class VIII kids are in their late teens. They all wear the school uniform, grey-blue ghos and kiras. Some of the smaller kids wear hand-me-downs, faded and splotched and miles too big for them. Pema Gatshel has both boarders and day students, and many of the day students walk for one or two or three hours to school each morning and evening. When it rains, they arrive at school soaked, and sit in their wet uniforms the whole day.

When the bell rings, we stand on the steps for morning assembly. The students stand in front of us at the edge of the playing field, in lines according to gender and class. The number of female students decreases steadily from preprimary to class VIII. The school captain, a class VIII boy named Tshering, leads the morning prayer and national anthem. From where I am standing, I can see the tip of a snow peak shining above a row of dark blue mountains in the northwest. I like to think that I am facing home, and wonder what Robert is doing right now, half the world away. It is yesterday evening there, and I picture him, with perfect clarity, in his apartment, reading the paper in his armchair, playing his guitar, cooking dinner. I wonder if he is thinking of me at the exact moment I am thinking about him. There is no way to find out. I am a million billion trillion miles away. Sometimes during morning assembly, my throat closes up and it hurts to breathe. Sometimes, though, I remember my book of Buddhist readings: feelings, desires, sorrows are all created by the mind. Everything in fact is "mind." If I remember this, I simply turn my attention back to the slow and stately singing, and the sadness drains away.

After the national anthem, a senior student gives a short speech in English or Dzongkha on an assigned topic: punctuality, honesty, respect for dear parents and teachers. Every English speech ends with the same breathless rush: " . . . and so my dear friends, I sincerely hope you all will be punctual/honest/respectful to your dear parents and teachers." The headmaster then makes a speech in Dzongkha; I know only the first word, *dari,* which means "today."

Dari, after the assembly, the headmaster informs me that I have been assigned to morning clinic, and will have to attend the first-aid course at the hospital starting on Monday. I have also been assigned to the library, he says, and gives me the key. I have already been to the library, a poorly lit room with a few very tattered picture books, abridged editions of *The Red Badge of Courage* and *Heidi,* and a great many Canadian readers published in the mid-1970s. How these came to be here, no one seems to know.

I like the headmaster and his wife, who has just given birth to twins. At first, I think he is very young to be a headmaster, but I change my mind when I see him with the students. He is sternly and completely in control. It is not so much his character as the Bhutanese way of being in authority, I think, remembering the officials we met in Thimphu, the Dzongda in Tashigang. Whatever it is, it elicits a fearful, unquestioning obedience from the students. With the staff, he is more relaxed, but I sense an undercurrent of tension between him and the Indian staff. The Indian teachers freely admit they are here because they could not find jobs in India, and they almost seem to resent the fact that they have to take orders from the Bhutanese. Last week, in the staff room, Mr. Sharma commented loudly on the uselessness of attending morning assembly if it's going to be in a language he doesn't understand. "Half the staff doesn't understand Dzongkha," he said.

"Well, half the staff does," the headmaster replied levelly. "Dzongkha is our national language." Mrs. Joy tried to give me a whispered account of "the problem with these people," meaning the Bhutanese, but I pulled away. I do not want to be a part of whatever factionalism is developing here.

Outside the door of my classroom, I pause briefly, listening to the clatter and chatter inside. It stops abruptly as I swing open the door. This is my favorite part of the day. "Good morning, Class Two C," I say. The entire class leaps up and sings out, "Good morn-ing, miss!" Twenty-three faces are smiling at me. Sometimes they shout it with so much conviction that I laugh.

I have a syllabus now, and the students have textbooks and thick notebooks, and pencils which they sharpen with razor blades. I haven't mastered the skill yet, and have to ask one of the kids to sharpen my pencils for me. Sharpening miss's pencil has become a somewhat prestigious task, but they were puzzled the first time, watching me almost slice off my fingers, and there was much whispered consultation in Sharchhop. "Where did they find this one?" I imagined them saying. "She can't even sharpen a pencil."

I teach English, math and science in the mornings, and in the afternoon, the Dzongkha *lopen* comes in to teach the national language. From the other classrooms I can hear the drone of students spelling or reading and reciting in unison: "h-o-u-s-e, house, c-a-r-r-y, carry, g-o-i-n-g, going." In the other classrooms, the teacher says something and the students say it back, over and over and over. I cannot think what good this rote learning is doing anyone. I ask the students to read out loud individually and they look at me as if I have lost my mind.

Often, attendance is the only thing we manage to accomplish in class II C. There are a thousand interruptions. A woman knocks at the window and holds up a cloth bag. The entire class rushes over. "Class Two C," I say, "sit down. There's no need for all of you to be at that window." Actually, there's no need for any of them to be at that window. "Who is it?" I ask.

"It is Sangay Jamtsho's mother," they answer.

"What does she want?"

"Sangay Jamtsho forgot his *jhola*."

"Sangay Jamtsho, go and get your jhola," I say. The entire class rolls toward the door, like ball bearings, but I am there first. "I said Sangay Jamtsho. Sit back down, the rest of you."

Sangay Chhoden comes up to my desk. Beneath her thick thatch of hair, her delicate features are screwed up in concentration. "Miss," she says so softly I can barely hear. "House going."

"What do you mean, Sangay?"

"Yes, miss."

I start again. "House going?"

"Yes, miss."

"Your house?"

"Yes, miss, my house going!"

"Now?"

"Yes, miss. House going now, miss."

"But why, Sangay? Why house going now? Now is school. Are you sick?"

"No, miss. House going now."

I sigh, exasperated. "Are you coming back?"

"Yes, miss. Coming."

"Okay, go."

Dorji Wangdi, the official assistant, tea-maker, and general all-round helper whose official title is "peon," knocks at the door. "Chit from Headmaster, Sir," he says, handing me a notice. It has been noticed that some teachers are "biasedly motivated" and all staff are kindly requested to follow the rules and regulations of the school and to attend to each and every duty including morning assembly without prejudice to their utmost ability for the smooth functioning of the school. This notice is for our "kind information and necessary action, please."

Sangay Dorji puts up his hand. His "stomach is paining," can he go to the toilet? Norbu's hand shoots up. His stomach is also paining. So is Sonam's! So is Phuntsho's! I tell them to wait until Sanjay Dorji comes back, but Sangay Dorji does not come back. I am so intent on explaining the difference between long 'a' and short 'a' that I do not notice until another student calls out, "Miss! Sangay Dorji is playing outside!" I look out the window, and yes indeed, there is Sangay Dorji, playing outside.

I send Karma Dorji to get Sangay, and we get all the way to long 'o' before I look out the window to see Sangay *and* Karma playing outside.

Mr. Iyya, Pema Gatshel's self-proclaimed bard, knocks at my classroom door. Originally from Madras, Mr. Iyya has been at the school for more than ten years. His curly black hair is slicked back with hair-oil, and he sometimes wears a spotted cravat. His everyday speech is a garbled mess of malapropisms, misquotations, and flights of fancy, and his poetry, which he pastes on the school bulletin board, is even worse. He is in charge of all English extracurricular activities—the school magazine, debates and plays. Underneath the genteel-poet guise, though, he has a terrible temper. Yesterday, I was horrified to see him break a stick on a class III boy's hand.

"Yes, Mr. Iyya?" I ask.

He bows deeply and says he would like to apologize to my ladyship for this untimeless interruption but he would like to humbly request me to borrow him my cane as he has the gravest misfortune of a broken one.

"My what?" I ask.

"Your ladyship's cane."

I stare at him. Mr. Iyya is definitely unhinged. I turn to class II C. "He wants one stick for beating, miss," one of them informs me.

"I do not use a cane in my classroom," I tell Mr. Iyya coldly, and close the door with a bang.

Dorji Wangdi knocks at the door. Another chit for my kind information and necessary action. There will be a *puja* at the school in a few weeks for the benefit of all sentient beings. All teachers are invited to attend.

Mr. Tandin, the class VIII history teacher and Store-in-Charge, comes to tell me that the School Store will be open for one half-hour. I go up to the Store and bring back twenty-three boxes of crayons. Class II C falls silent at the sight of them, and then erupts in a cheer. "Miss, I am very happy to you!" Sonam Phuntsho crows jubilantly. The crayons are magic. Class II C is very quiet as I explain that these are their own crayons, and they have to look after them, as it is highly unlikely that I will be able to persuade Mr. Tandin to release twenty-three boxes of crayons from his paltry store ever again. I tell them I will read them a story and then they will draw me a picture of the part they liked most. "Once a long time ago there was a mouse," I begin, but there is another knock at the door.

After school, I go up to the library and fling open the window. Everything is covered with a fine white dust. I begin to pull boxes off the shelves in an attempt to impose some sort of classification system, but there is hardly enough material to classify. I ponder various systems, but the most appropriate one seems to be: unreadably tattered, moderately tattered, and untouched (all the Canadian readers fall into this category). I lock the door and go home to find three students sitting at the top of my stairs, their ghos splotched with mud from an after-school soccer game. Karma Dorji and Norbu are back, and they have brought Tshewang Tshering, whose standing-up hair has recently been shaved off. "Are you waiting for me?" I ask stupidly. Of course they are. My Australian neighbor on the other side of the building, some sort of sheep or cow or horse insemination expert, has been out-of-station since I arrived. "May-I-come-in-miss?" they chorus as I open the door. Once inside, they stand uneasily. I usher them into the sitting room. They sit in a row on a bench, looking around, smiling at each other, dangling their bare, dirty feet above the floor. Finally, Tshewang Tshering asks me, "Miss, you have snaps?"

"Snaps?"

"Yes, miss. We looking snaps."

Snaps? I feel my face creasing up into a hundred lines of bewilderment as I try to guess what "snaps" could possibly mean. I have an insane idea that they want ginger snaps.

"Miss," Tshewang Tshering says. "Snaps. Mother, father, sister, brother."

"Oh, you want to see pictures! Snapshots!"

"Yes, miss!" They are nodding vigorously.

Oh hurray! I understand! I hurry off to the bedroom and pull out a Ziploc bag of photographs.

"This is my mother," I say, handing out the pictures which they seize eagerly. "My father. My father's house."

"This your sister?" Karma Dorji asks, holding up a picture of my brother, Jason.

"No, that's my brother."

"Your brother, miss?"

"Yes, Karma."

"He is lama!"

"A lama? No . . ."

"Why—why he is having long hairs?"

"Oh, because—because, hmmm," I search for an answer. "Just like that only," I finally say, and they nod.

Tshewang Tshering is looking at a postcard of the Toronto skyline. "Miss, this is your house?"

"No, that's a bank."

"This your house?"

"No, that's an office. All offices."

"This one your house?

"No, no! That the CN tower."

Another postcard, of Yonge Street. "This your village, miss?"

"Yes, Toronto."

"Who is this?" Tshewang Tshering asks, pointing to some tourists on the postcard.

"I don't know," I say, bewildered by the question. "Just some people."

And then I understand. I explain that there are two million people in Toronto, more people in this city than in all of Bhutan.

"*Yallama!*" they say softly, the Bhutanese expression for surprise or disbelief.

Karma Dorji is flipping through a stack of magazines and music books. "Miss, this your mother?"

I get up to look and almost fall down laughing. "No, that is not my mother!" It is Johann Sebastian Bach.

Finally, I ask them if they would like some tea. "No, miss," they say. But I know this is a Bhutanese no, so I go into the kitchen. They follow. Karma Dorji takes the pot from me. "We is making tea for miss," he says.

"Oh no, that's ok," I say. "I'll make it." I try to prize the pot away from Karma Dorji, but he won't let go. "You're too young to make tea by yourself," I explain. "My kerosene stove is very dangerous." They are reluctant to go, and stand in the kitchen doorway, watching as I pump up the stove. "Back, back," I tell them, gesturing wildly as I throw a match at the stove and push them out of the kitchen. They think this is hilarious. They have to hold each other up, they are laughing so hard.

"Not funny," I say crossly. "Dangerous. You boys wait in the other room."

"Miss, I am doing now," Karma Dorji tells me when he manages to stop laughing. "I am knowing this one. My house is having same-same stove." And before I can stop him, he is pumping up the stove. When it begins to hiss, he lights a match and deftly applies the flame to the stove. A strong blue light appears. I stand openmouthed as Tshewang Tshering fills a pot with water. Norbu is rummaging through the kitchen, pulling out packages of tea, milk powder and sugar. Karma Dorji shakes the cuff of his gho out and wraps the length of it around the pot handle. He pours steaming tea into the mugs. I follow them into the sitting room with a packet of biscuits. Karma tells me that he does the cooking at home when his parents and older sisters are working outside.

"What do you know how to cook?" I ask.

"I am cooking food, miss."

"What kind of food?"

"Food, miss," he says again. "Miss is not eating food?"

"Of course I eat food," I say. "What do you think I eat?"

"Miss is only eating biscuits, my father is telling."

"How does your father know?"

"My auntie is having one shop. She is telling miss is not buying food, only biscuits."

"Aren't biscuits food?" I ask, a little miffed that my eating habits have become news.

"No, miss. Food is rice."

"Ah," I say. "Rice. Well, in my village, in Canada, we do not eat very much rice, so I don't know how to cook it."

They obviously find this hard to believe. "What people is eating then in your village?"

"Oh, potatoes, bread, noodles."

"Miss," Karma Dorji says, his mouth full of biscuit, "I am teaching you how to cook rice. Just now, miss. You have rice?"

"Yes, but—"

All three of them are back in the kitchen. Tshewang Tshering is washing out the teacups. Karma Dorji has found the rice, which he pours onto a tin plate and picks through. I watch helplessly. Within minutes, the rice has been cleaned, rinsed and put into a pressure cooker on the stove.

"Miss." Karma Dorji is looking around the kitchen critically.

"Yes, Karma?"

"You is having onion and chili? I am making *momshaba*."

"Now wait a minute, Karma. The rice is enough."

Karma Dorji begins to chop up onions and chilies. Norbu is separating the spinach leaves he brought this morning and washing them in the sink. The pressure cooker whistles suddenly, sending me scurrying out of the kitchen. "What does that mean?" I ask from the doorway.

"Not finished," Karma Dorji says. "Three times then finished."

After the third whistle, they remove the pressure cooker and Karma Dorji fries the onions and chilies, and then adds the spinach leaves and some tomato slices. Tshewang Tshering pulls the little weighted knob off the pressure cooker lid and steam shoots out to the ceiling. I flutter around the kitchen, issuing unnecessary warnings—be careful, that's sharp, watch out, you'll get a steam burn. When everything is ready, I tell them that they must stay and eat. They protest, but I insist until finally they pull their tin lunch plates from inside their ghos. I am always amazed at what the upper portions of these ghos can hold: books, plates, cloth bags, a bottle of *arra* for me, rice crisps, dried apples, a cucumber, a handful of chilies to eat in class. Karma Dorji serves the food and we eat in silence. I cannot believe how good everything is, the rice sweet and unsticky, the spinach perfectly cooked, although extremely hot. I ask how many chilies are in this dish. Karma says ten.

"Ten! *Yallama!*" I say, wiping my eyes and nose. "How old are you, Karma?"

"Eight," he says and plops another serving of rice onto my plate. "Now miss is knowing," he says. "Now miss is eating food."

When they have gone, I write in my journal: "Anyone can live anywhere, even you. This is for your kind information and necessary action, please."

The End
of the Road

by Marybeth Bond

I had always wanted to go to the end of the road. I gave up my job, and with it the career I had worked so hard to build. I packed up my house, put all my belongings, including my car, into storage, and took off for a year-long sojourn through Asia. Now, perhaps, I could follow a road to its end. I found my chance on an excursion along the India-Pakistan border.

After three painfully hot days on the train from Delhi, I saw Jaisalmer rise out of the flat, yellow Rajasthan desert like a honeycomb. From the humblest shop to the maharajah's palace, the entire town glowed with the golden color of the sandstone from which it is built. Three centuries ago Jaisalmer's location on the old camel route between India and Central Asia had brought it great wealth. Today it is the end of the line. The air is heavy with the fragrances of jasmine, cinnamon and sweet curries. Women in flowing scarves and saris of saffron, turquoise and vermilion glide among camels, sacred cows and rickshas in the narrow unpaved streets.

Sipping tea in an outdoor café, I was enjoying the sight of three regal Rajasthani men in white tunics and pink and orange turbans when I noticed all eyes in the square were focused on me. Feeling uncomfortable, I gulped my steaming tea and slipped into the tangled maze within the old city walls.

Traveling in the summer, in the Indian desert, I thought I had left all Americans or Europeans behind, but at dinner my second evening, I met a French couple from Paris. Gerard was a professional photographer on his second trip to Jaisalmer. A year before, he had spent a month photographing the desert people. Now he had returned with his fiancée, Nicole, to show her his beloved landscape. Although he was very excited by the idea of returning to visit a friend, Farid, in his remote village in the Thar Desert, Nicole didn't seem at all enthusiastic. She had very little to say in either French or English; her bewitching green eyes, framed by long black eyelashes, never stopped scrutinizing me. Gerard, on the other hand, was elated to find an enthusiastic audience for his stories. What excited him about the Thar, he said, was that people still lived exactly as they had for centuries. Suddenly, without consulting Nicole, he asked me if I would like to accompany them on their visit to his friend's village. He added, probably without knowing how the words themselves would tempt me, "It is the end of the road."

The next morning at the intersection that served as the bus stop, Gerard introduced me to Farid, then squeezed through the bus's doorway to join Nicole in a seat. The vehicle was so crammed with passengers, pigs, chickens, baskets and oats that Farid looked at me and pointed to the roof. He formed a foothold with his hands. I caught at an open window and climbed atop the bus, which was piled high with trunks, baggage, livestock and humans. The only unoccupied space on the whole roof was on top of two filthy spare tires. Farid smiled and shrugged as we plopped down on the hot rubber.

The bus roared out of town. The blowing sand and grit stung my face and eyes. I put on my sunglasses and, following the example of the men around me, who used part of their red turbans to cover their mouths and noses, I wrapped my head and mouth with a scarf. The men's dark, penetrating eyes were left exposed. Clouds of dust unfurled behind us as we drove west, into the desert and back into time. Sheep and goats scurried from the road. A baby camel, unsure on skinny legs, looked up from where its mother stood guard as it ate from a single shrub clinging to a sand dune.

As we traveled deeper into the desert, I noticed that the village men were dressed more and more elegantly. They strutted about with their heads swathed in turbans. Thick black mustaches coiled on their weather-beaten cheeks. The women were no less flamboyant in brilliant, ankle-length skirts embroidered with sequins and minute mirrors that glittered as they moved. They wore tight-fitting bodices and on their foreheads, ears, noses, necks and arms they wore silver jewelry. Women and children running out to meet their returning men were like joyous visions stepping from Moghul minia-ture paintings. They came to life with grace and beauty against the parched land and the mud huts. I tried to imagine what their lives were like.

As we proceeded farther and farther into the heat and vastness of the desert, the bus slowly emptied; the road became less and less defined. Upon depositing several men at a cluster of mud huts, where no women came out to greet them, Farid leaned over to tell me: "No marriages have taken place in this village for over five hundred years."

I was startled. Then, not sure I believed him, and not knowing what to say, I stared off into the desert.

"The men in this hamlet never marry. Women who have no dowry end up here to be kept as community property." I glanced at the hamlet, then at him. He whispered: "Like brood mares." Then he too looked off in the desert as he added, matter-of-factly, "Female babies are suffocated at birth with a bag of salt."

I shook my head at his gruesome tale. I wanted to put my hands over my ears.

"Women who give birth to girl babies too often are also killed."

The bus started up with a lurch. I didn't want to believe Farid, but I had recently seen the tiny handprints young widows had pressed into the mud walls of the Jodhpur Fort before they burned themselves on the funeral pyres of their husbands. This custom, suttee, was outlawed in the nineteenth century. Just a few days ago I had read in a Delhi newspaper about the many "dowry deaths" of young girls. Wives often caught fire "accidentally" while cooking, thus freeing the husband to remarry, giving him a chance to secure a larger dowry.

We disembarked at the end of the dirt road, not far from the Pakistani border. Ten round, earth-colored huts with straw roofs were clustered together against the immensity of the desert. Women, children and barking dogs ran out to meet us. The bus soon turned around, leaving us in the dust. It sped back toward Jaisalmer.

Farid's younger brother, Abdul, greeted him with the hugs and kisses traditional among desert men, and proudly escorted us through the huts to their home. It contained a large room with open windows, several wooden cots and a table. The jingling of tiny bells from the rings on her toes announced their mother's arrival. Her bearing was regal, and her face was uncovered. She welcomed us warmly with nods and smiles.

Exhausted from our journey, we accepted an offer to stretch out on the cots. During our rest, curious children poked their heads in at the open doors and windows, sometimes giggling, but often just staring in silence. We were more strange to them than they to us. One tiny girl peered timidly from behind the legs of an older boy to assess the strangers. When she stepped into the light I saw a long red scar that ran from the corner of her right eye to her mouth. I gasped. The older boy, her brother, told Farid that a rat had bitten her.

After a short rest, we were invited across a courtyard to a tiny, unfurnished dining room, where we sat on the floor to eat a hearty lunch of rice, lentils and curried potatoes. There were no eating utensils so we, like the Indians, used our right hands. After lunch, Farid showed us into the family salon for tea. Shelves on the walls held flashlight batteries and empty pop bottles—rare items in the desert.

As Farid's mother served us tea, I noted that Farid and Abdul treated her with great respect. She did not fit the stereotype I held of an exploited Muslim woman. Farid told me his father had been killed in a border skirmish years ago and his mother alone had raised him and his brother. I wished I could talk to her in her own language.

When the heat abated late in afternoon, we went out to have a look around. Cows with ribs protruding from their dried-to-leather hides roamed the dirt paths. Through half-closed doorways I could see women, children and old men sitting in walled courtyards. Their eyes followed our every move.

At dusk, Gerard suggested that we walk to a small hill overlooking the water pond to photograph the village women. Nicole, saying she felt ill, declined to join us.

We heard giggles and laughter before we reached the summit of the hill, from which we could see the shiny copper vessels balanced on the women's heads. When they saw us they became quiet and covered their faces with their veils. They filled their vessels with the muddy water and, balancing them on their heads, glided back into the desert.

After a dinner in semidarkness (there were no candles to spare), Farid and Abdul joined us. Farid told us that, although the India-Pakistan border is officially closed, the desert people do a brisk trade in camels, cattle, goats and food supplies as well as radios, electronic goods, arms and drugs.

"Gerard," he continued, "was the first foreigner to come here before you. I doubt any foreigner," he was watching me closely, "has ever visited the surrounding villages. Would you," he flashed me a big smile, "like to see them?"

"But how?" My voice was more eager than I had expected it to be.

"By camel. There are no vehicles," Farid explained, "wagon, bicycle or car wheels get stuck in the sand. There are no roads beyond my village."

I turned to the others, sure they too would want to go. Gerard was intrigued, but Nicole greeted the idea with scorn. She reminded us how uncomfortable it was even here, and how much more unpleasant it would be riding on a camel and staying in far more primitive villages. Farid said he could arrange for the camels and would ask Abdul to accompany me as guide and translator. That night the thought of a camel trip into the desert wouldn't leave my mind. After hours of pondering the possibilities, I fell into a deep sleep.

Farid woke me with the first morning light, eager to tell me his mother had sent a messenger to ask a neighbor if he would be willing to interrupt his plowing and rent his two camels to us. And Abdul, he said, had agreed to come.

The bus, I knew, would not return to this village for five days. Five days would be time enough for at least a short safari. Or would I rather stay here and listen to Nicole complain? Five days! The idea of a solo adventure tempted me.

I was eager to move on, and yet, anxiously, I kept asking myself: Why am I doing this? If anything went wrong, there would be no one to help me. But the more difficult and frightening the journey seemed, the more alluring it became. Though I tried to be rational, I was already caught up in the romance of traveling the ancient trading route that had once been part of the Silk Road. More than a thousand years ago, countless travelers had journeyed along the 4,000 miles between Rome and China. I imagined their footsteps buried just beneath the blowing sand.

After dinner, while Gerard, Nicole and I were playing cards, Farid came in to announce proudly that the neighbor had arrived with his two camels. "And the camel owner," he said, "will accompany us so he can care for his animals."

I laid down my cards. "I've planned out a circular route," Farid continued, "which will take you into some Indian villages as well as others across the border, in Pakistan."

The sun had risen just enough to cast oblique shadows across the morning haze of the desert. I clambered onto the bony back of the camel to settle on a saddle composed of padded cotton quilts and wool blankets. My limited equestrian experiences had not prepared me for riding a camel.

As the beast rose, first on his back legs, I was thrown forward onto his neck. Then as he lurched up onto all fours, the ground suddenly seemed remarkably far away. Abdul, along with the camel owner, climbed onto the other animal. They led my camel with a rope attached to a wooden peg that pierced his nose. Our little caravan headed off into the desert. Gerard and Nicole waved. *"Au revoir! Bonne chance!"*

Perspiration immediately began to collect under my sunglasses and streak down my cheeks. With every drop of moisture that ran down my neck and chest, a portion of my energy evaporated. Within an hour I was drained and numb. Scant vegetation dotted the barren hills. Each tree or bush or clump of grass, no matter how small, became a focal point for my attention. Abdul and the camelman rode in silence. From time to time we passed a turbaned farmer shuffling behind a camel and guiding a wooden plow. The desert people grow millet, Farid had told me, which is ground into flour to make the flat chapatis that form the staple of the Rajasthani diet. We passed one shepherd tending a scrawny herd of sheep, a few skeletal cows and three goats.

As we plodded through the endless waves of sand, the landscape became more and more barren. My enthusiasm waned in the excruciating heat, in the unending wind that lashed my face with burning sand. My thoughts turned inward. Memories of sailing off the coast of Mexico filled my mind. Over and over again I imagined cool splashing waves rushing over my body. In reality, on camelback in the Thar Desert, I remained a stiffly rocking captive. Minutes seemed like hours. I hadn't worn my watch, nor missed it, since I left San Francisco, but now I urgently wanted to know the time.

Abdul spoke little English, the camelman none. My situation might have been comical if I had not been so miserable. The sun was directly overhead when we spotted the grass roofs on the horizon. Covered from head to toe in dirt, cranky from the heat, weak from dehydration, I was angry with myself for romanticizing the awful reality of a desert camel trip. This is no fun, I finally admitted to myself as tears filled my eyes and a lump grew in my throat. I was so drained of motivation and so uncomfortable I couldn't imagine continuing.

The village was devoid of life. My camel stopped and growled. He wasn't very happy either. As I climbed down, I was so weak I collapsed right into the dirt. Abdul came running. Gently, he helped me to sit up. My legs were stiff, my whole body hurt. I desperately needed to get out of the sun and drink liquids. Abdul led me to some shade and then he went in search of a family who might take us in and provide lunch. I watched him speak to several women. Then he returned and led me to a hospitable-looking hut.

Two pairs of colorful leather slippers with turned-up toes sat by the open door. I left my plastic thongs in line with the slippers and entered. Rugs were piled in one corner, and a small fire pit occupied another. Next to the hearth, clay pots three feet high and two feet in diameter stored the family's precious water. The rugs, cooking utensils, clay pots and two copper jugs for transporting water were the only items on the tidy dirt floor. There were no cans or bottles, no radios or TVs, no pictures, photographs or books—no printed material at all.

An attractive, perhaps thirty-year-old woman, dressed in brilliant red, green and yellow, fanned the fire in the semidark hut. Her head was not draped with a scarf, nor was her face concealed. Though her hands were wrinkled and leathery, her face was smooth. I counted eighteen ivory bracelets above one elbow, and thirteen on her forearm. Heavy bone bangles adorned her ankles; her toes were decorated with two silver bells. Her nose stud identified her as a married woman; the tiers of jewelry announced her husband's wealth.

Sitting on the floor, I watched her prepare the tea. She avoided looking at me. Neither of us uttered a sound. Across the cultural gap that separated us, however, I felt a kind of acceptance: I was alien but unthreatening. I would provide the family with a little extra income and I would become one of the stories she told to her friends at the well.

Fatigue overcame me, so I curled up on the floor with my pack under my head and closed my eyes. Within seconds I was dreaming of swimming deep under water. When I woke, lunch was prepared and Abdul joined us. We ate rice, curried potatoes and hot chapatis in silence. I drank cup after cup of hot, spicy tea to replenish my liquid-starved body.

After lunch I begged Abdul to call it a day and he, always gentle and kind, agreed. The woman cleaned up from lunch and left. I spent a quiet afternoon alone in her home reading, writing in my journal and napping. Late in the afternoon I explored the village. As I walked among the mud huts, dogs barked and children hid. The men, I learned, were in the field plowing, and the women had to walk more than an hour each way to fill their water jugs.

When the woman of the house returned with water at sunset, she immediately began to prepare dinner. Her husband, Abdul and the camelman joined us soon after dusk, but her four young sons remained outside. The men talked until dinner was served. The woman did not speak. Again we ate rice, chapatis and potatoes in silence. I was being treated as a male guest; the woman ate her meal with her children when we had finished.

Later with Abdul's help as interpreter, I complimented the woman on her exquisite jewelry. She was pleased by my attention. She joked with her husband and the men. I didn't understand her words but her humor was evident. She pointed at me and giggled. Abdul said she was teasing me because I wore no jewelry to proclaim my husband's wealth. When I said I had no husband, she indicated that she felt sorry for me. What would I do, she wanted to know, if I had no husband to give me jewelry and no dowry jewels to attract one? With a man for an interpreter, I didn't feel up to embarking on an explanation of American feminism.

What had been my saddle all day became my bed for the night. Abdul helped me spread the cotton quilts on the floor of the hut, and my pack continued to serve as my pillow. Having slept in close quarters with the local people while trekking in Nepal, I did not mind the lack of privacy.

However, the lack of washing water bothered me. But knowing that the woman had already walked hours to collect water for a family of six and three guests, I was unwilling to ask for more than the small bowl allotted to me. I stared into the shallow container. Should I brush my teeth? wash my face? my pits? or quench my thirst? I dipped my toothbrush in the water, then drank the remainder.

In the morning, I was honored by the woman of the house with an invitation to help cook the chapatis over the open fire in her tiny kitchen area. I was amused to think she was probably trying to show me some useful skills that would aid in catching a husband. We left when the sun was just beginning to rise.

The nasty discomfort of the first day repeated itself, and my fascination with the small mud villages vanished. They all seemed the same. The barren dunes stretched for miles as we crisscrossed the unguarded border between Pakistan and India. I could distinguish the Muslim women from the Hindu because the Muslim women kept purdah—clothed from head to toe in black, hiding from the eyes of all men save those of their families. The Rajput Hindu women, like my hostess in the first village, dressed in brilliant colors.

I thought of the lives of the Thar Desert women, the status that jewelry and marriage gave them, and compared it to my determination to live my life on my own.

Alone in the Thar desert with only blue sky and sand and two men more silent than I, I could find no escape from the tormenting truth. As I shifted my aching bones in the saddle, I knew that I alone was responsible for my maddening discomfort. It became clear to me that accepting responsibility for one's acts is a rite of passage for a woman. Suddenly I realized this trip across the desert had become my rite of passage. How much could I endure?

When our camels stopped in the village where we would rest the second night, it was already after sundown. With the last bit of my strength, I slid off the camel and stood by myself in the shadows.

Abdul and the camelman went off to arrange for fodder for the animals and dinner and lodging for us. I sat in the dirt and stared into space. It seemed like hours before Abdul returned. He apologized and said that no one was willing to allow me to sleep in their home. "A single woman," he said, "is suspect."

I reminded him that I would pay well for the honor of sleeping on someone's floor, but he told me money was not the object; a family's reputation mattered more.

I settled for the flat roof of the village schoolhouse. Having climbed the primitive wooden ladder, I made my bed for the night by spreading out quilts in a corner. Abdul gave me some cold chapatis he had been carrying with him in the event of not finding food. I ate them quickly to keep the howling wind from blowing sand into my meager dinner.

A tall, powerful-looking man climbed the ladder to our rooftop and spoke to Abdul. They looked at me, shaking their heads and discussing some issue of importance—perhaps Abdul had found a husband for me. But when Abdul turned to me he asked if I would like to hear some Rajasthani folk music. And would I care to taste the local home brew? If so, he could arrange it through this man, the village elder.

No food in the village, no place to stay, but they could play their music for me. I felt put upon, but I agreed.

Eleven men wearing orange-and-red turbans came to sit in the school courtyard below my perch. One man played a hand accordion, another the sarangi, a violin-like instrument. I learned from Abdul's translation that the melancholy songs were about love and battles. The charm of the repetitious rhythm soon wore off, and the white lightning of the desert, called *asha*, was too strong for my taste. I crawled off to my corner of the roof to be alone.

The wind began to blow ferociously. A crescent moon stood out in the pitch black sky. The stars seemed to compete with each other for space in the heavens. I was awed by the beauty of the desert night, but pleasure lay shrouded beneath fatigue and loneliness. Despite the suffocating heat, I huddled under my quilt to protect myself from the blowing sand and dust and tried to sleep. The entire sand floor of the desert seemed to be shifting across my bed. I could still hear the village men singing and enjoying themselves as I finally drifted off.

Danger!

I struggled awake. The crescent moon had set, the wind had stopped blowing, the night was dark and silent. I lay dead still, my heart pumping in my chest and a lump of fear rising in my throat. Someone was pulling on my cotton quilt. I smelled alcohol. Then I felt someone trying to crawl under my covers. A cold hand touched my bottom. Terrified, then infuriated, I kicked backward, hitting the soft part of a body with my heel. At the same time, I slapped over my head with one arm and screamed at the top of my voice, "Leave me alone!"

I flipped over to face my assailant. I could make out the shadow of the camelman as he crept across the roof and descended the wooden ladder. Where was Abdul? Despite the heat and the weight of my quilts, I began to shiver. Don't be hysterical, I reprimanded myself. Forget it. Go back to sleep. I was lucky, after all, that the camelman was a timid soul, for I was in no shape to fight off a determined attacker. As I kept shaking, I began to pray.

The camelman understood my cold glare and cool attitude for the remainder of the trip. Abdul, realizing something had happened, became more conscientious as my bodyguard.

The third day, as we entered one more village, where I was looking forward to a little exercise to work out the pains in my legs, only dogs came out to bark. But I could partly see and partly intuit that, as in other villages, eyes were scrutinizing us from behind the almost-closed shutters and doors. As Abdul descended from his camel, a group of men converged on us, shouting *"Pagal, Pagal."* One old man with a rifle threatened to shoot. Abdul did not utter a word, but, rapidly remounting, he prodded our animals to move quickly out of town. The men followed, screaming insults until we were far beyond their boundaries.

The villagers felt, Abdul spoke softly, that a woman traveling alone could only mean trouble. Such a woman must be either a lunatic or a witch. They wanted no part of me and my bad luck. My mood was such that I felt it almost an honor, a compliment, to be labeled mad and banished as a witch. I had had just about enough of questioning my own value.

Since Abdul wanted to avoid villages where he didn't personally know a family, we were forced to camp on the sand dunes the last two nights. Before retiring, Abdul scattered raw onion around. "It'll keep the *pena* at bay," he said.

"What's a pena?" I asked.

"It's a snake that comes out at night and crawls onto your warm chest. It spits venom into your nostrils." Fear of the pena didn't keep me awake. I was too tired to care.

On our last day, I caught a glimpse of two wild gazelles with twisted horns playing spiritedly in the distance, and I saw a single man in an orange turban, his back straight and his head held high, walking behind a camel. Arriving back in Abdul's village, we stopped at the water hole to give the camels a drink. The women, hearing us approach, ran to the opposite side of the pond. They giggled and pointed at me.

Abdul's mother welcomed us with genuine warmth and visible relief. I was happy to be back in the village at the end of the road, connected to civilization by motorized transportation.

I had realized my dream and glimpsed for a brief time life at the end of the road—and something else, as well. I had followed that quest despite its uncomfortable, even terrible risks, and had accepted the consequences of my choice. I had stood alone, an outsider, and returned with a new knowledge of myself.

Moonlight and Vodka

by Mary Morris

Train travel for me is the fictive mode. Trains are the stuff of stories, inside and out. From windows I have seen lovers embrace, workers pause from their travail. Women gaze longingly at the passing train; men stare with thwarted dreams in their eyes. Escapist children try to leap aboard. Narratives, like frames of film, pass by.

On the inside I have had encounters as well. I've met people who have become briefly, for the length of the ride, a lover or friend. A strange and sudden intimacy seems possible here. On the Puno-Cuzco Express through the Urubamba Valley of Peru I met a man I thought I would follow across the Andes. On the night train from Chung-king a woman stayed up half the night telling me the story of her life. On an Italian train I met a woman who pleaded with me to go to Bulgaria with her, saying she knew it was where I needed to be. I've been invited off trains into homes, into beds, asked to walk into people's lives, all I am sure because people know a train traveler will never leave the train.

My life even as a little girl was intimately tied to trains, with those fast-moving machines that raced across the Midwestern plains. When I was five, my parents concocted a train journey to Idaho, a family vacation at Sun Valley. My father was not with us on that ride. He would be joining us later, flying in after a meeting, coming for a short spell, his vacation time always being trimmed like lean meat.

So it was my mother, brother, and myself in our tiny compartment, my mother a frazzled woman, alone with these children on a long train ride, lonely I think, but dedicated, as mothers were then, to us. She didn't get angry about the toothpaste flushed down the toilet, the small suitcase that kept falling on her head. She wore lipstick and a blue dress and high heels to dine in the dining car and secured our water glasses with glove-covered hands as the heartland sped by. My mother's agenda was London, Paris, Rome, maybe Hong Kong, but we were en route to Boise, Idaho.

So I escaped and sat, hour after hour, beneath a glass dome, staring at the light over the cornfields. I sat—a dreamy, somewhat forlorn child of five whose father had too much work to do, whose mother was left with the unwelcome task of ushering us to a place of horses and duck ponds— watching the stars coming on like city lights, until my mother retrieved me back into the warm womb of our cramped compartment. Here I kept my eyes open, peering into the night at the passing towns, at the dark expanse of prairie, through a turned-up corner of the window shade as the world as I knew it receded and we moved into the West.

In the morning before daybreak I made my way, still in my night clothes, back to the domed car, to await the rising sun. Slowly it came as the train sped, never changing its pace, and the light opened on the plain. There before me suddenly stood the white peaks of mountains. I had never seen a mountain before and these shimmered—their glacial caps sheathed in sunlight—against the endless blue sky and the flat, green Midwestern plain from which they rose. There on that Union Pacific Railroad, carrying these reluctant travelers to our indeterminate destination, the mountains came upon me as my first truly complete surprise—the way the remarkable events of life have come upon me since.

As the train hurtled to those mountains, even my mother, as she came wearily to find me and try to coax me back to our compartment, paused for a moment in awe.

In the high-ceilinged, dark-wood waiting room for the Trans-Siberian Express, Chinese Muslims, the women with veils over their heads, sat on sacks of bulgur and rice. European students studied their travel guides or slept on their duffel bags. Eastern European diplomats in dark navy suits and shirts with frayed collars milled close to the doors. The noises were those of train travel. Announcements in Chinese blared overhead through static speakers. Anxious travelers—bound for Ulan Bator, Moscow, Warsaw, Bucharest, Belgrade, Berlin, London, and some even for Mecca—checked their watches or bid their goodbyes, though there was none of the frenzy I'd seen at the Chinese International Travel Services office.

I sat on my duffel and went through my papers as well. My ticket, Mongolian transit visa, Soviet visa. Everything seemed in order as I leaned into my duffel, once again suddenly overcome with fatigue as if I had sunk there never to rise again. But suddenly the doors to the waiting room were opened and a surge went through the travelers as we headed like an obedient flock for the door.

I moved slowly from the rear, dragging my duffel behind until I passed through the doors onto the platform. There it stood. An army-green train with perhaps a dozen or so cars, circa 1950, "Peking-Moskau" on its side, Chinese porters in red caps standing at each car, ready to show us to our cars. I stood amazed and thrilled.

I made my way to carriage number 3 where a very tall, very un-Chinese-looking porter, who would take care of our car for the entire ride to Moscow and who spoke enough English and French to make brief conversation possible, took my duffel out of my hand. He led me into the first compartment on that car. Dropping my duffel on the lower berth, he wished me a pleasant journey.

I stared at the lace curtains, the small lamp, the writing table with lace tablecloth, the chair, the small sofa that would convert into a bed. On the advice of a friend I had purchased a deluxe ticket, as opposed to first-class. First-class consisted of a hard bed and four people in the compartment. Deluxe was a soft bed and two people in the compartment. For six days, at a cost of two hundred dollars, I knew I had made the right choice.

I tossed my duffel overhead, pulling out just what I'd need for the day—the copy of *Anna Karenina* I'd planned to reread, my journal, some snacks, and a toothbrush. Then I inspected the compartment more closely. The sofa felt relatively comfortable and I thought that it would make an adequate bed. I opened the door to the semiprivate bath which consisted of a hose shower and a sink, so that at least I'd be able to bathe instead of taking what I'd come prepared for—Wash n' Dri sponge baths.

I sat down at the small table by the window. Travelers scurried outside. Porters helped them with their bags. My porter brought me a pot of tea and said that the samovar was always hot.

I breathed a sigh and settled in. I was opening my journal when Cecilia arrived. She sported a full pack and a loud Liverpool accent. "So here we are. We're roomies. Isn't this great!" She dumped her pack on the floor, hurled a few things onto the top bunk. She was large, a dishwater blonde with square features and a boisterous voice. In a matter of moments I learned that Cecilia was English, living in Singapore with her second husband and her two children, having marital problems, and also, she hinted, an affair. "Going to London," she said. "I needed a break."

I predicted rather accurately that Cecilia would not stop talking for the entire six days and that I'd learn more than I ever cared to know about her, her private life, her feelings for the royal family, her politics, and that if I wanted to think or rest I'd have to work my way around her, which did not seem very easy in an eight-by-six-foot room.

I got up to stretch and Cecilia took the seat at the table by the window, facing the direction in which the train was traveling. There she planted herself for the rest of the trip where she'd sit with her tea, her rock 'n' roll tapes, and the snacks she'd eat all day long, never seeming to have a meal.

I left the compartment and stared out the window. Soon there came a whistle, a brief announcement in Russian and Chinese. The wife of a Yugoslav diplomat who had the compartment next to ours stared out the window as well. When she heard the announcement she turned to me and said in English, "Now we are leaving." She gave me the only smile I would see on her face the entire trip. Suddenly the whistle came again, piercing and more insistent this time, and in a matter of moments I felt the tug of wheels, the power of engines as the journey began.

I found a jump seat at the window. I pulled it down and sat there for a long time. I watched as the residential streets of Beijing drifted away; the stream of bicycles receded, then disappeared. Rice paddies came into view. Farmers in broad-brimmed straw hats bent, legs in upside-down V's, planting in the sodden fields. Oxen pulled plows across the yellow-earth fields. I was oblivious to the other travelers, all with noses pressed to the glass, until someone shouted, "the Wall, the Wall." There it was, snaking across the mountains, crumbling here and there, careening down a ridge, only to rise again; the Great Wall of China wended its way like a mythological beast, fortified and useless against the ostensible fears. Then slowly it diminished until it was only a thin line, like a crack in the earth. And then it was gone.

The dining car looked more like a Chinese laundry than a restaurant—noisy, frenzied, boiling hot. Warm Chinese beer was being handed out and I grabbed one from a passing tray as everyone else seemed to do. The car was packed and I saw no seats, but then Pierre, the French saxophone player I'd met at the Mongolian Embassy, waved from across the room, pointing to half a seat. "So," he said, putting an arm around my shoulder, "you made it." He was sitting at a boisterous table of European travelers—Swiss, French, German and Dutch. They were all speaking assorted European languages, though French seemed predominant. When I joined them they switched to English but I told them French or German was all right.

A small fan blew overhead, the kind a secretary might put on her desk, but the heat continued to rise. Everyone was sweating. Plates of delicious fried meats, sautéed vegetables, rice, were being passed. "Open the window," Pierre shouted in French. Someone who spoke broken Chinese shouted the same thing. The soaking waitress ignored our pleas. Someone opened a window and the cook went wild, screaming in Chinese, slamming it shut. "Dust," he yelled which someone translated, "dust." We drank our warm beer and ate hot food as we baked in the sun.

The heat did not let up and felt close to a hundred and twenty at times. None of the Chinese porters would permit windows to be open. "The desert," our porter explained to me. But finally in our car protests were mounting. At last he let us open the windows in our individual compartments if we kept the doors shut. Cecilia had gone to the dining room to sit, for I don't believe she actually ever dined, and left me alone at the open window, dust blowing in my face.

The landscape had altered. From the farmlands and rice paddies we moved into a mountainous, more arid terrain as we crossed the Northern Chinese province of Inner Mongolia. Though we had yet to reach the desert, a scrub grassland reached to the horizon with occasional sheep grazing. I sat as the day shifted to evening and the heat subsided.

At eight-forty that evening we reached the outpost of Erhlien, the border town between Inner and Outer Mongolia. It was the gateway to Russia, Mongolia being a Soviet protectorate. The station was old-fashioned, like something out of the American West—a small, wood-slat structure. Chinese border guards came onto the train. After checking our passports and visas, they told us we could leave the train.

I stood on the platform, breathing the cool evening air. It was unclear how long our stop was, but to my surprise and almost fear, suddenly they took the train away. I watched as it receded, disappearing behind us. The Chinese Muslim men smiled benignly, but the Europeans seemed dismayed. Then I recalled the words of a friend who'd taken this trip before. "At the borders," he'd told me, "they take the trains away." They have to change the wheels because the track has a different grade, which in part makes international hijacking impossible across Asia and Europe. Also they take the train away because each country has its own dining car and now for Mongolia the new car must be attached.

I was happy to leave the train and walk in the cool night air. It was a lovely night now and a full moon shone overhead. All the travelers went into the station house, but I walked the platform. Chinese Muslim men strolled, but their women were nowhere in sight. In fact the Chinese Muslim women would never leave the train. They would not be seen in public. Instead they remained in their compartments, facing Mecca, eating from the giant sacks of food they had brought and cooking on small portable stoves in their compartments. I always knew where East was and roughly the time of day because the Muslim women would be facing East at specific times.

I went into the station where a small postal service was open. I bought stamps and began to write postcards from the border of Inner and Outer Mongolia, to many people seemingly the most remote place on earth, though in fact it was fairly accessible. I bought a bag of stewed apricots and a warm orange soda from a small stand. I sat in the station on a wooden bench, writing cards while border guards patrolled around me and a bolero of bullfighting music played incongruously on the overhead speakers.

On the platform an hour or so later, I ran into the Chinese Muslims I'd sat next to on the floor of the Chinese International Travel Services office. We greeted one another like long-lost friends. They laughed, happy to see me, and pointed to my pen which remained in my hand. One made a sweeping motion as if to wipe sweat off his brow, indicating how hot they had been. Then they pointed to the yellow moon over Mongolia, clasped their hands as if in blessing, and smiled.

At about midnight the train returned with new wheels and a Mongolian dining car and we crossed into the People's Republic of Mongolia. The temperature had dropped considerably and it was actually cool. I grabbed a sweater from my compartment. Then after perhaps half a mile the train stopped and Mongolian passport officials boarded. They had wide bronze faces, reminiscent of the indigenous peoples of America. Some theories of human migration say that these ancient Central Asian peoples crossed the Bering Strait and were the first inhabitants of the Western Hemisphere, the people from whom all the Native Americans descended.

But now their being part of the police state was clear. The train was thoroughly searched. Beneath bunks, overhead racks, suitcases were moved aside to search for contraband. Then, at 1:00 A.M., they left and we entered Mongolia.

I found I could not sleep so I wandered to the darkened new dining car, which, with arching windows, scalloped seats, red curtains, looked more like a mosque than a dining car. Pierre was sitting with two Dutch girls. The Mongolian dining crew—a man and his wife—were already setting up for breakfast. They worked noiselessly in the background.

Pierre ordered a bottle of Mongolian vodka and poured drinks all around. The man, who wore a small, brightly colored skullcap, and the woman, with a scarf around her head, both with sharp Mongolian features, wide, flat faces, brought glasses out and joined us. They raised their glasses and we raised ours. Then we sat in the darkened car, watching the beginnings of a moonlit Gobi rush by, drinking Mongolian vodka into the night.

The Longest Short Trip

by Pramila Jayapal

It wasn't a big trip, the eight-hour journey from Seattle to the Wallowa Mountains in eastern Oregon. In fact, compared to the traveling I have done in my life, this should have been downright easy. It was just a drive to a beautiful mountain home where I would spend a week writing by myself, a short trip with no changes in time or language or food or bodily functions.

I've traveled for most of my life, to remote villages in Africa and shepherd encampments in the mountains of India. I've traveled to places where the paths never stopped and the earth did not end. I've traveled to silently productive communities in the middle of deserts that mocked my previous notions of civilization. I've traveled with other people for companionship and as my own shepherd, trusting intuition over intention and chance over certainty.

At five years of age, I moved with my parents from India to Indonesia, a journey that seemed to my family like a brave venturing out into unfamiliar territory. I was too young to fear the journey but old enough to sense the excitement surrounding it. Some years later, my parents took a vacation to Europe and sent my sister and me, with identity cards on chains around our necks, from Singapore to India to stay with our grandparents. We were ushered from plane to plane by friendly flight attendants and kept occupied with stick-on airplane wings, decks of cards and cooing passengers. Perhaps it was then that we began to take for granted that we were safe in our travels and that we would always travel, whether to see our family or to journey on our own.

And so the travel continued, first on family vacations and later, in high school, with friends, on class trips and singing tours. I flew with my friends to Bali, to the forests of Java and Sumatra, to desolate places where only our propeller planes could land and we were to sing to isolated expatriate families who worked for oil companies. What may have seemed adventurous to someone else felt quite normal to me.

It was when I was sixteen, however, that I made what I consider to be my first real solo trip. I was going to college in the charmed land of America. It was the first time I would travel alone, but it was more than that. I was setting off on something, a new chapter of my life that I would have to forge myself. My parents would be thousands of miles away and I would see them only once a year, during the summer. My closest family would be my sister in Philadelphia, a few hours away from my school in Washington, D.C.

I arrived in America with two suitcases of cotton clothes, no socks or closed shoes, and sixteen years of very limited wisdom. As I would realize much later, the aloneness of the physical journey was miniscule compared to the aloneness of the trip I would take over the next fourteen years in America. This was a journey no one could travel with me. I would have to slither through unknown spaces and unexpected turns by myself, exploring a new country and culture that often seemed as strange to me as mine might have seemed to others.

I've analyzed and explored my first solo journey at length, a fourteen-year trip that came to an end only after I returned to live in India for two years at the age of thirty. In my mind, I rolled my time in America around like weighty Chinese hand-massage balls, trying to understand the feelings and experiences I had had of assimilating and differentiating. Only when returning to live in my birth country did I realize that in order to know the place we end up, we need to know the place we come from.

I realize now that travel is not just about physically going somewhere, but about conscious exploration. The physicality of aloneness pushes some people toward this conscious exploration of their surroundings and themselves. Being alone physically—not having someone to share your adventures with as they unfold, having to make every decision, big and little, being able to relax only by yourself or with strangers and never with a trusted friend or lover, waking up by yourself—does make you understand aloneness, the freedom and the pain associated with it.

But for me, there was no real edge to aloneness because I had become used to it. Sometimes I missed being with someone, but the independence I had developed from leaving home at a young age carried me well. Most important, I was always emotionally connected to the partner I had left at home. Knowing he was there allowed me to enjoy aloneness without being lonely.

My second real solo journey began when I separated from that partner of twelve years. The extending I would be forced to do this time was different. Making the decision to leave was excruciating and took over a year. In separating, I was challenging not just our relationship but the cultural values of my heritage: I was the first in my family to leave a marriage.

I was not going easily this time, and often not even voluntarily. I hadn't paid for my tickets because I wasn't sure I wanted the trip, but I was pushed along by the crowd of choice, fate and time. Even before starting the journey, I was aware of moments when I cowered from myself, refusing to be either the sheep or the shepherd.

As I travel this path alone, I tell myself that stillness is as much a part of travel as motion, and then I fight with the silence. There are moments of wonder and possibility when I think about what I might discover in this new territory ahead, but I'm without the consuming excitement I've had when I've ventured off alone before. Perhaps, as with the arranged marriages that my mother tells me about, there's less to be disappointed with this way.

My separation occurred one year before my Wallowa Mountains trip. In the agonizing back-and-forth of letting go and holding tight, and the frenzied conversations of what was and wasn't, what could be and couldn't, there had not been time for me. My ex-partner and our four-year-old son were to go to New York for Thanksgiving, so I accepted an invitation from a friend to use her house in the Wallowas for a week of writing and healing.

For a woman who used to travel alone to remote places for many months of the year, a simple eight-hour drive and one week writing alone should not have caused the panic it did. But the fear was keen, more acute even than the sense of danger I have had wandering by myself through deserted city streets in strange places late at night. Travel abroad was a world I knew. This journey, this aloneness, was completely unfamiliar.

I reassured myself by dwelling on the limited nature of the trip and on my competence as a traveler. I tried to forget that it would be Thanksgiving—the first one I would spend by myself since arriving in America (there had always been friends before my partner)—and also our anniversary. I had been married on Thanksgiving Day nine years earlier. I ignored the way my stomach churned with every new logistical twist and resisted the desire to run into the largest, noisiest crowd I could find.

The gracious owner of the house to which I was going sent me an e-mail saying that snow had fallen and I should expect difficult driving over mountain passes. The journey would likely take more than eight hours, she warned. Bring snow tires or chains, warm clothes, a thermos of hot drinks. Keep the number of my friend near the Oregon border in case you are stuck in snow and need to stay the night.

To be sure I was prepared for an unexpected night in the car, my friends brought me sleeping bags and blankets, while I fished out a full bottle of Scotch. They advised keeping fresh fruit and vegetables handy, while I shopped for Pringles and Doritos, foods I hadn't eaten since I was a freshman in college.

One close friend finally confronted me. Why, she asked, was I insisting on a long, snowy drive alone on a holiday that had meaning to me as a time of celebrating relationships, when I didn't particularly like driving, considered snowballs a novelty, had never attached a pair of chains and had a car with a reputation for slipping and sliding across ice?

Why, indeed?

I knew I *needed* to go. I needed to know I could. For all my travel, I felt like the sixteen-year-old that had arrived in America, but this time without the child-like naivete about what it means to be alone. I had spent the last twelve years of my life with one partner, given birth to a gorgeous child and yet, here I was, alone again. Like the intrepid traveler who has reached one place and isn't sure she wants to stay, I had to find a way to move on. By myself.

Three days before I left, I called a friend in a panic. Would she come with me? She had made the mistake of gently telling me that it would be okay not to go, that when she had split up with her long-time girlfriend some years before, being alone was the last thing she would have been able to do. Give yourself time, she had advised softly. You don't have to confront all of it right now.

My call to her was too late. She was teaching until the day before Thanksgiving, and as much as she wanted to go and understood my panic, she couldn't.

I focused on the driving, which was my outward sign of terror. If I could get through that, I thought, I would be okay. I packed up a shopping bag full of CDs, a variety that could satisfy my wildly vacillating moods: Bob Dylan and his scratchy whine on love lost, old favorites like

Talking Heads and Elvis Costello, soulful women like Cesaria Evora and Shawn Colvin, Anoushka Shankar's sitar music and Native American women singing to the spirits. There were other shopping bags too—ten of them to be precise—along with several bags of just-in-case supplies. The haphazard plethora of shopping bags was a sharp contrast to my typical minimalistic and ordered packing.

I had planned not to bring any books. For a reader like me, this was the equivalent of running into the middle of a charging group of tigers, but I had been wanting to try writing without reading at all, to see if I could hear my writing voice better that way. At the last minute, I caved in. I threw in a bag of about twenty books—poetry collections and new novels, heavy non-fiction treatises on incomprehensible subjects and three months' worth of unread magazines. This was not the time for brave experiments.

I woke up early the morning I was to leave. I planned to depart by 8:00 A.M. and drive without stopping to the Wallowas. If all went well, I would make the trip in daylight, before darkness fell, roads iced over and mountain passes became treacherous. I glued myself to The Weather Channel on television, laughing to realize I had never before checked the weather prior to a trip. The report was terrible: icy roads, accidents all over the highways out of Seattle. Don't drive unless you have to, intoned the weather reporter. Wait until the fog lifts and the sun comes out.

I waited. I ate three satsumas and drank multiple cups of coffee. I checked and rechecked my bags, reread the instructions on the snow chains I had bought the night before and made sure my cell phone battery was fully charged. When there was nothing left to pack or unpack or check or recheck, I spread out my Washington and Oregon maps on the dining table to look again at my route. From Seattle, I would head east over Snoqualmie Pass, through the apple orchards of Yakima and the dry, rolling Horse Heaven Hills. I'd continue south through Prosser and the Tri-Cities area, crossing the border into Oregon. Just south would be the Blue

Mountains pass, over three thousand feet. Then I'd head east off the main highway towards the edge of the state and into the small town of La Grande and, finally, to Joseph, Oregon, where the road ended.

I'd stay in Joseph, a small village cradled at the base of towering mountains, named after Chief Joseph and home to the Nez Perce Indians. The Wallowa Mountains, a little-visited part of Oregon, were spectacular, I already knew. I had been there the summer before to teach a writing workshop and had been stunned by the grandeur of the scenery. This time, though, I would see it in winter when the lake outside Joseph would be frozen and snow would cover the massive mountains.

The sun finally showed itself at about nine-thirty and I quickly jumped in the car and left. As I crossed the bridge out of Seattle toward the mountains, I found my shoulders dropping a little. I actually heard the music that was playing and began moving to the song. A sense of excitement and adventure that felt familiar and wonderful, like an old friend lost and now found, surged through me.

As I drove, I noticed my surroundings with the sharpness of sudden vision. The trees were bare and stark. Stalactites gripped sheer rock face, frozen in motion. Shadowed fog lifted off the hills and mountains, and scattered sprigs of snow rested languidly across trees and branches. I was driving further out, into unfamiliar terrain.

I drove too fast along the highway, Bob Dylan wailing loudly and the yellow lines of the road flying in my face. The road wound around tall skinny poplars standing like pilgrims praying with straight arms to the sky. Next to it, towers like steel men carried power lines up the hills beside bristly, snow-dotted clumps of green and brown bush. I climbed up and up and up the Blue Mountains, now with Tracy Chapman's melodious voice both keeping me company and allowing me to feel my aloneness. There was freedom here on the highway, a sense of beginning something new—even if it meant that for the first time in almost two decades, I was not sure with whom I would share my stories. Next to me, snow molded the Blue Mountains like white thimbles. The valley and canyon walls ran alongside streams and rivers turned to glittering hard ice that shimmered in snatches of sunlight.

With the sun on my face and the wind whistling through the cracked window, I suddenly remembered something a friend had written me when I had first separated from my partner. "You'll get through," she wrote. "It takes forever, but the balance of the day shifts back into your favor. And one day, you find yourself in mildly recognizable but mostly unfamiliar terrain and you realize you're even happy." Yes, I felt that, the first sense of some deep joy that pierced through everything else. Fleeting as it might be, it was something to hold on to.

I reached Joseph by four in the afternoon, stopping first at Chief Joseph's grave to give silent thanks for allowing me to use his land for this solo journey of mine. I felt a lifting of spirit, a release of anguish and tension and fear as I entered a lovely barn house with wood-beamed rafter ceilings, a burning wood stove and a view of silhouetted mountains in the darkening sky.

I sat on the floor in the middle of the room in front of my burning stove, listening to the crackle of wood and smelling the stick of incense I had lit. *You'll get through,* I echoed to myself. *You'll get through—and maybe, even more.*

The house was a two-story building with unexpected vaulted ceilings and, at the very top, a steep set of stairs that led up to a charming meditation room. Linda, the owner, had been a student in my writing workshop and had offered me the house as a thank-you for the class. Her generous and gentle spirit infused the house. There were incense sticks and candle holders, essential-oil diffusers, beautiful pottery and glassware, and a lovely bronze statue of a woman that graced the living-room table. The wood stove sat against a brick wall and radiated heat and comforting crackles.

I established a routine that depended on no other person. I would wake up early, around six, when it was still dark except for the faint blue outlines of the distant mountains against a slowly lightening horizon. I'd lie in bed in the room upstairs, looking out a floor-to-vaulted-ceiling wall of windows. After a quiet meditation in bed, I'd pad downstairs and light the fire. I'd have my coffee on the couch in front of the fire, drinking in the warm liquid and the gorgeous views, watching the deer frolic outside my window. Then, I'd sit at the big wooden dining table and write. I wrote well, focused on the words and undistracted by phone calls or emails. At about eleven-thirty, I would stop, stretch and go for a long walk through town or out to Chief Joseph's grave or to the lake below. I'd come back and take a hot shower or bath, eat lunch, and then write again for several hours. If ever I couldn't take the unending silence, I'd turn on the television and listen to the equally unending analysis of the Florida recount of the 2000 presidential election. I did not read and did not want to—other people's words and stories felt like clutter to me.

Sometimes, during the days, loneliness flew in and surprised me, blanketing me in cold and shutting out the warmth. But, consistently, it was the evenings that felt longest: it was then I had to face my aloneness. Silence rang loudly in my ears and stillness set in like an aching cramp. Unlike my other travels, there was no talking companion to search out in a nearby café, no new sight to be seen. I ate the Pringles I had brought and then bought some more. I cradled my rapidly diminishing bottle of Scotch and turned music on and off when the memories evoked by a song unexpectedly sent me into tears. I lay awake at night gazing at the bright stars through the glass windows across from my bed and feeling the empty space next to me. On Thanksgiving Day, my ninth wedding anniversary, I heated up a four-cheese pizza and polished off more glasses of red wine than I'm able to remember. As I read somewhere recently, the truth will set you free but it's hell in the meantime.

Writing well and feeling my aloneness were inextricably linked. I wrote stories that tapped into those feelings of fear and isolation, of uncertainty and fragility. I wrote, cried, laughed and played with an intensity that left me exhausted. In getting through and even thriving on some days, I felt as if I were pushing the boundaries of what I thought I was capable of in the same way we do as travelers in new countries. And, finally, I allowed myself to accept a truth I've always wanted to escape: that we are ultimately alone.

By the time I was ready to leave the Wallowas, I had two completed stories, the start of a novel, several empty bottles of Scotch and beer, and fifty burned-down stubs of incense sticks. I heard on the radio that a big snowstorm was due to pelt Washington and Oregon, and travel advisories were out for later in the day. I wanted to leave early, but by the time I packed up, it was already ten in the morning. I armed myself with an enormous cup of coffee, two fresh, homemade sweet pastries from the neighbors and an apple. I looked for Pringles and Scotch just in case I got stuck somewhere, but it was a Sunday morning and the stores were all closed.

The weather was beginning to gray, the radio warned of heavy snow, the winds whistled around me and forced me to grip my steering wheel tighter. I had to drive slowly, with no music to distract me from the narrow canyon roads out of the Wallowas. The Grande Ronde River next to me was surging along, creating white foam as it went. On the road, black ice hid in the curves and turns. The trucks had already been along, scattering salt, but the roads remained treacherous. When I finally made it over the Blue Mountains, I breathed a sigh of relief. Visibility was still poor, but I was on a highway now.

Unfortunately, the trip did not speed up. It took me six hours to reach a spot about thirty miles east of Snoqualmie Pass in Washington. Snow had started falling furiously, the flakes getting smaller and smaller as the snowfall increased. There was no turning back, nothing to do except sit with the hundreds of other stationary cars at the eastern foot of the pass. I sat there in almost the same spot for two hours, watching evening come, darkness fall and snow blanket the roads. I was stuck, this time in the midst of cars and people, but again, alone.

I've always liked the concept of snow but not the reality of it. Running around in it for a few minutes is one thing, but driving in it is another. Every time I tried to move an inch, my car slipped, veering dangerously into the narrow space between the road and the side railing. With the road as narrow as it was and cars packed bumper to bumper, there was no room to put on my snow chains. This was a blessing and a curse. Truthfully, I would have traded in a flash trying to put on snow chains in the dark for finding my way from Senegal to Ghana or crossing the Mekong from Thailand to Laos. Those I knew how to go about; this I didn't.

It took me three hours of slippery, tension-filled driving to travel a mere ten miles. In my earlier confidence, I had forgotten to recharge my cell phone. It died in the middle of a call to a friend to get reassurance and company.

In my overly dramatic mood, death seemed certain to clasp its black, suffocating paws around me. For the next hour and a half, as I crawled some few miles, I thought of all the people I wished I had said goodbye to properly, the fights I had left unresolved, the son I adored and would never see again. Most of all, I thought about how I desperately wanted companionship in the moment, someone to turn to and rely on. I pushed down the tears that were welling up, took some deep breaths to relieve the tightness in my chest and angrily blared Elvis Costello's "Alison" twenty times in a row. Fear and loneliness bring out the obsessive-compulsive in me.

I finally reached a place where the road widened and I saw some people putting on chains. *They'll surely help me,* I thought with relief. I pulled over and walked through the cold, snowy night to each of three cars. The other drivers barely cast a glance at me, saying both in words and gestures that they were too busy and cold to help me with my chains.

Down on my back next to my car, fingers frozen because I had misplaced my gloves, I felt like I was trying to push a square peg into a round hole. I was halfway through my work when I heard someone next to me: "*Hola!* Do you need help?" It was a Latino man with his wife, who was shivering in open-toed sandals with thin cotton socks. They spoke little English, but help requires no common spoken language. If I felt like a stranger in America after fifteen years in the country, this couple recognized the fear and aloneness as their own. Together, we attached my chains and chatted for a few moments. Were they okay, I asked? *Sí, sí,* they nodded vigorously. We shook hands and I thanked them with inadequate words, knowing that they understood anyway.

I clanked along the road, hearing the chains cut through ice and slush. The road was dimly lit with car lights filtering through thick fog. When I reached the bottom of the pass, I took my chains off with ease and enjoyed the silence of driving. Around me, stars twinkled in the dark night sky and it was as though I had never gone anywhere at all.

I reached Seattle twelve hours after leaving Joseph. My house, quiet and dark, was heavenly. It didn't matter that it was quiet—I welcomed the aloneness, this time in a safe place I called home. I poured myself a tall, cold beer and started a hot bath.

As I collapsed into the lavender-scented bubbles, I had a sudden thought: my third solo journey was about to begin.

Redeye to Thai

by Michelle Kehm

Freeing myself from the shackles of India, I hopped the redeye out of Delhi and arrived in Bangkok sick, thin, travel-haggard and hungry. But in a way it was perfect, because my tired, depleted state made everything I was to experience that much more sensually and spiritually satisfying.

I went to my usual Bangkok guesthouse. I slept all day, then went to McDonald's and gorged American-style on French fries and a hot fudge sundae before heading to see the *X-Files* movie with Thai subtitles. I was in a whole new world, appreciative of the world I had left behind in India, but glad to be where I was now.

I wanted to go to an island, a *ko*. A couple of years before, I had traveled up and down the south coast of Thailand, where the most plentiful and popular kos are situated: Ko Samui, Ko Phangan (famous for X parties), Ko Tao. But the islands down there are pretty cosmetic and meat markety, and I wanted a paradise in the rough. I just wanted to be.

I chose Ko Chang, a little piece of paradise floating in the Gulf of Thailand, within a stone's throw of Cambodia. I knew that a lot of locals went to Ko Chang for the holidays, and I love to hang out with the Thai folks. I also knew that accommodations on Ko Chang were somewhat primitive by Western standards, which meant no blow-'em-up movie nights, Internet cafés or curling-iron travelers. Plus, the trip was only five hours from Bangkok, and after India, that seemed deliciously easy on the ass.

I bought myself a bunch of new tapes for my Walkman (Bangkok is literally crawling with bootleg booths that sell tapes for a buck apiece), a couple of books, a $10 bikini, and I was ready to ko.

To Ko

Fact: Ko Chang is the main island in a national marine park that comprises fifty-two islands. Chang has a few villages supported by fishing, coconuts and smuggling, but the other islands are pretty desolate.

The Bangkok minibus picked me up at 11:00 A.M. It was a hot, rainy day, and it was pure luxury to sit back and listen to my new tapes and look out the window and not have to talk to anybody. After being crammed on Indian buses with no shocks and sometimes no seats in 100-degree-plus weather, this little cushy-seated, air-con'd eight-seater was absolutely dee-vine.

About five hours later, the bus dropped us off at the docks in Trat, the launching pad for Ko Chang National Marine Park. There was a restaurant and several little cheap-cheap shops selling all the last-chance items any tropical island farang could need or want: sandals, sunscreen, snorkeling gear, Thai whiskey. I bought my ticket for the boat and stared out at the green sea. I could see Ko Chang—a big lump of coconut trees and rolling mountains, maybe a quarter-mile off shore.

All I could think about was how absolutely delicious it was to be back. It had been two years since I was last on the shores of the Thai sea. There's something about it that is so beautiful, peaceful and slow—it's as if every moment comprises a lifetime. The warm sea air smells thickly of salt, burning coconut fields, fish sauce and other spices from the food carts everywhere. And somehow even the piercing, polluting sounds of the third-world boat engines slicing through the calm green seawater seem serene, nonviolating.

The boat was overloaded with vacationing locals, people bringing rice and fruit from the mainland, and a few farangs like myself. I found a place to sit among the salty ropes, live chickens and rice bags. Then the engines fired up, cutting out all human communication; people hid from the sun, dozed off or gazed at the water. I sat back against my pack and marveled at the view. Thick forests, raw beaches, coconut groves. No beachfront condos, no Coney Island stalls, not even a sandcastle half-eaten by the sea. I felt adventurous. Raw. Real.

We docked forty-five minutes later, and everyone jumped onto a truck that drove along the island's one road to a beach with accommodations for travelers. I had no idea where I was going. I just got off when all the other backpackers did, and walked straight to the sea's edge. I was at White Sand Beach, and, judging by the number of sunburned, thonged farangs lounging everywhere, it was clearly the island's hot spot.

I walked along the beach, kicking the warm sea, checking out bungalows; everything seemed too populated for me. People were baking in the sun, playing guitars, bodysurfing. I walked about a mile to the end of the beach and still didn't find what I was looking for, but I was tired and sweaty, so I decided to stay at White Sand for one night. I'd swim, rest and continue my search for the perfect beach the next day.

Khlong Phrao

The next morning I hitched a ride a few kilometers down to Khlong Phrao beach—a beautiful, quiet bay with snow-white sand and a couple of islands just off the coastline. It looked perfect: quiet, desolate. I started walking.

But Khlong Phrao accommodations turned out to be mostly highbrow resorts priced at $100 a night—outrageous for Thailand. I spent the morning walking down the beach (it's a very long beach) in search of a place I could afford.

Then, around ten or so, the sun started searing. It was about the time all the locals head inside to fan themselves and gossip, and I was out on the beach lugging a twenty-pound backpack, sweating profusely, refusing to stop until I found a place to call my own. I kept feeling these little stings up and down the backs of my legs and arms. I knew there were sand fleas on the beach because I could see them, but as far as I knew the only biting sand fleas were white and bit at dusk and dawn. These were black and it was midday, so I thought I was safe.

On my last trip to a Thai island, I had been eaten alive by sand fleas and faced such an unimaginable form of itchy purgatory that I had made a mental note to stay off the beach during biting hours next time. But were these fuckers biting me at straight-up noon? If they were, there was absolutely nothing I could do about it. I was in the middle of a huge beach with nowhere to go. I tried to tell myself it was the salt from my sweat crystallizing in the thick heat. Right. I was the lunch special of the day.

For the next three days, I huddled in a cheap Khlong Phrao bungalow, covered in flea bites, hiding from the beautiful but flea-infested paradise outside my door, paralyzed with fear by those little black biting dots. I was trapped. I felt like a rabid animal, my mind wigged out from an overdose of flea poison and nonstop, hair-raising, head-to-toe itchiness.

Being covered in flea bites is an experience that you can't adequately describe to somebody who's never had the extreme displeasure. It's excruciatingly frustrating. Your entire body screams, demanding to be itched, but itching is the one thing you know you shouldn't do. It's the ultimate test of mind over body, and one your mind always loses. Even the most innocent scratch or accidental brush of fabric against skin packs such a wave of orgasmic pleasure that once you get a little taste, there's no turning back. Five minutes later you awaken from your pleasure-trance scratch-dance, covered in blood, with pieces of skin all over your sheets, and what's left of the skin on your body is raw and ON FIRE. This is exactly why flea-bitten beach varmints have no fur.

I had my flea-bite routine down: cold shower, pasty pink calamine lotion, prickly heat powder (a Thai staple, it contains cooling menthol and feels great), then a dab of a special fiery yellow oil some Thais gave me right on my bites. This oil is the local secret brew. It comes in a tiny bottle half as long as your pinkie—just a touch and shazam! That spot is on fire! After I completed my full flea routine, my whole body would combust for half an hour, sometimes just long enough for me to fall asleep. But of course, I'd wake up in a scratching frenzy in the middle of the night and . . . just . . . couldn't . . . stop . . . it . . . felt . . . so . . . good.

I was a mangy mess. I looked ludicrous covered in pink calamine lotion and caked up with prickly heat powder. The locals whispered to each other about me—"Oh! The poor farang!" I had to get away from that flea-infested beach. And I had this painful little lump under my right arm to boot. I knew I had to see a doctor, but none of the locals spoke English so I didn't know where or how to find one. Finally, I charaded "doctor" to a couple of locals, and, once we understood each other, I had them write the word down in Thai on a piece of paper. I took it up to the road and hitched for two hours, showing it to anyone who stopped, trying to get a ride. But they would just shake their heads apologetically. Nobody would take me to a doctor, and I had no idea why because I couldn't understand what anybody said. (I found out later that the road was washed out due to heavy rains.)

So, with all the pride of a hairless beach stray, I tucked my tail, itched and hitched my sorry ass all the way back to where I started—flea-free White Sand Beach.

I got off at the first bungalow in the mile-long row of beds-for-hire. I wanted to be at the very end, where I thought it would be quietest. That first bungalow was called La Plaloma. I had been, again, stubbornly prepared to walk around to find a good place, but once I met the folks at La Plaloma, I didn't leave for two weeks.

The Gates of Heaven Open

I walked into La Plaloma's restaurant area and met the man who owned the place. He was Swedish and spoke perfect English. Bonus! He could help me find a doctor! He said he had seen me before, when I first arrived. I asked to see a room, and it turned out to be a beautiful bungalow with an attached bathroom, tile floors and a patio, all overlooking the ocean. Big boulders lined the beach and the sound of the waves breaking against the rocks was like liquid thunder. And best of all, there was no sandy beach right out front; hence no packs of sunbathers, and no sand fleas! It was secluded. Quiet. Perfect. They gave me a room for $6 a night. I knew I had arrived.

I unpacked and hung my things out on the clothesline to be freshened by the sea breeze. Took a shower. Slept. Woke up. Went for a swim at sunset, my favorite time to swim in the sea, when the foam is orange and pink and the water is magically, iridescently green. The saltwater felt great on my raw, scratched-off skin. But I still wasn't feeling very well. I had put myself on antibiotics for the lump under my arm. I knew it wasn't life threatening and was trying to kill it with pills (antibiotics are over-the-counter in Asia). Unfortunately, the antibiotics killed my energy level, too.

My first night at La Plaloma, I sat out on the porch and wrote in my journal by candlelight. The warm winds were blowing, and the sea crashed against the rocks not a hundred feet away. And for the first time in almost two months, my stresses melted. I exhaled India, where everybody wants something from you, and inhaled Ko Chang, where nobody wants a thing. Nobody wanted to know me. Sell me something. See me naked. It was just me. The sea. The island.

Surgery, Thai Style

After a couple of days, I realized that the painful little bump under my arm was not going to go away. The antibiotics were doing nothing but making me tired, leaving a bitter taste in my mouth and making my sweat smell pharmaceutical. I knew I had to go to the mainland and have a doctor look at it, possibly even cut it out.

Early one morning I headed back down to the Chang dock. I caught the first boat over and hired a taxi on the other side to take me to Trat Hospital. The owner of La Plaloma had told me that the hospital in Trat was very good, so I wasn't too worried. I was just anxious to get that lump taken care of.

I checked myself into the hospital while my taxi guy waited outside. The hospital was very clean, very Western in terms of medical standards, and I was impressed. The doctor took one look at me and told me that it was an infected ingrown hair, very common in hot, muggy, dirty climates. He had me lie down on a cold metal table, gave me a local anesthetic and cut it out of me on the spot. Can I just say "Ouch" ? He told me I couldn't swim for a week.

Looking oh-so-stunning in a tank top with a huge white gauze bandage under my left armpit, this farang again tucked her tail, taxied it back to the dock and hopped onto the afternoon boat to Chang.

The surgery turned out to be the easy part. The real pain didn't start until I had to go to the Chang island clinic to have my dressing changed every couple of days. You know the pain when you rip a bandage off a wound? Let's just say the skin under your arm is very, very sensitive, and an open surgical cut doesn't help much. The first time I had my dressing changed, I was writhing in pain, yelling obscenities at the poor Thai nurse. The simple procedure was so painful, it left me wobbly-legged and tired afterward. I had to go through that pain, that ripping of skin, three times; and then my wound started to heal and I was allowed to dress it myself, in the privacy of my own bungalow. Oh, the price I pay for paradise.

Khlong Phlu and Beyond

One day, I rented a moped to go to Khlong Phlu waterfall, about five miles away—which came with a big bunch of bananas the owner had picked in his yard. I explored the west road for a bit, dodging huge potholes, sliding in the wet red clay that was everywhere and watching for quicksand. A girl I'd met told me she had stepped in quicksand and it had sucked her shoe right off! And she'd reached into the puddle up to her elbow and gotten her shoe back! She said it was really thick liquid, like water, but dry. How cool is that?

It was raining off and on as I putted toward the falls, so I had to pull off the road and squat under palm trees a lot. I love how it will just pour so hard that all life seeks shelter—then twenty minutes later, the sun comes back out, people reemerge, and everything dries up so quickly in the intense sun that it's as if it never even rained. When I was hiking on the footpath that led up to the falls, a rain spell was close. I could smell it. I was too far in to make it out in time, so I just kept going. And at the exact moment that I first laid my eyes on the beautiful Khlong Phlu falls, the rain came.

For a few minutes, I just looked at the falls, which raged due to the rains. Then I took off my shoes (thongs are way too slippery for hiking when it's raining) and walked back barefoot through the thick, green rainforest. The red clay earth was slick and soft under my feet, and there were warm rain puddles filled with tropical leaves. The only sounds were the raging river and the heavy raindrops smacking off thick, tropical leaves into puddles below. Clay oozed between my toes. I wondered what my friends back home were doing at that exact moment. No doubt they were wearing shoes.

I didn't really do too much on Chang. It rained a lot. Every night it stormed viciously, beautifully. Roads flooded. Beach rivers overflowed and blocked beach access. The Thais played frisbee in the unusually huge waves. Dinner-plate-size jellyfish washed up by the hundreds and made the beaches a gelatinous minefield. I read everything I could get my hands on, and when I ran out of books and magazines, I read every single classified ad in the week-old *Bangkok Post* someone had left in the restaurant area.

Most days, there was nowhere to go but inward. I had just spent a month in India, where I was lucky enough to attend a seminar on Tibetan Buddhism taught by His Holiness the Dalai Lama. He had spoken about the importance of letting go, about how holding on to material objects and emotions leads to nothing but suffering. This was plenty for me to ponder on a rainy day. I was nervous about returning to the States, where people have everything and nothing at the same time. I knew I would have to face the reality I had left behind, the realities I had fled: rent, job, personal relationships, a judgmental, material society. This scared me to death. I had transcended that on Chang. I was living every moment of my life with absolute confidence, no regrets from the past, no plans for the future. I was existing solely in the moment, and I didn't want to lose that. So I read and reread my journal from His Holiness's teachings. I thought things through so thoroughly, I got to a point where my rationale overcame emotional attachment, and I felt ready and able to overcome anything I might face back home. I felt so strong. Fearless. Wise. Whole.

This is from my journal, my last night on Ko Chang:

Now I'm getting ready to go. Into what, I don't know. I'm living moment by moment these days, and I have only feelings leading me into tomorrow, not specific ideas. I believe this exquisite intuition I possess now, this moment, is because I have slipped into the Eastern world long enough to adapt its energy, its way of life, and it feels so good. It's easy to see why the Thais are so happy with what they have— because what they have at any given moment is enough to be happy. I just want to say thank you, Ko Chang, for sharing it with me.

Jewel of the Seychelles

by Wuanda M. T. Walls

We carry with us the wonders we seek without us:
there is all Africa and her prodigies in us.
—Sir Thomas Browne

Mahe, 14 February

Dear ReVonne, My Starfeather,

This is it! I'm in paradise. Finally, after traveling for nearly thirty hours, with layovers in Paris and Jidda, I'm here. So, my friend, you can breathe easy now.

All the flights were smooth. To tell the truth, I had almost forgotten the joy of flying Air France. But, listen, before I bend your ear about the perks of Air France, I must say, I knew I was headed for Europe when I saw passengers carrying their beloved mutts in their arms. Those small vicious lap dogs ever ready to snarl and show off. You know the type. Nothing like your wonderful Dalmatian, Measles, or the terriers I adore.

Girl, my memory was awakened and I immediately remembered how appalled I was when I saw dogs dining in the finest restaurants in Brussels in the seventies. Some were even dressed for the occasion, decked out in sparkling collars and soft, woolly sweaters. They sat so proper and upright on their hind feet with front paws daintily placed on linen tablecloths, I felt as though I was in a scene straight out of *Animal Farm*. It was weird, and I was numb with disbelief watching those dogs being treated like humans. And my host, a noble Frenchman, ever so sensitive, instinctively settled my mounting alarm with a glance that said, "Now, princess, when in Rome act accordingly." Anyway, I still find this custom bizarre and appalling, yet I'll admit that I'm equally amazed to see the animals comport themselves with incredible gentility.

Across the aisle from me was a well-groomed black man traveling with his poodle, and the flight attendants made a fuss over him. The little poodle ate it up. When the dog quickly glanced at me, my blood ran cold, and I wanted to kick him from here to the kingdom. Really, I don't quite know what came over me, for you know I'm not a mean person. In any case, I believe that crafty mutt read my mind.

Well, the plane was packed with students, tourists and travelers of all colors, shapes and sizes. I was seated in the *Le Club* section, a few steps above the American version of Business Class. Before the magic carpet took off, the drama began. A tall, medium-build, plain-looking, mature woman handed out international newspapers and those wonderful French magazines we love. While flipping through the pages of *Marie Claire Maison* I was served champagne and fruit. Figs, cheeses and flaky croissants followed. Next came rich, aromatic Colombian coffee and the menus, pretty enough to frame. After we ordered our meals, we were given cosmetic cases filled with a fragrance from Givenchy, a toothbrush, toothpaste, mouthwash, wet wipes and eye covers. As you can imagine, the meal was delectable. And so was the after-dinner brandy. Oops! The *calvados*.

A far cry from the tasteless fare served on those trusty American airlines. No wonder they rank low on the international ladder. I was in doggy heaven—oh, excuse me, I meant to say seventh heaven.

It has only been three hours since I arrived and, although I was exhausted, I could not resist changing into something tropical. The colorful skirt Mercedes made with the floral fabric I bought weeks ago, along with a Colombian T-shirt, made me feel and look soignée. Besides, I wore the combination to honor Mercedes and her South American homeland, as promised.

With camera in hand I left my lovely suite to inspect the grounds of the Seychelles Sheraton, a stately edifice jutting out into the aquamarine Indian Ocean. It was midmorning on a glorious, blooming day, sweetly scented with patchouli, vanilla and cinnamon. The softly scented sea breezes blew gently as I walked toward gigantic tortoises (the same species found in the Galápagos) near the hotel's entrance, torpid next to posing tourists. My heart cried out for them. Minutes later, I changed my course and made my way to a huge boulder at the edge of the bay. I sat on it facing the sun, and the rays were so soothing, warm and seductive, I started to remove my clothes.

The sound of the surf beckoned and the cream-colored sand was so inviting that I was spellbound for a moment. My eyes were wide as apples, looking at coral and small shells scattered on the beach. Then I noticed small Therese Island across from me. I inhaled as I turned and looked behind me at the soaring green mountains covered with masses of palms, cinnamon, mahogany and majestic *sangdragon* (dragon's blood) trees. A tropical verdure lush with rare orchids, thickets of ferns, fragrant fruit (*choux choute, guava, jamalaque* and *corasol*), medicinal plants and flora found nowhere else in the world. At that moment, I felt extraordinarily whole, healthy and happy.

At once, the sound of men's laughter broke my reverie. I turned slowly to see barechested, honey- and chestnut-colored men walking towards me. Their curious stares and polite expressions told me they were reserved. Nothing like those assertive, sweet-talking Caribbean brothers we know so well. I carefully avoided looking directly at them as I turned away.

When I glanced down at my feet I saw tiny opalescent fish shimmering near my toes. How sweet of them to greet me, I thought. Then, out of the blue, I heard a boat approaching. I looked up and assumed it was the one that takes tourists to Therese Island. As the boat rolled in, three of the laughing men walked along the beach to meet it. Two stayed back, and one of the two, Charles, casually made his way over to me. He politely asked if I was waiting for the boat. When I said no, he offered to bring me a coconut to drink.

I was taken aback by his direct yet nonchalant manner, and felt thirstier than ever. The cool, sweet nectar of the coconut was so tasty, I had to restrain myself from guzzling it down. The liquid was like a refreshing stream flowing through my body, stirring up coconut memories of Bermuda, Colombia, Brazil and Panama. Charles stood, patient and silent, as I savored the last drop. Then, with a little more enthusiasm in his voice, he invited me to walk up the road to meet his family. I handed him the empty shell and followed in his footsteps.

It was lunchtime and I could smell the pungent aromas of exotic spices, fresh-baked bread and seafood simmering in what I thought smelled like curry wafting from the kitchens. Only a few cars sped by and the road was clean, no litter anywhere to tarnish the beauty of the picturesque scene. The cooking aromas became laced with the scents of jasmine and the intoxicating *paille-en-quene* orchid. Every house we passed had a terraced garden shaded by jackfruit, ylang-ylang and the flamboyant scarlet spread of bougainvillea. Litchi, frangipani and hibiscus attracted colorful birds that sang and alighted on low branches. Starfeather, I spotted my beloved doves in the company of bright red Madagascar fodies. Oh, what an enchanting scene! I'm sure they're probably a different type, but they were as calm and peaceful as any other doves, cooing under a casuarina tree.

When we entered Charles's home I was greeted with sunny smiles. The spacious split-level house was airy and cozy, and the walls were painted ocher and turquoise. I read once that those colors were found in stately seventeenth-century French villas.

Charles's mother, sisters, brothers, nieces and nephews were so gracious and curious. Their warmth and beauty touched my heart. Each face represented a kind of global brotherhood/sisterhood, if you will. Jewels of Africa, Europe and Asia (including Indonesia, India and Malaysia) blended together. Observing the family's diverse physical beauty and natural courtesy, it was easy to understand why the Seychellois are reputed for interracial mixing and racial harmony. Charles's sisters reminded me of Filipinas I had met in Spain many moons ago. The same round faces, almond-shaped eyes, glossy-black straight hair and flawless, amber-colored skin.

So, now you want to know about Charles, right? He's quite handsome. A virile African of average height and slender build, a beautiful, sculpted face with high cheekbones, a button nose and full, moist lips.

At the table, he was gallant. And I was amazed at the amount of food, although I realized that here, as in Spain and South America, the heaviest meal is eaten early. I tasted a bit of everything, and couldn't get enough of the meaty heart of palm, breadfruit, paw paw, *brede* (a green vegetable) and the shrimp and octopus cooked in curry. The *bourgeois* (a deep-water red snapper that is larger and meatier than its Atlantic Ocean cousin), marinated in lime juice and cooked with ginger, garlic, red peppers, onions, thyme and nutmeg, melted in my mouth. Starfeather, you must try this dish, and serve it up to your fans.

Red Snapper Seychellois

2	pounds of red snapper fillets
1	red pepper, cut into thin slices
1	green pepper, cut into thin slices
3	cloves of garlic, chopped finely
1	medium red onion, chopped coarsely
2	tablespoons of ginger, minced
1	teaspoon of freshly grated nutmeg
3	sprigs of fresh thyme, minced
4	limes, squeezed
2	tablespoons of olive oil

salt and cayenne to taste

Marinate the fillets in lime juice and nutmeg for one hour. Drain and pat dry. Sauté fillets in oil, brown on both sides. Remove before completely cooked. Set aside. Sauté garlic, onions, ginger and peppers, stirring frequently until peppers are soft (approximately 4 to 7 minutes). Remove the vegetables. Place the fillets in the pan and cover with vegetables. Add salt and cayenne to taste, and cook over medium heat for 3 to 5 minutes. Squeeze lime juice over the dish and serve with rice.

Serves 4

After lunch, Charles took me on a mini-tour of his village, Port Glaud. As we walked along the narrow road, he told me that I had landed on Mahé, the largest of the granitic islands (the Seychelles are the only midocean granitic islands in the world), which is seventeen miles long and five miles across, beginning with the capital of Victoria. Of the 115 islands that comprise the archipelago, Mahé is the most mountainous and 90 percent of the 70,000 residents live here. Most of the islands are uninhabited and continue to be preserved by the Seychellois for future generations. There are more nature reserves and marine parks in the Seychelles than any other place in the world.

I can just imagine what you're thinking: Why are you allowing that man to give you the facts when you have read everything there is to know about his country? Really, what always amazes me is how proud, patriotic and knowledgeable others are about their countries, compared to Americans. Besides, I enjoy hearing things from the horse's mouth.

As we strolled past the school (literacy is high and children are fluent in French, Creole and English), the clinic (health care is free) and the cemetery (in full view of the wooded hills and mountains of Morne Seychellois National Park), Charles named the different plants and flowers. The sweet-smelling ones used for perfume, and those used for aches and pains. When I asked about plants used for magic, Charles smiled and asked if I was an anthropologist. Still curious, I replied, "No, I'm not. I read that sorcery was banned in 1958, and I'm just interested in healing plants, voodoo and sacred African beliefs." He looked somewhat serious and stared at me, briefly and intensely, before saying we would discuss it later.

Everyone we passed greeted us with warm smiles and sun-filled eyes. A few men and women carried exquisite, bright flowers, beautiful and aromatic, to be placed on graves. Children ran ahead of their parents, laughing, singing and playing, as all happy children do, their beauty as dazzling as the flowers. I noticed that the men and women walked in the same casual, rhythmic manner as Charles—relaxed, balanced and imbued with a tropical aura elevated by harmony and peace.

From Charles, I also discovered that there are no poisonous snakes, and the islands lie outside the cyclone zone. I knew there was no need for those horrible shots because tropical diseases are nonexistent. However, what really got my juices flowing was learning more about President France Albert René's strong commitment to the republic's land, citizens and wild-life. Largely due to his policies, there is no air pollution, and the residents are extremely healthy. Life expectancy at birth is seventy-one years, and cancer and other degenerative diseases are virtually unheard of. I have visited many places, but no place where the government practices what it preaches, if you will. What a tribute to Gondwanaland, the forgotten con-tinent that broke up into India, Australia, Antarctica, Africa and South America 130 million years ago, the continent many scientists and others believe was part of Africa and separated when Asia began to drift away. Today, Mother Africa claims them all, and the island nation of the Seychelles is Africa's smallest. By the way, dear friend, this is a matriarchal society, and the women not only rule the roost, they enjoy the legal, political, economic and social rights equal to men. And, it is quite common for a woman to have more than one man in her life, and children belonging to different fathers. Puritanism has no home in this paradisiacal society, an-chored by women unencumbered by obstacles.

When I left Charles, I headed back to my abode. Once inside, I hung the *Ne pas déranger* sign on the door and opened my welcome basket. It was filled with all types of goodies, and I decided to open a bottle of Seybrew.

I looked at myself in the mirror as I listened to the sound of waves crashing against the rocks below my balcony. My face was serene and vibrant. I walked onto the balcony and disrobed. The warm breezy air, perfumed with earth and sea, caressed me. Then I stretched my nude body in a lounge chair. The kiss of the equatorial sun was luscious. I succumbed and closed my eyes. For nearly thirty minutes, I was in a state of bliss. Slowly, I got up and leaned over the balcony to stare at the sapphire sea. It was a sight to behold. I turned to look above me, and, to my surprise, there was a man ogling me, wide-eyed and grinning. Startled, my first impulse was to shake my tits, but instead I slowly stepped back, then said, loud enough for him to hear, "What a lucky chap you are."

Before dinner, I decided to introduce myself to the manager and thank him for the lovely basket. On my way to his office, I ran into Mr. Rubio, the food and beverage manager. Our meeting was surprising and wonderful. Señor Rubio is Colombian. I can't wait to tell Mercedes. I know she won't believe me, but the warm, friendly gentleman had noticed my T-shirt and wanted to know if I was Colombian. Life is grand.

Love,
Angel

for Jean Walden and Ed Smith

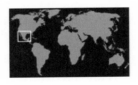

Sylvia One
and the Guided Pilgrimage

by Louise Wisechild

When I was a child, I was fascinated with the idea of miracles after hearing about them in Sunday school. Miracles were about magic, the complete and merciful transformation from debility to wholeness, from blindness to sight, from hunger to nourishment, from lameness to vigor.

Supernatural wonders happened to ordinary people in those stories. I longed to experience the extraordinary, to touch the divine. But I was told that miracles didn't happen in the modern scientific world, as if we didn't need them now.

In rural Mexico, where life is less modern, people still seek divine intervention. My friends in Oaxaca told me that when they needed a miracle, they went on a pilgrimage to Juquila and made requests to the Virgin there. They said that to visit her you traveled far, through the mountains. It was a place not listed in my guidebook. When I found it on my map, it was a barely visible dot.

I had seen many images of *La Virgen de Juquila* around Oaxaca, in houses, churches and in the stalls of vendors selling religious icons. In gold plastic frames her image was displayed next to Guadalupe and Jesus on altars: her delicate deep brown face surrounded by a cloud of obsidian-black hair on top of which rested a golden crown, studded with stars. She wore a white embroidered cloak with a European design though she herself was undeniably of Mexico, her skin the color of coffee, her face serene and peaceful. Her eyes were closed, marked by fine black lashes. My friends called her *La Virgencita,* the little virgin, because, they said, the actual image of her is small.

One friend told me her brother had been diagnosed with a serious condition and needed an immediate operation. He went overnight on a pilgrimage to Juquila and then returned to his doctor, who was ready to schedule his surgery. "But when the doctor examined him, he was completely well," she said. All of my Mexican friends had visited this site at least once with their families. Most of them had taken the bus, a seven-hour ride through the narrow ribbons of roads that cross Oaxaca's mountains.

I arrived at the vast second-class bus station my usual half-hour early, which normally set me apart from the Mexican travelers who saunter aboard within three minutes of departure. So I was surprised to board the bus and find it full of dressed-up families, smelling of the oranges they were passing among themselves to go with the tacos and tamales vendors peddled in the aisles.

There were only two empty seats, so I squeezed toward the one in back. I was used to riding with people who were on their way to the market, as buyers or sellers, the buses loaded with bundles and sometimes livestock. I'd ridden with Mexicans returning to their pueblos for a fiesta or to spend Sunday with their families. I'd taken buses headed toward the border, full of men with silent intent faces, concentrating, I imagined, on the perils of crossing. But this bus was like stepping into a fiesta in progress. Men and women leaned across the aisles, talking and laughing; little kids stood on the seats to talk with those sitting behind them. The luggage racks were overflowing overhead. I put my bag under the seat and nodded at the teenage boy next to me, who nodded back. I was the only person alone and the only foreigner. I took out my journal and started to write, content in the privacy that comes from being alone in a crowd of people who all have significant others.

The bus pulled away with a huff and I wrapped my *rebozo*, the long handwoven shawl of Mexican women, around my head and shoulders as the chilly early morning air blew in through windows that were stuck open on the old bus. The motion of the bus lulled me into a peaceful doze while my neighbors ate more oranges and the driver turned up the music. A couple of hours later the bus stopped on a street lined with thatched-roof open-air restaurants, banana trees and palms rising in the jungle behind them. The driver announced we would be here for forty minutes and everyone disembarked and scattered to different cafés. I followed the driver into the restaurant in front of us and went over to stand by the counter, behind which three women in aprons tended cauldrons of chocolate, *café* and *mole*. I ordered coffee with hot milk and a couple of tamales. As the woman turned to make my food another one of the passengers approached me.

"*Hola,*" she said, looking directly into my eyes. She was tall with impressively erect posture. "Are you traveling alone?" she asked in Spanish.

"*Sí,*" I said and nodded.

"My sister-in-law and I are traveling alone too," she told me, waving at the shorter, more rounded woman standing behind her. She meant they were traveling without their husbands. Both women, it turned out, were named Sylvia. I thought of the tall one as Sylvia One, not only because I met her first but because she stood straight and tall like the number one, with tight curly hair on top for emphasis. Sylvia Two was softer and more rounded, resting like the number two on a platform of ground.

Sylvia One did all of the talking while Sylvia Two listened, which I imagined was usual when they were together. She told me they were from the city of Puebla and had already been traveling for twelve hours on buses. She, Sylvia One, had made a pilgrimage to Juquila several times before.

I introduced myself and we all shook hands. Sylvia One's hand was strong and dry, though the grip was Mexican—a soft resting instead of a squeeze. Sylvia Two's hand was more tentative.

My coffee came and I went to find a table by myself. I was enjoying my solitude and wanted to write more in my journal. Lining up to get back on the bus, I greeted the Sylvias, who were sitting in the front row, and resumed my anonymity in the back. The road was windy and those of us in the back suffered, some of us more than others, as several people began vomiting. Everyone on the bus began emptying the contents of the plastic bags in their possession and passing the bags back to the afflicted. I put on my Walkman and listened to Mercedes Sosa instead of the sound of retching. Later, Sylvia One told me the people throwing up considered the agony of motion sickness to be part of the sacrifice they were making for the Virgencita de Juquila, just as her spending thirty-four hours coming and going on a bus to the pueblo of Juquila in order to spend less than twelve hours in the home of the Virgin was part of her sacrifice. Each step of the journey was part of the pilgrimage.

I had ridden in buses and passed pilgrims who were walking to the shrine of Guadalupe at Tepeyac. It might take them a week to get there. I'd witnessed others climbing the granite steps up to Guadalupe's shrine on their knees. Outside San Miguel de Allende, I'd visited a church known for ceremonies of self-flagellation. The church housed statues of bleeding saints holding flagellation whips. This mortification of the flesh made me uncomfortable. I believe we don't honor our bodies enough, that nurture and pleasure are pleasing to the divine. I like to think that the divine would rather we expressed our devotion in singing, dancing and the construction of beautiful altars. Surely if the divine made our very bodies, they wouldn't delight in our tearing them up.

"Thank you that I am not nauseated," I whispered to Juquila. I considered the mysteries of the trip ahead. I wanted to be respectful of the traditions that I might find. "Show me what to do, okay?" I added to my prayer.

The approach to the town of Juquila was slow, as the buses that had poured into town from other parts of Mexico crawled up the tiny one-and-a-half-lane road. Along the sides of the street crude signs advertised the availability of a shower or a room. Throngs of people were visible everywhere I looked. I began to wonder how I was going to find a room for one in what appeared to be a small Mexican town overrun by visitors, all of them traveling in groups.

I was relieved to see that Sylvias One and Two were waiting for me outside the bus. My American need for privacy and separation had quickly melted in the utter volume of Mexicans on pilgrimage. Sylvia One led us off through the crowd at a stiff pace and I saw with relief that there were several hotels. The first one looked large and promising but it was full. As were the second and third. Finally we landed a room with two beds—the Sylvias would share one and I would have the other. I sat on my bed, relieved to have found it. I imagined I'd unpack and then set off on my own, maybe meet up with the Sylvias for dinner.

Sylvia One proceeded to take off her clothes in the middle of the room, with no embarrassment whatsoever. She had an athlete's body—strong calves, muscles arranged tidily against her almost militaristically erect spine, surprisingly rounded breasts kept firmly in place with her bra, and muscles instead of a tummy. She replaced her jeans with a pair of shorts and a clean T-shirt and informed me that we were going to the church first. She was carrying a large wooden cross.

I hesitated slightly in responding, but she motioned toward the door and said, "You are ready. Let's go." I looked longingly toward the bed where I'd anticipated a short nap and time to clear my head from the bus, but I picked up my daypack and followed them out the door, trying to accustom myself to the idea of taking a group, instead of a solo, excursion. Sharing a room was one thing, but I hadn't planned on sharing my pilgrimage. I liked to travel alone.

I enjoyed the freedom of lingering when I felt inspired and moving on when I was bored. Solo travel matched my own rhythms and gave me unlimited permission to satisfy my own curiosity and be attuned to my own responses. This seemed particularly important in visiting a place of miracles. Traveling alone sharpens my attention and creates an inner spaciousness and receptivity. Too often, journeying with others, I would make their company my focus or would squelch my own inclination in deference to the group's preference. In Mexico City I'd gone with a group to Tepeyac, the site where the Virgen de Guadalupe appeared miraculously. I stood with my group in front of the miraculous cloak far longer than I would have chosen, only to find myself deeply moved by the magnificent bronze statues tucked away on a hillside, but alas with only five minutes before I had to meet the group. I promised myself that this time I would linger wherever I needed to, even with the Sylvias.

The church was simple compared to the other gold-encrusted Mexican churches I'd seen. It lacked the foyers of the larger churches, which held various saints and Marys and even relics, bits of saints' bones nestled into life-size statues, which reclined in glass coffins. This church had plain, whitewashed walls with rows of pews until the nave, overflowing with arrangements of flowers—all of them the same, orange birds of paradise and white mums. High on the front wall, in an alcove, was the tiniest statue of a *virgen* I'd seen in all of Mexico. In reality, she looked less like a statue than an Indian doll wearing an extraordinarily ornate robe. Her niche was outlined in blue neon and on top was a yellow neon crown with a blue cross. I stared up at her. All around me Mexicans gazed at Juquila with adoration and whispered fervent prayers, crossing themselves in the rites of Catholicism. Sylvia Two stood next to me.

Sylvia One had dropped to the floor in the central aisle and was progressing on her bare knees toward the front of the church, staring at the image of Juquila and holding her cross, which had a circle at the intersection of the wood. Even walking on her knees she kept her back tall and straight, her face determined and intent but betraying no discomfort. The vast majority of pilgrims stood upright.

We had all bought candles outside from one of the vendors, who sold them next to rosaries and pictures of Juquila lit with one large red or yellow Christmas tree bulb and sparkling with gold glitter. A small door to the side of the altar led to a room blackened with smoke and illuminated by hundreds of candles that covered three granite slabs, the flames lengthening upward toward the divine. Sylvia One, whose knees were red from crawling to the altar, pointed to an empty spot and we all deposited our candles. La Virgencita seemed tiny next to this evidence of the magnitude of need and want. I tried again to pray in this room full of candles, to whisper my fervent longing, but I didn't feel inspired. I had expected to feel moved at this place so many had come to, but all I felt was curiosity.

The candlelit room had filled with a new rush of supplicants and I looked around for the Sylvias but I didn't see them. I headed toward the nearest door and circled the church but they were nowhere to be found. I went back inside the sanctuary, certain I would find them looking at La Virgencita. But they weren't there either. I scanned the aisles of vendors selling photos of Juquila and others selling peanuts, tacos and ice cream. I looked everywhere. The Sylvias had vanished.

I thought I might as well go take a nap and wait for them to show up sometime before dinner. Sylvia One had the key, of course. If there had been a map she would have had that, too, I thought impatiently. I planned on getting an extra key from the desk. Maybe the Sylvias were even at the room. They weren't. "No," the clerk said flatly when I asked for another key, "there is only one key to that room and your friend has it."

"But what about the master key," I persisted, as if I were at a Holiday Inn. The clerk looked at me and shook her head. "No other key," she repeated and shrugged. I climbed the steps near our room and sat on the top step, waiting, trying not to think of lying down on my bed. I took the journal from my pack and stared at the blank page. Finally I gave up and walked back toward the church, willing energy into my body.

The Sylvias stood at the top of the road. When she saw me, Sylvia One marched toward me, hugging the cross in front of her chest. "We have been looking for you," she said sternly.

"You've been looking for me?" I asked with exasperation. "I've looked all over for you. I was even waiting for you at the room. Where did you go?"

Sylvia One ignored me and shook her head disapprovingly at me for getting lost. "You must keep better track," she said. Sylvia Two stood behind her sister-in-law, looking tired and undoubtedly wondering why Sylvia One had insisted on adopting me, although I suspected I might be relieving her from the brunt of Sylvia One's need to control. Having reached the end of her lecture, Sylvia One stepped into the road and hailed a taxi, hustling us all inside.

I wasn't sure where we were going as the taxi left the town behind for rolling hills and then, for a tense moment, hugged the edge of a jagged drop-off in the road caused by a recent hurricane. Sylvia One was talking about her family, her relationship to Sylvia Two and how her first visit to the site of Juquila, three years before, had been all to the good for her family. I only half understood much of what she said, but felt I was getting the gist of it, when she leaned over the cross in her lap so that her face was about six inches from mine in the back seat of the taxi and said, "Okay, you understand what I said? Then tell me back exactly."

I was dumbstruck by this challenge, which was both beyond my memory and my level of Spanish. The many Mexicans I had met were patient and unfailingly polite about the imperfection of my Spanish. I had often regretted their reluctance to correct my pronunciation and grammar, feeling I would learn faster if they would be less tolerant. But still, I was tired, hot, hungry and on the way to an unknown destination. I considered telling Sylvia One to back off, that I wasn't up to a foreign language class at just that moment. Then I told myself that pilgrimages were about accepting those who come across your path and seeing them in as compassionate a light as possible. Sylvia Two was quiet and beatific in the front seat. I attempted to emulate her sweetness. I explained carefully to Sylvia One that I thought I had understood most of what she said, I would be sure to tell her if I didn't, and I hoped she would correct my Spanish as we spoke. She looked at me intently. I figured her husband must be a brave man to withstand the scrutiny of that gaze.

The taxi deposited us at the bottom of a wide, rutted and dusty road that led up the mountain. Sylvia One explained, in slow, precise Spanish, that part of our sacrifice would be to walk to the top. I told myself that exercise was a good antidote to tiredness. Twenty minutes later we had arrived at the crest of Pedimento, the mountain of petitions. Juquila was said to have first appeared in these high, rolling hills. It was here, Sylvia One told me, that people asked Juquila for what they wanted. "But if you receive it," she continued, looking at me fiercely, "you must return within a year to thank Juquila for your miracle." That was why she was carrying the cross, which was engraved with a message of gratitude and the name of her family. Indeed, there were thousands of crosses visible in the hills in front of us.

I wandered over to a vendor who was selling *milagros,* the metal charms that often accompany prayers in Central America. There were the usual representations of body parts—hands, eyes, ears, stomachs, arms, feet, breasts, lungs—as well as metal images of boys, girls, cows, dogs, chickens, donkeys, corn and beans. But they were not only for health and agriculture, there were milagros in the shape of cars and houses as well as bundles of miniature play money for prayers that involved the need for cash. I scanned the display in front of me. And there, at the bottom, was a milagro of three miniature brass books connected together as if on a shelf, with tiny etched-in bindings. It was because of books that I had kept my belief in miracles. Stories relied upon extraordinary events, leading me across boundaries of culture and time, accompanying me through the terrain of despair and then illuminating possibility. I paid three pesos for the milagro and went to stand behind the Sylvias in the long line of pilgrims.

Slowly we moved forward toward two stone statues illuminated by rows of candles. The larger statue was carved from granite with a rose hue; the smaller one was black. They were both of Juquila, but their faces were bolder than her image in the church. Here, Juquila's eyes were wide open and looked right at us as we approached. Her body was stone, solid and ancient. Prayers clothed her in hundreds of milagros dangling on red thread, occasional notes of real and fake money, and sheets of notebook paper with inked entreaties next to photographs of children and adults. Sylvia One told me I could bless my milagro by holding it in front of the statues as some of the women ahead of me were doing. When I received my prayer I could bring it back as part of my offering to Juquila. Ahead of me I could hear murmured prayers and watched as each person stood before the statues, looking into the eyes of Juquila.

Then it was my turn. I stepped in front of the statues. Immediately everything fell away—the people waiting behind me, the woman next to me saying her prayers, the presence of the Sylvias. It was as if I had entered a vortex where energies ran so powerfully that thought ceased, leaving only pulsing goodness. I closed my eyes and reached for my deepest breath. I felt the living power of the rising mountains that stretched fertile around me. My blood hummed in my ears. The darkness behind my eyelids was golden like sun and dirt mixed together. I became rock, primal, enduring, a piece of the mountain. Near my core, beside the inside of my spine, I felt a surge, like water let loose—water sweeping up from the plate of my sacrum, traveling against gravity—the fluid rush of my spirit stretching up and out of its dispirited puddle. The perfect sky blue of encouragement slipped into my mouth like a rare fruit, falling ripe through my throat, spreading from my stomach into my organs.

I opened my eyes, which fell upon the smaller, darker statue. "Oh thank you, *gracias,*" I said. I held my milagro by its red thread near her belly. A charge ran through my fingers, a tiny electric blessing.

I stepped to the side as a young woman in a tank top and jeans replaced me. The sun was slanting and making shadows in the mountains and the crowd had thinned. Once more, the Sylvias had disappeared. Still feeling relaxed, I followed a family to the back of the shrine. Sylvia One beckoned to me from among the offerings of crosses and flowers slightly down the hill. Even though she reminded me of a drill sergeant, I welcomed the sight of her. Among so many families, it seemed natural to be with the Sylvias instead of being alone.

Sylvia Two had placed her cross against a nearby tree where it joined the legions of other answered prayers. She was squatting in a cave, scraping the sides of the wall with a plastic spoon and putting the dirt into a plastic bag. I stooped to enter the cave. Sylvia One followed me in, handed me another plastic spoon and together we filled half a sack with dirt. Then Sylvia One poured water from a bottle into the plastic bag of dirt. She mushed it efficiently with her fingers. Around us kids and grandmothers, teenagers and couples worked the mud and prayed once again, this time with their hands. Some fashioned mud bodies with prayers for health, others sculpted hearts hoping for love and harmony. Most common were mud circles the size of tortillas, affixed to the wall outside of the shrine, etched with pictures of houses and trucks, animals and families.

Sylvia Two made a car, complete with plastic caps from bottled water for tires. I fashioned a heart and drew a path with a book on it. I wrote *esperar,* to hope, on my path by etching on the mud with a stick. Around me people were laughing and playing in the mud. A couple of little girls walked by holding hands. No one seemed to be suffering. Rather, it was more like an intergenerational playschool where we were invited to embody our prayers and dreams in clay.

On the way down the mountain Sylvia One bought small sticks of wood resinous with sweet-smelling pitch. She gave me a piece for a *recuerdo,* a memory of my visit. We rode in a taxi back to town. I figured it was time to eat, and I was ready for an extended sitting, but Sylvia One, as usual, had other ideas. She led us to yet another line, which snaked around the side and finally to the rear of the church.

As the sun turned the afternoon orange and then rose-pink, mothers nursed infants and toddlers, then rewrapped their rebozos so that the children were securely cradled against their bodies. Fathers carried older kids on their shoulders and held their hands as the line processed forward in the growing darkness. We went up a stairway and into a back room of the church, behind the altar. Sylvia One told me that two hundred years ago this church had burned to the ground and been completely destroyed except for this image of Juquila, which had been found in the rubble, untouched by the flames. One by one we touched our hands to the glass behind the doll-like image of La Virgencita. But when my hand touched the coolness of the window behind her I found myself in memory, standing in front of her wide-open eyes on the mountain. I wondered if the church had burned down because Juquila prefers being outside.

Sylvia One towed us back to the vendors so we could buy tiny plastic jugs, which we filled with holy water and blessed oil available for free in back of the church. "When you feel sick, you use some of the oil and drink a sip of the water," Sylvia One told me, pantomiming shaking some in her hand and applying it to her stomach and her throat. Our hands full with little jugs, flowers and the pictures of Juquila we'd bought from the rows of vendors, Sylvia One at last led us toward our hotel and supper. We had chicken mole at the same restaurant that Sylvia had frequented on her other visits. By this time I was exhausted, not only from our pace but from Sylvia One's continuous correction of my Spanish. "I bet if you had children, you would make them march and would never allow them to meander," I remarked over dinner. Sylvia Two sniggered and nodded her head in agreement. "She is like this all the time," she added, and we laughed together while Sylvia One rose up even straighter in her chair.

That night, just as I was ready to embrace the long awaited privacy of sleep, Sylvia One informed me we would attend mass before we headed for our separate buses. After much repeating of exact words, I was sure we'd be getting up, *levantarse,* at 6:00 for the 7:00 A.M. mass. It was startling, then, when Sylvia One's alarm clock went off at 4:00 A.M. and the overhead light blazed on a minute later.

"*Qué pasa?*" I asked grumpily.

"It's time to get up for mass," she explained brightly.

"But it's four in the morning!" I said.

"Mass is at five," she responded firmly.

"But last night you said it was at seven," I protested, but trailed off as she loomed over me, eyes dark and imperative.

"You can have the first shower," I said politely.

We were the first people at the dark, locked church. I glared at Sylvia One, who this time carried a thick, four-foot candle. Ten minutes later the enormous wooden doors were unlocked and by five-thirty the church was filled to overflowing and hundreds of people stood outside, receiving mass from loudspeakers.

I didn't understand a word that was said, what with the distortion of the amplification and the addition of Catholic Spanish words, but the service involved the congregation in multitudinous signs of the cross—the fleeting touches of fingers across the body in the rites of Catholicism. There was a small version that encompassed the face and a larger version involving the shoulders. At the end, people kissed the tips of their thumbs. Not having been raised a Catholic, I had invented my own version of the blessing, lighting my fingers on my face and shoulders and bringing my thumb to my lips at the end—worshiping in my own individual way and "passing" among the more devout.

Sylvia One, however, caught my blurred motion from the corner of her eye and turned to stare at me in shock and disapproval. I smiled, shrugged my shoulders and whispered, "*No soy católica*" (I'm not Catholic). Sylvia One looked at me sternly and stuck her thumb between her first and second fingers, motioning for me to imitate her. She went through it with me several times, each time observing me intently as I crossed myself. If I succeeded she nodded once, firmly. But, of course, under her examination, I often misplaced my fingers and then she instructed me all over again. Sylvia even had me do it twice more when the mass had finished, just to make sure I'd learned.

It was with relief that I boarded a bus to the coast and waved goodbye to the Sylvias from the window. We had traveled about an hour when the bus broke down. Suspended in the ovenlike heat for a couple of hours, I took the opportunity to say a prayer to Juquila, thanking her for shaking me out of my solitude and providing the Sylvias, without whom I surely would have missed the mountain of Pedimento and perhaps would have ended up on the street without a bed for the night. And, I added, if Juquila wanted to count my being stranded midday in full sun as part of a requisite sacrifice for her blessing, I offered it fully up to her. But mostly I hoped I would return some day in order to thank her. And then I would string the milagro on a red thread and hang it, along with the other miracles, on the belly of her statue.

Turkish Delight

by Margaret McConnell

In travel, it's not just an itinerary you can change your mind about; you can change your mind about a country too. I had heard for years that Turkey could be a dangerous place for any traveler, but especially for women. No one I knew even mentioned the possibility of a woman traveling there alone. I had considered these warnings early on, giving them some credence, but with time found them suspect. I had begun to change my mind about Turkey, and it was about to be changed forever.

I traveled solo to Istanbul. By the time I arrived, I had cast off any worries about tall tales I had heard. I was able to take in the myriad sights, smells and sensations without inhibition. I walked through the small smoky airport and noticed how it differed from others I had traveled through. Gone were the sunglasses, suntan lotion and inexpensive paperbacks of airport shops in sunny American and European locales. Instead there were kiosks that sold spices, sesame cakes and amulets to ward off the evil eye. Western dress seemed to dominate, but it was a version I know only from old photos—black suits in a straight 1950s cut. Workers wore short-sleeved collared shirts, matched with somewhat formal trousers and locally made sandals. Here and there I spotted people in more traditional, flowing Islamic dress, but these people seemed to be visiting from abroad, as I was.

I walked outside into the welcoming midday warmth. I was armed with two Turkish words to get me started on my voyage: *merhaba* (hello) and *te, sekkür ederim* (thank you). I approached a taxi driver, opened with my "hello," presented a slip of paper with my hotel name and address and, as my bag was thrown in the trunk, I closed with the "thank you." This was received with an appreciative nod and smile. With this first accomplishment under my belt, and a warm breeze passing through the taxi, I relaxed into the drive.

In earlier travels through Western Europe, I had expressed my desire to visit Turkey some day. Other travelers told me in earnest about the "dangers" of this country, which involved robbery at best and kidnappings into the slave trade at worst. I had decided over time that a complex recipe including fear of the unknown, romantic notions of the Orient Express and, sadly, a touch of racism, must have led these travelers to tell such stories. I trusted that urban street smarts would suffice to protect me on this new adventure and, as it began, my theory was immediately put to the test.

My taxi ride seemed to continue ad infinitum on a desolate highway. My travel book said nothing about an extended distance between the airport and the city. Time passed, and low rolling hills passed, but no major metropolis appeared on the horizon. I wondered with a chuckle if my fated abduction could really be underway so quickly and efficiently. I decided I would check with my hotel before paying the cab fare, in case this was the more expensive scenic route reserved for travelers like me. (Later, when I did this, the taxi driver was so genuinely offended to have his honor called into question that I decided it might be a good idea to take my street smarts down a notch.)

Naturally, with time, the cityscape did appear. It was a postcard-perfect sea of domes and minarets sloping down to the sparkling Bosporus. At closer inspection, the streets were not so unfamiliar. We first drove through a newer area of the city, which looked much like any other in Europe, with traditional street level shops and accommodations above. There was a modern tram traveling down the center of the street. And yet, to my left there was a man with a small boy, walking a large black bear along the sidewalk. *That seemed a little unusual.*

We began to wind into an older part of town and were now traveling slowly through narrow streets. I realized we were immersed in that sea of domes and minarets—in fact, it turned out that my hotel was across a narrow road from the Aya Sofia (a domed Byzantine church, later converted to a mosque, and now functioning as a museum), and my room looked out at its terracotta walls. I settled into the hotel patio and listened to Jim Morrison. His voice was projected through the hotel speakers and competed with the call to prayer, which was projected through hundreds of more distant speakers throughout the city. "Texas Radio" was playing: "Listen to this and I'll tell you about the heartache—I'll tell you about the heartache and the loss of God." The cry of the imam wove through these words. I sat there satisfied; I had finally arrived.

Istanbul enchanted me. The mosques, museums and palaces can fill days of sightseeing. I enjoyed visiting these places and was steeped in my share of history, but it was the smaller, more personal aspects of the culture that colored my idea of the city. I loved that each morning I could buy from the moving street vendor a cucumber, which he would peel, salt and pop on a stick for me. This was all he sold—cucumbers. I enjoyed watching a young Turkish couple, who appeared to be on vacation themselves, carefully photograph their young son who stood proudly in front of the Blue Mosque in a formal black suit.

Other favorite moments were spent in the marketplace. Some of the bazaars of Istanbul are a shock to travelers with romantic notions, because these days they sell more gold, furs and T-shirts than traditional wares. However, the Misr bazaar is a marketplace for foodstuffs, and here my senses really came alive.

The spice shops, with their open barrels of aromatic goods, were a treat for my eyes as well as my nose. Shops were small and dark, just crowded enough to convey a sense of endless abundance—a lifetime supply—of powdery magic in each shop. Even the ceilings were densely hung with full burlap bags. The spices themselves were rich in color and texture. Fresh turmeric, cayenne, paprika and saffron peaked in small mountains of intense reds, yellows and oranges. I was filled with the illogical impulse to dive into the barrels and swim through that wonderful sea of color. Other shops specialized in Turkish Delight—flavored cubes of gelatin in every pastel shade and every flavor imaginable—which filled barrel after barrel. It was a virtual heaven of sugar and gelatin and powdery confection.

I found my own Turkish delight in the carpet shops, where serious buyers and looky-loos alike are welcome to spend hours sipping tea as the merchants spin carpets up into the air like pizza dough, to come floating down one upon another. The travelers who come "just for fun" make purchases as often as those who arrive intent to buy. Shop owners know this from experience, and a social afternoon is provided for all visitors, in an atmosphere rich with the potential for sales, and flowing with the sweetness of Turkish tea and hospitality.

As the days passed, I met other female travelers in Istanbul. I even met two women in my hotel who had traveled solo. We spent a few evenings together, including one at a traditional Turkish smokehouse. Sophia was American and enjoyed turning heads with her petite tomboy look. She wore shorts and a sleeveless shirt around town, and had purchased a traditionally male Turkish cap to wear on top of her short, curly black hair. She believed the men were too stunned by her bare-armed boyish look to hassle her. Chifon was a tall and voluptuous Swedish Australian with long brown hair, who wore flowing pantsuits that covered all her skin. In spite of her more conservative look, she was getting unwanted touches each day, which I was very surprised to learn. My look was somewhere in the middle; I had come with clothes that covered my arms and legs, but they were tomboyish like Sophia's. The attention I received was benign. I heard occasional comments like, "Is it me you are looking for?" or "Why are you so beautiful? Is it because you are French?"

As we three entered the smokehouse, we must have been quite a sight for the predominantly male clientele. We were given a table and were immediately joined by three young Turkish men. They seemed to be presenting themselves as guides, or possibly chaperones, and quickly assisted us in ordering a hookah, tobacco and tea. We were not smokers, and consumed much more tea than tobacco. One of the young men even said to me, "I can tell you are not a professional smoker." Yet the opportunity to sit in this lush male environment, designed for the political and philosophical exchange of ideas, made it well worth the attempt at smoking.

Chifon seemed to enjoy her time in Istanbul and was unruffled by the male attention; Sophia was happily defiant. So I was very surprised when I learned that neither woman wanted to travel outside the city. It wasn't that time or itineraries restricted them, they just didn't believe it was safe. But I simply had to venture beyond the city.

Two years earlier, I had bought a calendar of Turkey and hung it in my workspace. That year of pictures allowed the country to seep slowly into my unconscious—to become a part of me. Each month I would turn the page and a new breathtaking sight would reveal itself to me. The colossal stone heads of Nemrut Dagi fixed their collective stare upon me for thirty days. This image was relieved the next month by turquoise waters, so clear and bright as to compete with any paradise I'd ever seen. Other months, the architecture of Greek, Roman and Ottoman empires would lure the history buff in me, to be relieved by blue waters again—this time the sky-blue, calcium-rich mineral waters of Pamukkale, pooled and cascading over descending white formations of stalactites. I didn't know I would one day soak a sore toe there as the sun set, bringing out the intensity of that heavenly blue color. I just flipped my calendar, and gazed at the next delight—volcanic spires in the valleys of Cappadocia, hollowed out by Christians and turned into churches.

A year is a long time to think about a country. Now it was finally time to venture into that collection of beautiful photographs. I had come to know Turkey visually, and I wondered what I would encounter culturally. As I began my travels outside of Istanbul, I was greeted with a warmth that I found disarming. I was invited frequently to sit and "practice English," and was included in two wedding receptions. Because village people rarely own cameras, I was often asked to photograph families. The subjects of these photos would carefully write out their addresses and request that I send copies for their mantelpieces. One woman rushed to grab a newborn lamb that she held proudly for her photo. Three young girls, about eight years old, asked for their photo and explained by holding up fingers that it was very important to send three copies. On my way to the Roman library at Ephesus, I walked down a shady lane and was followed by a group of enthusiastic children who called, "Hello! Hello! Where are you from?" And always I was offered tea.

Tea is the cornerstone of social life in Turkey. While there are cafés for the express purpose of sitting and sipping from tulip-shaped glasses, a traveling tea vendor is never more than a phone call and five-minute walk away. Once, as I visited an empty museum, the curator followed me around attempting to provide a personalized tour of the exhibit, acting out, when necessary, the purpose of each antiquated piece. He made what looked like a quick but important business call, and in a matter of moments the tea vendor had appeared. We walked and tried to talk as we sipped our social elixir, each of us pretending to understand more than we actually could. This desire to share culture, and to share a moment, was repeated often in my trip and especially on my favorite day of the journey.

After several weeks of travel, I had reached the village of Goreme in the Cappadocia Valley. The valley is sprinkled with villages that nestle in and around volcanic formations, many of which have been adapted as dwellings throughout history. In the scorching summer heat, these churches, old homes and even hotels are not only interesting, but a comfortably cool respite too. In Goreme, I stayed in a comfortable $3 pension. I fancied the tablecloths there, and was told I could buy some like them in the neighboring village, which also happened to have a volcanic castle. In this remote village of Goreme, where women in black travel atop high haystacks, I was able to purchase a walking map from a little office called Green Turtle Tours. Walking tour #2 sold for the fair price of $1.50 and promised to take me to the neighboring village of Ushinar and my coveted tablecloths.

The walking tour was really more of a hike that led through the local hills. The directions were very clear, but there was a jog in the trail at one fatal point, and I found myself scrambling up a hillside trying to get back on track. Eventually I turned around to retrace my steps and met two women who had also lost their way. Together we found the trail, and then parted company again, once the village was in sight. I was surprised by what I saw. The village, and its main road, crawled slowly up and around a conical volcanic hill, peaking with the castle.

I rested for a short while and then began the circular climb, but soon heard the sound of a tractor pulling up behind me on the narrow road. The elderly and weathered driver signaled to me to climb up, using hand signals to say that it was too hot for walking. There was only room for one on the high-perched seat, so I climbed onto a step and held the handrail as we started to travel upward. The road was lined with small homes, and at times we narrowly missed collisions with flowerpots and pets. Old stout women came out of their houses, waving and laughing at the sight of this local man and his new tourist friend. We both waved back and laughed. At the top of the road I disembarked, and my driver bid farewell and drove off.

I wandered toward the town center, asked directions, and was immediately invited to have tea and "practice English." The tea break led to very good directions, and within no time I had found my tablecloths. The castle seemed like the next obvious stop, but when I learned the admission price, I decided to enjoy it from the outside. The castle guide was in a state of disbelief that I would pass up a chance to see the structure (a crudely carved collection of rooms and lookout towers over the valley). As I began to wander away he came and took me by the arm, and without an admission fee took me through the whole castle, pointing emphatically at all its attributes. He spoke no English, so I learned very little about the castle, although I felt I learned something about this man's pride of country, culture and hometown.

There was a lovely view from the top of the castle, and I spotted a main highway that seemed to provide a more direct route home. As I walked this road a taxi pulled over, full of Dutch travelers. I had met the driver days before and miles away. He had given me his card as I sat in a café, and suggested I use his affordable taxi service, rather than the bus, when I traveled to the next town. Now he recognized me on the road, and had a good laugh at having caught me not using his services. He had me squeeze in, dropped me at my hotel, and waved goodbye without charging me, concluding my favorite day in Turkey.

By the end of my trip, I had visited most of the locations on my calendar. When I reached Pamukkale and soaked my toe in those cascading mineral waters, I realized I was on the other side of that old work calendar. Rather than gazing at photos and wondering about Turkey, I was in one of the photographs, looking out at my old life. I no longer feared Turkey. I had fallen in love with it.

Color Locale,
Bedouin Style

by Bernice Notenboom

We sit to drink a cup of tea with the Bedouin camel drivers, who have come by caravan from Saudi Arabia. The desert is tranquil, vast and beautiful. Being a responsible camel rider, I turn to check on my transportation, but am puzzled by my camel, whose behavior seems unusual. She closes her eyelids with their double rows of eyelashes, folds her hairy ears against her head, and I see two flashy plugs close off her nostrils. Just as I bring the scalding glass of sugary tea to my lips, Hamoudi runs to me, pulling the fabric of my *kouffieh* scarf completely over my face. He then throws a sheepskin blanket over the rest of my body.

"*Aashifa* is coming," he says anxiously.

Then we wait, sitting quietly in the middle of the Wadi Rum desert of southern Jordan, braced to endure the coming of a sandstorm. A thick murky cloud approaches with the speed and sound of a freight train. I hold my breath as the first grains of sand pepper my back.

I have been traveling for six days through the deserts of Petra and Wadi Rum, accompanied only by a Bedouin named Hamoudi. We set out from his village to ride our camels through the complex of *wadis* (canyons) that surrounds the ancient ruins of Petra, the capital of the Nabatean Kingdom. We have crossed the hot sand flats of the Wadi Araba desert to arrive at the massive rock escarpments of Wadi Rum, on the Saudi Arabian border.

My reason for being here is simple: to experience the stillness and grandeur of the desert through the eyes of this traditional nomadic culture. I have always been fascinated by nomadic cultures. They have little concept of roots, home and belongings, a way of thinking so foreign to our Western cultures. I wanted to travel with them, alone, to absorb this nomadic culture to its fullest and to be humbled by the lack of Western comfort. I was curious to sample a simple life in a harsh environment.

The Bedouin raise their sheep and goats in the *Sagrah,* the lands of endless sand. They live in tents of black wool, which they usually pitch in remote wadis, close to springs. Bedouin are the ultimate lightweight campers. They can pack all their worthy possessions onto their camel caravans in less than fifteen minutes and be off to the next suitable grazing spot.

Before we set out, Hamoudi unfolded a map of the desert and pointed at the places where we *might* find water during our six-day journey. The springs were the farthest apart during the hottest part of the trip, when we would cross the Wadi Araba desert.

"We go camel way," Hamoudi said that first morning and pointed at my duffel bag. "Camel way and Bedouin way same." My duffel bag was left behind. I headed off with just the clothes on my back.

"We eat with Bedouin, sleep under the stars and drink water from springs, Bedouin way," explained Hamoudi as he tied a kouffieh around my head.

"Now, you Bedouin woman." He smiled. Then he commanded the camel to kneel, and I climbed onto her sturdy back. We left the village and entered the bare, arid desert. Suddenly, I realized I was completely reliant on Hamoudi for food and water. I had no change of clothes and was sleeping in camps of people I had never met. What was I thinking? Had I let my thirst for adventure get the better of me?

At dusk, after trekking the whole day through wadis and over mountains with grand views of the Wadi Araba desert, I wondered where we would spend the night.

"When shadow stop, we stop too," said Hamoudi, as if he could read my mind.

A small herd of camels greeted us at the spring of Wadi Mousa. Just beyond I saw the silhouette of a Bedouin camp between big boulders. A lantern lit the interior of their large tent. Chickens, camels, sheep and goats picked through the scraps of a previous meal, oblivious to the presence of strangers. Hamoudi dismounted and kissed the *sheikh*—the leader of this camp—three times on the right cheek. The shy women quickly drew their *mandeel* over their faces, covering up their amusement at watching me wobble on camel-sore legs to the guest quarters of the tent. Inside it, a curtain separated the men and their guests from the women.

The women immediately went to their quarters, where they store food and clothes, weave, do laundry and cook. I followed the women but was instantly ushered back to the men's. Apparently, I was the guest of the men. I asked Hamoudi if I could see the women later. He looked confused and must have wondered why a guest wanted to visit the women's quarters.

The oldest woman had a tattooed face. When she caught me admiring the intricate designs on her forehead, she quickly grabbed my chin and forced open my mouth as if I were a horse. Curiously, she examined my teeth and was excited to see that I had a gold crown. She returned a warm approving smile that revealed her front teeth—all capped in gold.

I asked Hamoudi how many children the sheikh had.

"Twenty-seven children," he said proudly. How could anyone remember twenty-seven birthdays? my practical Western mind wondered.

In the mysterious way of the desert, our host had known of our journey to his camp. By the time we arrived, a goat, freshly slaughtered in our honor, had been cooking for three hours to absorb all the flavors. Baked in hot, dried yogurt, topped with fried pine nuts and served on a bed of rice, this traditional dish, called *mansaf*, is eaten by rolling the meat, rice and yogurt into small balls with the thumb and fingers of the right hand (never the left!—this hand is exclusively reserved for sanitary duties). We huddled around the big platter, the food almost too hot to touch.

I could not help but stare at the culinary centerpiece of this feast: the goat's tongue, displayed on its own throne. It is a Bedouin tradition that this "delicacy" is always reserved for the guest of honor. I must have had my eyes closed when I finally swallowed the last bite of this tasteless, hairy piece of meat. I imagined I was eating a juicy filet mignon to help process the goat's tongue on its way to my stomach.

At sunrise, we found our camels already packed with freshly baked *shrak*—Bedouin bread—goat cheese, tomatoes, oranges and lots of *hisheh*, the local tobacco that is necessary for any long and hot journey across the open Wadi Araba desert. As we left the sheikh's encampment, I asked Hamoudi about Bedouin hospitality.

"How long exactly is a guest welcome for?"

"Three days," he said with a laugh. "That is how long it takes for all the food the host gives you to pass through you."

In the middle of the day we arrived at Wadi Sabra, the connecting valley and a popular trade route between Petra and Jerusalem. In the distance I could see the white shrine of the Prophet Aaron perched on top of Jabal Harun, the highest summit in Petra at 4,430 feet. Aaron, brother of Moses, is believed to be buried up there, having died while Moses led the Israelites to the plains of Moab. To this date, the shrine is visited by Muslim, Christian and Jewish pilgrims.

Pieces of pottery were scattered in the Wadi Sabra wash. The benches above me showed the ancient remains of well-engineered water cisterns, tombs, a Roman-style theater and Nabataean dwellings fronted by ornate columns. The Nabataeans, a tribe of nomads originating in western

Arabia, were the first people to live here. Petra, where many of their incredible architectural achievements are visible in stone buildings, water-works and tombs, has been named a World Heritage Site by UNESCO.

We had now traveled a far distance from Hamoudi's village, camping with Bedouin families along the way. Petra lay far behind us. The land ahead looked hostile and uninviting; a yellow haze shimmered in the south. We had arrived at the edge of the Wadi Araba desert.

The shadow of the day was long gone, but we plodded ahead. Our camels were tired after trekking all day in the hot sand. We had not seen a single Bedouin camp the entire day. As we climbed over a little pass in the Wadi Araba, the desert sprawled below us. The fiery sun was mirrored against the Red Sea, hazy in the distance—a surreal red glow in the lower western sky. Suddenly, Hamoudi's eyes twinkled as he extended his arm to the brightest star in the southern sky.

"Bedouin star," he proudly said. "We go with Star of Bethlehem!"

Stories of Christmas filled my head and I could just imagine the three wise men coming over the sand dunes from Syria.

We marched in a daze through wind-carved dunes. The dunes revealed prevailing winds in lines of ridges. Hamoudi read the sharp lines like the points of a compass and steered our camels in their direction.

"How can anybody keep their course in this desert with no land-marks around?" I asked Hamoudi.

"No secret mountains, only sacred ways," he explained. I later learned that this knowledge was handed down from his forefathers, who have been traveling this desert for many generations.

The Bedouin have twenty Bedouin songs that they sing to keep their mind off the thirst, heat and soreness of riding their camels. We sang them all during the two days it took to cross the Wadi Araba.

When we arrived in Wadi Rum, I felt like I had entered another world: a timeless and tantalizing desert landscape of sand and rock, punctuated by majestic *jebels* of granite encapsulated in petrified sand dunes. As our camels trotted through the rose, red and white sand, we heard the mesmerizing sound of the *rababah*, a stringed instrument played by Bedouin. We had encountered a caravan journeying from Saudi Arabia. Pots of seeping tea were boiling over a small fire. Men were singing, clapping, laughing and chatting. We joined them for a cup of tea. The oldest man pointed at a mountain in the distance.

"Lawrence of Arabia," he whispered as if that were secret information. The mountain consisted of seven columns. Of course this was probably Lawrence's inspiration for his book of Arab life, *Seven Pillars of Wisdom*. I looked out over this vast and magnificent desert landscape and understood why Englishman T. E. Lawrence had bonded with the Arabs and their desert. Lawrence had supported the Arab cause of revolt and helped Emir Faisal, king of the Hashemites, defeat the Ottoman Turks in Syria in 1918.

All of a sudden, an avalanche of sand hits me like shattered glass. The turmoil of the storm makes me dizzy. It lasts a few seconds, then it vanishes, leaving silence in its wake.

I am hesitant to open my eyes, uncertain of what to expect. The sandstorm certainly made an impressive appearance, but now stillness has reclaimed the desert.

The Bedouin take up their song again, as if nothing has happened. Hamoudi sips his cup of tea, now partially filled with sand. He smiles mischievously when he sees the shock on my face. He opens his mouth and shows me his yellowed, worn teeth.

"Sugar, sand, same same," he says.

The Heat, the Moon, the Dance

by Holly Smith

The sidewalks of Córdoba radiated the 100-degree heat. Sweat streaked my face, and I wondered if the clothes in my twenty-two-pound pack were getting wet with the perspiration that plastered my back. Now I understood the summer heat in Spain mentioned in the guidebooks. I stopped for cold drinks and directions—*Dónde está la mezquita por favor?*—and, following the aim of pointed fingers, spent an hour wandering before I got to a hotel and peeled off my pack. I had been traveling for two months, and while my sense of direction was generally reliable, the heat-filled afternoon had only intensified the fact that I was alone; that I spoke no foreign language; and that each stop consisted of finding a cheap place to stay, somewhere to eat and the sights that had drawn me there in the first place.

After renting a room near the *mezquita* (mosque), I took a refreshing shower in the shared bathroom, then made my way to the tourist office. It was there that I overheard a conversation spoken in a mixture of Spanish and English and understood enough to learn there would be a concert with flamenco dancing at the Orange Center of the mezquita starting at 10:00 P.M. that evening. The cost was 1,000 *pesetas*.

That night, as I walked through the walled compound into the mezquita's courtyard, my senses were filled with a mixture of ancient and contemporary Spain. In the eighth century the Moors added to an existing structure to create what eventually served as the largest mosque in the world. In the thirteenth century Catholics gained control of the area and, during the following three centuries, built in and around the mosque, which became a cathedral. They enclosed the normally open worship area of the mosque and built a bell tower around the minaret. Through the open cathedral doors, I could see the red-and-white-striped Moorish archways; directly in front of me was the bell tower. A centuries-old pebbled pathway snaked its way through the courtyard, around large open spaces now filled with folding chairs, among an orchard of orange trees and through colorful beds of summer flowers.

There was seating for at least three hundred people, and I chose a chair on an aisle about fifteen rows from the front. The atmosphere was electric; smiling people entered the courtyard offering double-cheeked kisses to one another, calls of *buenas noches* sang through the air. Looking around I was reminded of sandpipers scurrying on the beach—people popping up from their seats to shout to friends across the way, women snapping open their fans with a perfected flip of the wrist to cool themselves, the flash of a spotlight being tested, a quick *uno* spoken through a microphone on the stage.

I noticed a man with a warm smile, sparkling blue eyes and an English travel guide, looking for a seat. I waved to him, pointing out the empty chair next to me. Ian was from England; on his fortieth birthday, four months ago, he had quit his job and spent the next three months traveling in India. He was now two weeks into a seven-week stay in Spain. We were soon laughing together, swapping travel stories and talking about our mutual anticipation of the performance.

We had both heard of the excitement and drama of flamenco, that famous Spanish art form full of *espíritu* (soul). Though its history is a bit elusive, its origin is commonly agreed to be Andalusian, strongly influenced by Gypsy and Moorish cultures. Its key components are singing, dance and the guitar. *Canto hondo,* the deep, tragic songs of Andalusia, are sung with raspy, full-throated voices. The dancers' movements exude tension and emotion. Improvisation sets the dancers apart from one another, with the interaction between the dancers and the musicians being a vital element of a performance. We were both familiar with flamenco guitar, the extemporaneous strumming and finger-picking that make these guitar players some of the best in the world. The intricate rhythms of the castanets and the handclapping add to the drama of the music. We were ready for something wonderful.

She floated across the stage in a lime green flamenco dress—large ruffled sleeves, tight from shoulder to knees and a series of ruffles below the knees that ended in a three-foot train. She turned and with a quick kick of her heel whipped the train around. Though she was only a teenager, her voice was strong and passionate as she sang songs of *amor.* The crowd applauded appreciatively.

She was followed by a group of about twenty people singing somber, earthy songs. Two singers performed a duet of what must be a well-loved Spanish song, for the audience joined in. The crowd shouted exuberantly to all the singers, encouraging them to hold a note, applauding while it reverberated through the night air. I glanced behind me and saw an orange moon, one day short of being full, rising over the mezquita. I showed it to Ian and we exchanged a shy smile, nodding our heads in shared delight.

After their performance, our verbose and enthusiastic announcer returned to the stage to introduce the headliner. Superlatives flowed from his mouth—*bonitísima, preciosísima, perfectísima, maravillosísima*—while behind him, two guitarists and four men took to the stage. When the guitarists began to play I closed my eyes to feel the music flow through me. One of the men began to sing, and the others backed him with a deep, solid palm clap. Though the words were foreign to me, there was a familiarity in the tone that brought back memories of other travels. Simultaneously I was hearing the music from a funeral procession I had happened upon in Malaysia and a gamelan orchestra practicing in an Indonesian village. And although it was a Spanish song, I heard the muezzin calling the Muslims to prayer. Suddenly, sitting outside in this ancient courtyard, it all made sense. I heard history come through in music and felt the mark we humans leave on one another. Ian gave me a concerned look when he saw the goose bumps appear on my arms.

Then she appeared; our eyes were riveted to her black flamenco dress and the circling of its train as she wove her way through the musicians and singers on stage, acknowledging each of them individually. The fringe of her red embroidered shawl mirrored her movements; her red lips and hair ornament were bright against her dark braided hair. When she finally looked at us, it was with just a hint of defiance in her eyes. With our mouths agape, Ian and I squeezed each other's arms.

She began her dance slowly, taking over the stage with large, full steps. The hollow sound of the clappers rang out in unison with the clicking of her shoes. Her agile arms and swaying body amplified her presence. As the beat of the music quickened, her arms dropped to pick up the bottom layers of her dress, revealing her amazingly nimble feet. Then she stopped, sauntered around to one side of the stage, hesitated, then began again to a furious rhythm. Faster and faster she danced, reaching a magnificent crescendo, when suddenly she brought down one foot and . . . the music stopped. A brief moment of quiet, a gasp; the applause exploded.

She returned in a red dress, fitted over her torso, with layers of chiffon instead of bouncing ruffles. She made more eye contact with the audience, and when the church bells chimed, she glanced at the bell tower, threw her head back, danced steps to the bell's rhythm, and laughed at her own ingenuity.

It was then that I noticed the dance within a dance. The round spotlight on her also highlighted the round Moorish arches behind her. Her graceful, fluid hand movements became shadow plays on the back wall. A calm filled me as I watched her hands for a story, remembering shadow plays at odalans, temple celebrations in Bali. The layers of chiffon on her dress lifted and separated in response to a gentle breeze. Ian turned and softly touched my cheek. It was disorienting when she again quickened her pace, then stopped suddenly, turned, and sat on a chair at the side of the stage, done. The audience erupted into a chorus of *olés*.

We barely had enough time to catch our breath before one of the men on stage began to dance. There was no slow or easy beginning for this man with receding gray hair and trim body. His feet were like lightning; his eyes twinkled with his smile. Abruptly, he pulled out his handkerchief and waved it at the crowd, and then, laying it tenderly over his shoulder, he gave his final bow.

A second, younger man moved to center stage. His booted feet sounded like galloping horses. He whirled and twirled and seemed not to breathe. With a quick turn and a nod in her direction, he stepped back and she rose off the chair to dance once more.

The audience sat up a little higher to watch her. She demanded our attention with the reverberating stomp of her foot; she held us with her eyes. She danced with abandon; she consumed us with her gestures, and then cast us to the heavens. Again she brought us perilously close to the edge; again she calmed us with her grace. And when she was finally finished, though we were spent, our gratitude came, long and loud, from our hearts.

After sitting silently for a few minutes, Ian and I decided to have a beer. As we made our way to the makeshift counter he said, *"Un momento por favor,"* and pulled something out of his money belt. He told me that last week he had spent an afternoon in an olive grove among wild poppies. He had pressed a few flowers, thinking there might come a time when they would be nice to have. As he presented one to me, he said that although he wished it were a rose, he thought it was still an appropriate memento of this amazing evening; then he lightly kissed my cheek. Amid the celebratory atmosphere of the crowd, we had a quiet conversation. We looked around and admired the women's exquisitely embroidered shawls, the men's perfectly creased shirts and trousers. When I said that I too was wearing my best, Ian raised an eyebrow. We had to laugh at ourselves, me in my cotton print skirt, and him in his shorts and T-shirt. Ian commented that after an evening like this he felt he could go back home, and a part of me agreed, the satisfaction of the night fresh in my mind. But I knew that I would be traveling for five more months, and my spirits soared as I imagined future adventures. Whom would I meet? What would I see, hear, taste, smell and touch? Oh, the freedom of traveling alone, so open to chance encounters, with every sense heightened. In parting we toasted the moon, now high overhead, and kissed each other on both cheeks.

My feet seemed not to touch the ground as I walked back to my hotel. I exchanged *buenas noches* with the other concertgoers in the street, and we all shared a good laugh as I tried a couple of those dance steps.

Solo in Samarkand

by Ena Singh

Browsing one day through dusty rusty shelves in my college library in Delhi, I found an illustrated history of the Mogul dynasty. Standing right there in the stacks I read about the early life of Baber, the first of the Mogul emperors. A descendant of the ruler Tamerlane, Baber first conquered Samarkand in 1497, when he was fourteen. He lost the city three times before he gave up and turned his sights eastward, to India. Baber wanted Samarkand not only because it had been Tamerlane's capital and a rich city at the crossroads of the Silk Road, but because of the glittering beauty of its mosques and gardens. I was riveted by the color illustrations, though the book in my hands was faded and dusty. Page after page showed glistening blue domes. Familiar with the quiet grace of the white domes of the Taj Mahal, I found these cheeky, tantalizing. I hungered to see them, especially because someone had once looked at my grandmother's high cheekbones and said, "Hmm, Mongol blood." Perhaps on their way down the Khyber and through the Punjab, Tamerlane's soldiers had mingled with my ancestors.

Over the next fifteen years, my education, my work and my wanderlust took me through many parts of India and America, often alone. But I never went to a place as closed and mysterious as Central Asia. The opportunity came four years after the breakup of the Soviet Union, when a friend of mine posted in Moscow told me he could get me into Uzbekistan: With a Russian visa, I was allowed three days in the former Soviet republic without an additional visa. I was thrilled. My family was apprehensive. I was determined. They gave in.

Three days would give me a day and a night in Samarkand, and possibly a day in Bukhara. A night in Samarkand was a must, so I could see the domes by moonlight. My family tried once more to dissuade me. It was crazy to go alone, not knowing the language, not knowing anyone there, they argued. And they all thought, but dared not mention to me, the family feminist, that it was particularly unsafe for a woman on her own. I was not listening. The place beckoned, and I responded.

A flight from Delhi to Moscow, a few days in Russia, and then I was on an overnight Uzbekair flight to the capital, Tashkent. A friend of a friend had arranged rental of a car and driver to Samarkand, which was a three-hour road journey from Tashkent. Sasha, the driver, was ex-Russian Army and I was assured I would be safe in his keeping. Clearly, everybody was more worried than I about my safety.

It was late afternoon on a warm summer day when we drove out of Tashkent, heading southwest, driving through flat green country. It was fertile land, and people were out working on the farms. Patches of corn stood golden in the fields. Horses trotted about, looking busy, and cattle stood by grazing, lazy. I lounged comfortably in the back seat of our light blue sedan and enjoyed the smoothness of the road, which cut through the countryside, straight to the horizon, without a twist or a bend.

A little over two hours out of Tashkent and we were in the mountains. From a distance the mountains looked worn and wrinkled, but closer up they were soft-cheeked, with a thin layer of green and yellow grasses. The valley widened, and cherry trees lined the road, with deep orchards beyond.

Occasionally, we passed a factory. Although not a wealthy area, some of the adobe homes and shops had a trimming of blue Samarkand tiles.

I asked Sasha what was made in the factories we passed. He smiled in answer and I was startled by a row of golden teeth. (I learned later that this is a traditional way of storing wealth.) When he didn't answer my question, I realized Sasha spoke no English. As I spoke no Russian, much of our communication through the rest of the journey was by gesture.

When I asked Sasha for a drink of water, he pulled up by the side of the road, flashed his golden smile at me again, and replied, "No problem." He served me water out of a flask with a tin cap that said Made in China. I smiled my thanks. The car needed a drink too, and it was watered before we drove off again.

The sun was beginning to set; men rode home on their mules, bringing back piles of hay. Mothers tried to hustle their children indoors, but they were enjoying their play, and loath to return home. The women were dressed in satin pajamas, with long shirts down to their calves, a garb much like the Indian *salvar kameez*. Their hair was wrapped in bright scarves, and they had Mongolian features and light skin with rosy cheeks.

We passed a sign: Samarkand 22. I started to fantasize about the blue domes. I would soon be in the city that had so fascinated Baber, and that I, too, had dreamed of for over a decade, ever since I saw the pictures in my college library. In a few minutes I should spot the Khazret Khizr, the mosque of the Saint of Travelers that my guidebook told me stood welcoming visitors as they entered the city.

Samarkand 5, said the milestone. Instead of a mosque, I spotted a police patrol. A cop stopped us, and asked for Sasha's driving license and the car registration papers. He was a tall Uzbek in a smart navy uniform. After checking the boot of the car, he gave our bags the once-over. Before I knew it, he had my wallet, and was examining the thick wad of notes with interest. He asked for my passport, flicked its pages, and asked for my visa, first in Uzbek, then in Russian.

"She doesn't need one," Sasha explained in Russian. "She is in Uzbekistan for less than seventy-two hours, and has a valid Russian visa. That is all she needs."

"Not if she wants to go to Samarkand," the policeman informed us. Two or three more policemen joined the discussion. Sasha bravely, patiently, repeated himself. Meanwhile, the policeman kept my passport clutched in his hands. Sasha glanced at me and said, in English, "Little problem," at which point they all moved away from the car, and a heated exchange took place beneath a tree some distance away. I waited in the car, accustomed to Indian bureaucracy—in which sound and fury generally preceded a settlement. I was confident that Sasha could resolve the situation.

The sun had set, and I watched a full moon rise silver above the horizon. In the distance the discussion continued, with interruptions as other passing cars were stopped, checked and waved on their way again. Sasha came back to the car and took a bottle of whiskey out of the glove box. "Problem," he muttered, and vanished again behind the trees. The discussion continued out of earshot. My confidence slipped a little.

It was now nearly an hour since we had been stopped, and I struggled to keep anxious thoughts at bay. I had visions of languishing in jail. Perhaps I had been foolhardy not to pay heed to the warnings of my family. How could I have forgotten this was the land of Tamerlane and Genghis Khan? I wanted to be safe at home in Delhi. Even back in Tashkent would be fine. Even Moscow.

The men returned. I looked at their faces, searching for an expression that would hint at freedom for me, but they gave me no clue. "Problem, problem," Sasha muttered, half to himself. A fat policeman opened the car door and slipped into the seat beside me, where he stroked the navy-and-gold lion emblem on my passport with his chubby fingers. No one explained what was going on.

We drove into the city, my fantasy of a blue-domed paradise quite shattered, and entered the compound of what looked like police headquarters.

Jail, then? Sasha and the officer went in but I was told to wait in the car. Perhaps it will be okay after all, I guessed, else they surely would have taken me in, too. I imagined myself recounting my adventure to my family and friends back home in Delhi, but stopped myself—better not to start on that train of thought just yet.

When the men returned, Sasha looked more relaxed, and was smiling. The fat policeman was with him, still clutching my passport in his chubby hands. Another police car, with a siren and red lights on its roof, drew up and parked next to us. More conferencing. Finally, one of the officers came over and peered at me through the window. "You are a tourist?" he asked in English. I nodded. "Okay, you can go," he informed me, and handed back my passport, which I grabbed with relief. Sasha and I made our escape through the high iron gate of the compound as quickly as we could. A five-minute drive brought us to our hotel. I was at sea about why I had been stopped, and why I had been let go, but had to hold my curiosity until someone could translate for us.

We checked into Samarkand's Intourist hotel—a dull, square, characterless concrete building. A legacy of the Soviet Union, Intourist was the official tourism network that kept control over foreign tourists. We dined on the terrace, beneath the stars, ordering *shashlik kebabs* and *lepioshkas,* unleavened bread cooked in a clay oven. It was late, and we were the last of the diners. My appetite, frightened away by the cops, returned as the fragrance of kebabs wafted across our table. I chewed in concentration, comparing the taste to kebabs I'd enjoyed at home. Uzbek kebabs, I concluded, put more emphasis on the meat, while the ones at home were camouflaged with delicate spices.

Before turning in for the night, I decided I must see at least one of the monuments by moonlight. With the Gur-Emir mausoleum only a five-minute walk away, I could not resist the temptation to explore, even at this late hour. But since my courage was flagging a bit, I asked Sasha to accompany me, to which he replied "No problem."

Since the encounter with the police, the word "problem" had become an important part of our vocabulary. Choosing between "problem," "little problem" and "no problem," Sasha and I communicated effectively through life's adventures.

The street was dark and empty, but for a few stragglers. Houses on either side were set back from a wide pavement, their lights off, their residents asleep. A soft cool wind made music in tree leaves as we trudged along the sidewalk. In a few minutes we arrived at an open square and ahead of us the fluted dome of the Gur-Emir gleamed blue-white in the moonlight. In its compound, steps led down to a large courtyard patterned with bricks. A guard showed us around, lighting the dome to reveal glittering gold and blue patterns, and nine graves in the mausoleum—of Tamerlane, his grandson, his teacher and others. This tomb was intended for the grandson, not Tamerlane, so it is the child who lies at its heart, and Tamerlane is by his side, an afterthought. Tamerlane died unexpectedly on his way to China, and the mountains between him and his home in Shakhrisabz were covered with snow and impassable, so he was edged in with the others. He lies now in a grave of jade, beneath a dome blue as the skies, golden as the sun.

We hurried back to the hotel, because they locked their doors at 11:00 P.M. My room on the first floor was basic, but clean and comfortable, with a door opening out onto a balcony. I stepped out into the wind, and spotted the dome of the Gur-Emir rising up against the sky, other domes and mausoleums visible in the distance. I could have been back five centuries, but the city lights surrounding the domes punctured that illusion. Even so, I felt the tug of the beauty that had pulled Baber to this city.

Anticipation had me up and dressed early the next morning. We ate fried eggs, cheese and lepioshkas in a spacious dining room, bordered by a garden. I watched the breeze dance in the trees through white net curtains that let in the light, but kept out the glaring brightness of the summer sun. In a while, bored with the garden, the breeze wrapped itself mischievously in the curtains, which billowed out and shook the wind loose again.

The English-speaking guide was late, so Sasha and I watched the guests greeting one another, bowing with the right hand upon the heart. At last Tanya arrived and we set off behind her turquoise high heels.

Our first stop was the Registan ensemble. Registan in Uzbek means sandy, as it does in Urdu. It is a plaza, bound on three sides with two large *madrassahs* (colleges) and a mosque with a noticeably crooked minaret. The madrassahs are large square buildings bordered by rows of student rooms with arches opening into the central courtyard. Classic blue domes crown the buildings, and mosaic covers every available inch of wall space. The second madrassah, its imposing arched entranceway decorated with star motifs, was named after Ulughbek, Tamerlane's grandson and an astronomer. He believed in teaching more than theology in the madrassah, and the star motifs are a statement of his determination—amidst opposition—that science and astronomy be taught there. In the rooms lining the madrassahs now stand souvenir shops stacked with rugs, jewelry and other tourist attractions.

From the Registan, Tanya took us to Ulughbek's hilltop observatory. At its entrance stands a statue of the man for whom the observatory was named. A wise man, Tanya reported, who ruled well for over three decades. Mulberries had fallen from the trees surrounding Ulughbek's statue, and had stained the courtyard around him purple. Tanya informed me that a string of six observatories stretched across Eurasia along this parallel, and that this observatory and Ulughbek's Table of Constants were famed for their accuracy. But this observatory was destroyed in an invasion soon after it was built, and only the base of the sextant survived, buried beneath the rubble. How fortunate that the learning that had thrived there survived and spread, though its physical home was in ruins. Nearby, a small museum contained maps of Tamerlane's empire, which had stretched all the way into Northern India. Maps of the Silk Road charted the pathways taken by travelers, with a major crossroads shown at Samarkand. I was reassured to see so many crisscrossing roads being collectively referred to as the Silk Road, since I had always been confused about where exactly the Silk Road lay.

During the days that Samarkand was on the Silk Road, Tanya told me, a colorful bazaar had flourished around the Registan Square, with traders from different countries selling their wares. What exotic items must have filled the bazaars of Samarkand at that time: shimmering silks and soft muslin, sun-baked pottery and delicate porcelain, lustrous pearls, jewels and gems, gold, carpets and spices. I imagine a market bustling with caravans and camels, shrewd merchants, adventurers and intrepid travelers. Quite obviously, even our ancestors had a penchant for "imported" goods, and would go to great lengths to obtain them.

Sasha then drove us to the Bibi Khanym. We had to park some distance and walk through a bazaar, where I enjoyed watching food-shop owners cook snacks in *tandirs,* clay ovens like the ones we call tandoors in India. The mosque loomed large over the bazaar: It was awesome in its scale, and I got a crick in my neck looking up at the main entrance. Tamerlane's wife had had the mosque built in his absence, as a surprise to welcome him back from his victories. But the scale was too grand, and it crumpled under its own weight. It has been under renovation for some time now. The compound of the mosque was quiet, with no visitors, worshipers or tourists. Amidst an overgrown garden was a large Koran stand: a marble base angled to hold the Holy Book. Measured with my outstretched arms, it extended beyond my fingertips. As we sat in the shade of a tree, an old man walked up to us and showed us a flower-shaped blue and yellow tile, similar to the tile border at the base of the dome of the Bibi Khanym. He had helped himself to a piece during the renovation, and was now offering to sell it to us.

Our next stop was the Shakhi Zinda, a necropolis a short distance away. Thirty-odd steps, called the Steps to Paradise, led to the ensemble of tombs. Anyone who counted the same number of steps on the way down as they had on the way up was a good soul, and would be assured a place in heaven. I climbed to a narrow passage. Noble ladies of the royal house were buried on either side, each in her private mausoleum capped by its own dazzling turquoise dome. Only women are buried here, under protection of the saint buried nearby. Here lies Tamerlane's niece, said to have been as beautiful as the moon, slender as a cypress and clever as Socrates. If he had met her, Tanya said, Solomon himself would have been confused, so distracting was she. The face of each tomb was a mosaic in rich blue and luminous turquoise, interspersed with bright yellow and white tiles. The original pieces were intricate, the renovated ones of simpler interlocking geometric patterns, but the effect is a mesmerizing glitter, like a sparkling sea reflecting the sun. The tiles of the mausoleum repeat the colors of the heavens, cloud-white, sun-yellow. I wondered if it was the blue that made the domes so graceful? Or the grace of the domes that heightened the beauty of the blue? Blue dominates the city. Color of water and of life. Blue of heavens, and so of death.

I returned through the passage, down the Steps of Paradise, counting carefully. The result: a different number than I had counted while climbing up. No heaven for me. But a pilgrimage to Samarkand served as well. Elsewhere in the world, light from the sky shines down upon the earth. In Samarkand, they say, it shines from the earth up to the heavens.

Was Samarkand heaven now? I asked Tanya what she thought of the recent changes in the country. She had welcomed perestroika, she told me, thinking that morally, they would live better. But now inflation was killing, and she no longer knew what to think.

Tanya was from Leningrad. Her father, an Austrian communist, had migrated to Russia, where he had married her Jewish mother. Though he was a communist, Stalin's regime had been suspicious of him, and had picked him up one night. She did not know what had become of him, whether or not he was still alive. Tanya and her mother had been sent to Samarkand. Although it had all happened long ago, her eyes moistened as she spoke. Tanya, divorced from her Ukrainian husband, now lived with her mother. Her son lived near the Latvian border with his Russian wife. It was difficult for him to make ends meet, and he could not visit his mother often. His last visit, two years ago, had only been possible because Tanya had paid half the fare. She could not leave Samarkand because it was too expensive for her to live elsewhere. And for many Russians like her, this was home. As this new country sought to define its identity, so did many people within it, seeking new selves, learning to be Uzbek. Their roots may have been elsewhere, but now, for better or for worse, this was where they would stay.

Tanya was anxious about my safety. Her own experiences had given her a dread of the militia and any disorder in official paperwork. I was more relaxed because in my country a brush with officialdom resulted in delays and theatrics, not jail or exile. But I couldn't deny that uniforms and badges in this country inspired a certain uneasiness even in me. The Soviet Union no longer existed, but an official culture of intolerance is not easily erased, and my experience driving into the city was a reminder of what stood in the shadows.

Sasha drove us to the vegetable market to gather ingredients for lunch. With a red plastic bucket in hand, we went shopping. The food bazaar was spread over an acre of land, in the heart of town. It had a makeshift roof to keep out the hot sun, but in places was open to the sky. Men and women stood behind rows of rough counters with buckets and baskets of fruit, vegetables and spices of every imaginable variety and every possible color: pomegranates, luscious peaches, yellow lemons, sharp red chilies, shiny green peppers, deep yellow turmeric, sticky brown dates and mountains of white butter. I counted cherries in four colors, some as large as crabapples. Everybody talked loudly and simultaneously, but didn't quite succeed in drowning out the clink of money. I loved the general air of commotion, and felt right at home. People were dressed as they would have been five centuries ago, speaking the same language, eating the same food. The changelessness was reassuring, a guarantee that the patterns of daily life, the comfortable ways of ordinary people, can survive even if leaders and their mausoleums, regimes and their officials, come and go.

Sasha and I selected one kilo of jet-black cherries from large tin pails, a kilo of apricots and one large lepioshka. Armed with our lunch, we said goodbye to Tanya and headed back toward Tashkent.

A half-hour later, Sasha turned off the highway into a leafy by-lane in the midst of an apple orchard. We got out of the car and he placed his briefcase on the ground to serve as a tabletop. He washed the fruit and then pulled out tomatoes and cucumbers, some bread and a tin of beef. We lingered over our picnic in the cool shade of the orchard, breathing in the clean clear air of the still afternoon, its silence disturbed only by our shuffling.

Back on the highway, the countryside rolled by. Mountains circled the valley of Samarkand. I wondered why they were so dry when the valley was so lush. I could see snow streaking a distant mountain. The land was rich, but the people looked poor: Men and women both were out working the land, in spite of the hot sun beating down on their backs. Children splashed in pools and troughs of water to stay cool. We came across roadside stalls of fruit and vegetables, tempting travelers to stop and buy.

Sasha stopped the car. "Little problem," he said. Something under the hood of Sasha's "machina" needed fixing. Sasha shuffled between the boot and the hood, going from his tool bag to the carburetor, hammering and tightening, filing some component to make it fit better. Sasha found a temporary solution to the engine trouble but needed a mechanic, so we took a detour, stopping in a small town. While Sasha went into a mechanic's shop, I sat in the car watching people sitting in the shade of their houses. Two old men lounged beneath an archway, busy at a board game, a teapot and cups of green tea at their elbows. A woman worked busily in a nearby tea stall, while two of her customers sat on their haunches, waiting to be served, just as in a chai shop in the back streets of Delhi.

Sasha returned. His temporary solution got us to Tashkent late that night.

A hotel, a cool room, a cold bath and a rest. Bliss. The next morning, I got an English translation of my adventure with the passport. The man who came with us in the car to Samarkand had been a police major, and the building we'd gone to was indeed Police Headquarters. The arguments had been over payment of a hefty fine. There was little chance of my being handcuffed and thrown into a dungeon to rot for the rest of my life—an explanation that came as a disappointment. I would rather have paid a hefty fine and gone on to Bukhara, but I was touched by Sasha's concern for my financial well-being.

As I flew out of Tashkent the next day, I gazed out of the airplane window to the land below, the land with which India shares so much of its culture: aspects of its language, dress, food. The domes of the Taj Mahal have their home in this land. As do my grandmother's high cheekbones. I was returning with a deeper understanding of my history, and quite pleased at having finally seen the blue domes I'd admired in the faded book long ago.

The views expressed herein are those of the author and do not necessarily reflect the views of the United Nations or of UNFPA.

Wagamama

by Jennie Peabody

Junko's come down with a cold. I was hoping my solo travel days were over for a while, but she's decided to recuperate at Temple Thirty-three an extra day. I try to hide my disappointment, but I can feel it on my face. Traveling companions come and go on the *henro michi* (pilgrim road), but meeting Junko at dinner last night, after hiking the past fourteen days completely alone, felt like a gift from Kobo Daishi, an end to my isolation. She is the only other woman walking *henro* (pilgrim) I've encountered thus far and is close in age, twenty-six to my twenty-three years. I showed her the photographs of my family and friends taped to the inside cover of my journal, an effort to substantiate my existence beyond this immediate, unfamiliar one. She gave me some Japanese hard *ame* (candy), her favorite. These simple exchanges felt monumental to me. We carved a memory beneath the superficial *Hello*s and *Thank you*s I've found so hard to push past, three weeks into my pilgrimage.

Unlike most pilgrimages, where one travels to a specific destination to worship and then returns home, the pilgrimage I am walking consists of eighty-eight temples honoring holy man and scholar Kobo Daishi

(774–835 A.D.). The temples form a rough circle around the island of Shikoku, Japan, Kobo Daishi's birthplace. One begins and ends at the same place on the map, but time and experience alter the traveler forever.

Kobo Daishi is best known for founding the Shingon (or Esoteric) sect of Buddhism, though only a small percentage of today's henro are Shingon priests-in-training. The majority of pilgrims on Shikoku are laypeople, not necessarily well versed in Buddhist doctrine, but committed instead to the fulfillment of a personal goal. For centuries henro made the thousand-mile journey—over mountains, through farmlands and villages, along the coast—to pray for cures for their own illnesses or those of family members, to atone for sins, or to indulge in the exploration of thought that solitary walking day after day can provide. I am here to photograph the temples, to learn about a culture very different from my own by diving into the heart of a Japanese legend.

Henro dress in white, the color in which the Japanese traditionally bury their dead, since historically either you survived the arduous journey and became stronger in the process, or you died and were buried along the way. A wooden walking staff (available for purchase at most of the temples) is carried by all henro and is the symbolic manifestation of Kobo Daishi, believed to be making the journey alongside his pilgrims. I feel his presence strongest on the henro michi—foot paths that take me off the asphalt roads and highways that have been carved across Shikoku in the past half-century. This morning, side-stepping puddles, blessed by the raining heavens, I set out alone once more for Temple Thirty-four, Tanema-ji.

Tanema-ji is where pregnant women go to pray for safe childbirth. Upon arrival, a woman presents the priest with a newly purchased wooden ladle. The priest punches out the bottom of the ladle, symbolizing an unobstructed passage through which the baby may now enter the world. The woman then takes the ladle home and places it on the family altar for the duration of her pregnancy. When her baby is born safely, she writes her name and age on the handle of the ladle, and returns it to the temple. Hundreds of these ladles are nailed to the wooden shelter outside the temple before me, stark silhouettes against a white sky. Staggered—one ladle high, the next low, the next high—they remind me of those wooden safety gates that parents straddle across stairwells to protect toddlers from inevitable accidents.

Sun replaces rain the next day, and casts light through the trees onto virgin journal pages. The path over the mountain from Temple Thirty-five to this secluded green oasis was ideal except for the cobwebs. They stretch across the trail between trees and bushes directly at face level. I don't want to destroy them, so I try ducking under. More often I see right through them and take one in the face. Once removed from my lashes the web membrane still clings to my hands. It's a minor inconvenience I'll gladly bear to exit the paved road for a few hours.

The stream below my feet jabbers senselessly on its way to grander waters. It's funny, I write letters to friends and family back home about how lonely I am and yet, lingering here in the woods, I want to postpone my return to civilization as long as possible. My minimal Japanese, learned in a six-week crash course, inhibits my ability to converse with people beyond conveying my basic needs: buying food, finding a bathroom or making reservations to sleep at temples or inns—and even those exchanges are challenging. Alone, I can justify feeling lonely, but if I feel isolated surrounded by fellow human beings, then surely there's something wrong with *me*.

But return to civilization I must, and at Temple Thirty-six I find a seemingly endless group of elder bus henro—primarily retired Japanese pilgrims who typically breeze from temple to temple by motorized means rather than the rarer, traditional way of walking. As they crest the final steps on their way to the *hondo*, the inner sanctuary of the temple where one ritually goes to pray upon arrival, a man not more than four feet tall catches my eye as he hobbles past. Judging by the frequent glances he keeps sneaking over his prayer book towards me, my six-foot stature must intrigue him as well. When he finishes worshiping, he comes very close to me. Pointing a gnarled finger at his nose he offers, *"Boku wa kyūjūyon-sai. Hachijuhachi kasho mairi wa, hajimete."* (I am ninety-four years old. This is my first time on the eighty-eight-temple pilgrimage.) He then reaches into his satchel and begins hunting for something but comes up empty-handed. I reach into my own bag and pull out one of my name slips with my name written phonetically in *katakana*, a spelling he can read.

On the pilgrimage, a name slip is traditionally deposited at each temple to symbolically notify Kobo Daishi that you have passed through in search of him and his blessing. Gesturing that my offer is too much, the little man tries to give back my name slip, but I insist he keep it. He clasps it with both hands and bows humbly. I ask to take his photograph individually, apart from the group, and he straightens up proudly. I'd like to ask the man a dozen questions about what brings him to Shikoku in his ninety-fourth year, but even if I could get a question out, it is doubtful I would understand his answer. I must accept and be thankful for the interaction as it exists, a genuine effort to break through the staring curiosity more commonly cast my way.

As I turn the corner into the inn's dining room that evening, I am astonished to find Junko glancing up from her meal. Registering a similar look of surprise on her face, I determine that she must have covered my two-day route in just one—a notable feat, she jokes, since her legs are so much shorter than mine. Junko smiles further when she notices that I now close my *yukata* right flap under left. The first night we met, she told me I was wearing the light cotton robe the wrong way. I didn't know there *was* a right or wrong way to tie a robe, and was too embarrassed at the time to ask why.

"The other way," she explains, "is how we bury you when you are dead."

✼

Up before dawn, I watch dense indigos of the night sky and ocean absorb brilliant pinks of the rising sun as Junko and I search for a ferryboat to carry us across a small inlet towards the next temple. The dock is so hard to find that even Junko has to stop for directions several times. I'm certain I would have missed the boat had I tried to find it alone.

Later that afternoon, I spot an abandoned bicycle on a henro michi shortcut. Fatigued and aware of how much farther we still have to walk, I suggest we steal it. "I'll drive and you can ride in the front basket."

"Like E.T.!" Junko chimes in without missing a beat. Shared laughter infuses me with the energy I need to push on the rest of the way.

We decide mutually to rest at Temple Thirty-seven an extra day and spend the afternoon at a bookstore in town. I find a book on Marlene Dietrich, my idol since high school, and Junko tells me her *aidoru* (idol) is Madonna at the height of her *Blond Ambition* tour. Marlene and Madonna—strong women who stretched boundaries of how women are perceived by society. Before meeting Junko, I believed the prevailing stereotype of Japanese women as docile and ultra-feminine; but Junko has shattered that myth. She is an independent and opinionated individual.

We've hiked all the way to Temple Thirty-eight at Cape Ashizuri today. On my own, I probably would have gone only half as far. After dropping my backpack at the *minshuku* (temple inn), and leaving Junko to start her laundry, I take a walk to see the view from the Cape. A low, walled-in platform gives the illusion that I am safe on top of the sheered-off cliff. This temple is infamous for suicides. Gazing below me and at points all around, I understand why. The ocean pulsates back and forth, gently taunting the shoreline before sending a deadly wave to crush the jagged rocks in its path. The sight hypnotizes me and I wonder what it would feel like to fall from this height. The safest solution is to physically remove myself from the threatening temptation. The wind on the Cape is as powerful as the waves and almost blows me over a couple of times—

especially because I'm balancing precariously on a pair of *geta* (wooden thong sandals) that the temple has provided for me.

Leaving the coast, a mountain road takes us up and up and up, winding forever. When we finally descend, we have only 1.5 kilometers left to hike but they are against gale-force winds that wrench my pack away from my body. My back and legs ache when at last we stumble into the guest quarters at Temple Thirty-nine.

The next several days bring long distances on narrow roads shared precariously with fast cars and trucks, and miserable rain which dampens spirits as much as clothes and skin. I am in a bad mood by lunchtime on the last day. Junko picks up on it.

"Jennie very quiet today. Homesick? If you have problem, talk to me."

Dancing around the issue, I tell her, "In America, I take pride in being fairly independent. It's very hard for me to always be asking for help in Japan, and then not always being understood when I do ask for help. I'm learning dependence and humility."

"Before I met you," she shares, "I didn't like Americans. But you are"—and she points to the word *otonashii* in my dictionary—"gentle, obedient. You have very good Japanese manners."

The truth is, I'm uncomfortable with how dependent I've become on Junko. I no longer worry about making overnight reservations without understanding what's being said on the other end of the line—she makes the phone calls. And with her as a liaison, I'm participating in dinner conversations with other henro more confidently. However, I now feel obligated to travel on Junko's schedule (she's on a deadline to get back to work), which has us hiking twice the distance in a day that I would have hiked on my own. The pace is exhausting and will put me in Takamatsu too early to meet my mother, who is coming to hike the last two weeks with me. I wonder if I shouldn't put more trust back in myself and Kobo Daishi and continue on alone.

During dinner that evening at Temple Forty, lightning, thunder and rain battle outside. The storm makes me smile but Junko frown, as we've agreed that if it rains, we'll stay an extra day. Ultimately Junko's entreaty to the weather gods is more potent than my own—the squall stops as abruptly as it started. I'm almost hoping I'll be sick so I can't go with her tomorrow, the way she opted out the day after we first met. I realize I should just put my foot down and say I'm staying. We're not obligated to each other, after all. Where is the confidence that got me here, on this 1,000-mile solo hike in a foreign country, in the first place? I just can't find the strength to willingly separate from Junko. I keep hoping she'll offer to stay an extra day. And I pray for rain.

Over breakfast the next morning, I am more direct with Junko than I have been and explain I would feel much better if I stayed at Temple Forty one more night.

"Fine, stay," she says abruptly.

"But I don't want to separate."

"Fine, come along."

The memory of the emotional isolation I experienced while walking alone is still too close. The threat of being an absolute outsider again overshadows any physical exhaustion I might endure. And so I relinquish to Junko's lead once more. On my way back from the bathroom, I bump my head on the eternally too-low doorjamb and immediately try to read some greater meaning into it. Is it a sign I should stay or am I being punished for challenging Junko's schedule? I am desperate for guidance from a higher power.

I go to mail a letter at the post office just down the street from the temple. On the way back I shoot photographs of multiple henro crossing through traffic on their way to Temple Forty, a contradiction of past and present distinguished boldly by white robes and linear crosswalks against black cars and asphalt. When I finally put my camera down, I spot Junko, irritated, waiting for me by a tree, ready to go. I put my pack on quickly and we start walking. Though I was tired when I first woke up this morning, I find new energy on the road, inspired by the pictures I've just taken and thinking about the letters I've recently received from home.

Hiking with Junko, I usually set the pace several yards ahead of her. Agreeable to both, the system allows us to fall into personal rhythms of walking and solitary thinking while still being together. I often slip into a minor meditative trance, as we keep most of our thoughts to ourselves, but today it isn't long before I start to feel an evil glare piercing through my backpack from Junko behind me. When I can't shake it off, I turn around and ask her, "Are you mad about something?"

"Mad?" she queries.

"Angry?" I clarify.

She laughs halfheartedly and assures me she isn't. We keep walking, but I'm not convinced.

We stop for a snack and Junko observes, "You don't seem so tired anymore."

"Yeah, I'm surprised, too," I smile. "I think the letters from home really cheered me up."

"Well, if you're happy, I'm happy. But," she adds, "I was a little angry earlier."

"*Gomen nasai,*" I apologize.

Laughing, she teases, "You are *wagamama.*" I look up the word in my dictionary, and find "selfish, big ego" next to the entry. It feels like a slap in the face. I sober up quickly and become instantly quiet, wondering, *Why is it that I'm selfish for wanting to stay an extra day, but Junko's not selfish for insisting we go?* Yesterday I was "gentle and obedient," today I am "selfish with a big ego."

We walk further and a young man stops his car, waves his camera, and asks to take a picture. We oblige and then I hand him mine to take one for me. Junko points out that my lens cap is on, which triggers the realization that all the pictures I shot this morning are nonexistent. I mention this to Junko and she immediately quips, "Kobo Daishi," as if to suggest this is his spiritual practical joke, rewarding her wishes over mine. I turn my back on Junko, so she can't see the tears that are overtaking me, and start to walk again. I wonder then if Kobo Daishi *is* working on my behalf and means for me to turn around right there and walk back to Temple Forty to take the photographs of henro arriving that I missed this morning, to make this *my* pilgrimage, *my* journey, on *my* terms. I feel so frustrated and unclear as to how to behave in this culture. I am American, after all, and believe that some selfishness in terms of independence and individuality is good. And yet, when I try to assert myself with Junko, I feel I am hitting a wall. I must back down, retreat, give up.

Stopping for lunch, Junko encourages an extended break because, as it turns out, our minshuku is only forty-five minutes away. "Don't you want to hike further," I ask, "change our reservation?" because this morning I thought she said this particular inn was too close.

"No," she answers, "relaxation is good." After a brief pause she adds, "Don't you have more free time? You should take more free time."

She has me completely confused by her contradictions, and yet in retrospect, it's really quite simple. I received the compliment of "gentle and obedient" when I was dancing around the issues, in good Japanese form. I received the criticism of "selfish, big ego" when I was direct and, in her view, outright rude. It is a painful illustration of the famous Japanese saying, *"Deru kui wa utareruîó"* (The nail that sticks up gets hammered down). I played the nail to Junko's hammer, but I must have played it well—for in granting a slower pace, perhaps Junko is acknowledging her own wagamama tendencies.

We arrive at our destination for the night—a delightful seaside resort, halfway between the last and the next temple, with rooms overlooking oyster farms in an inlet backed by mountains, and, most notable to me, a showerhead tall enough to stand under. When asked if we want separate rooms, Junko shouts *"Hai"* (Yes) enthusiastically. My first reaction to the private accommodations is rejection—Junko seems excessively happy. She brings me canned juice as a peace offering, though, and we go sit on the dock to watch the sunset together.

Through broken *Jenko-go*, a term we've coined (from the first syllable of my name, the second syllable of her name and *go*, the Japanese suffix for "language") to describe the half-Japanese, half-American language we use to communicate, I ask Junko what inspired her to walk Shikoku's pilgrimage. "I was in a slump," she confides. "I decided to go to India for a change of pace. Living there, I saw many things that were different from Japan. Situations that I thought would be resolved through common sense were not so obvious to the people I met in India. It made me think more about my own background. I wanted to know more about Japan. I still needed some time alone and I remembered my grandmother telling me about *hachijūhachi kasho* (eighty-eight-temple pilgrimage). So here I am."

Here she is, a strong, spirited individual living in a society that doesn't readily reward independent behavior. A fundamental paradox of traveling to a foreign land is that in observing another culture, one discovers a mirror reflecting back upon oneself. I realize I came to Japan thinking naively I was here to learn about the Japanese way of life, and yet what traveling with Junko has begun to teach me about myself exceeds what I'm learning about her and her culture.

With the onset of autumn, Junko and I are changing colors like the *momiji* (maple leaves) at the base of the mountains. We've traded stereotypes. The bold, independent American and the polite, obedient Japanese no longer exist. Yesterday's wagamama episode was a trial of wills, some sort of instinctual contest to see which woman would dominate. There's greater ease between us now—a camaraderie that strengthens with each incident.

The path along the base of Temple Forty-five parallels the course of a river. It's a beautiful trail, meant to be meandered, but Junko and I run it. The sun is setting and I'm hoping to photograph the temple before dark. Unfortunately, the light is too low when we arrive, so we go straight to our room.

At breakfast the next morning, Junko says I called out in my sleep, *"Hayai! Yukkuri!"* (Fast! Slow!) and then mumbled more in English that she couldn't understand.

"Bikkuri shita!" (You surprised me!) Junko added. "Very loud. Wake me up *mayonaka gurai* (around midnight). Little smile, but you still asleep."

Ironically the phrase can be translated two very different ways. Either I called out in typical frustration, "We're going too fast! Let's slow down!" or I shouted, "Hurry up! You're moving too slow!" which would satisfy Junko's desires. In truth, we are both doing a little give and take to stick together until we get past the steepest part of the pilgrimage, near Temple Seventy-three. This morning, Junko insists I take as much time as I need to photograph before we hit the road.

Iwaya-ji, Temple Forty-five, is a magical place, built high in the mountains. Even the bus henro must leave their vans in the parking lot far below and climb the dozens of stairs that lead from riverbed to mountain peak. Once there, a narrow wooden ladder points to a still higher altar carved into the towering rock face. Few henro are brave or agile enough to make the final ascent. Junko agrees to the climb only after I go first. Gazing down on fellow henro milling about the temple grounds, I feel a subtle euphoria. In this special alcove I understand why gods tend to mingle in the heavens. Here a boundless tranquillity exists. It begins to dissipate the closer one falls to earth.

Weeks later, getting down the mountain from Temple Sixty takes longer than I expect it to. This area was hit hard by typhoons. As the henro michi becomes an obstacle course of fallen trees, I am humbled by the storm's power—power I had naively ignored in the early days of my pilgrimage.

Junko and I climb over or crawl under most of the downed tree limbs with a little extra effort, but one leveled pine tree completely obstructs our path. The only way around it is to scramble up the embankment for several yards, cross over the tip of the tree, and then scoot down the bank on the other side.

The henro michi eventually dumps us out on a steep road. Zigzagging to save our knees, Junko and I joke about how we ski: snowplow straight across perpendicular to the slope, stop, turn around, snowplow straight back, stop, turn around. I'm reminded of the older bus henro I taught to navigate a difficult descent near Temple Twenty in much the same way.

At the base of our "ski slope," in place of a cozy lodge, we come upon a huge, austere, granite-faced building. I think perhaps it is a museum, but it turns out to be Koon-ji, the richest temple on Shikoku. The monstrosity houses ornate statues of appropriate deities on a stage before rows and rows of auditorium seats. No kneeling until your legs cramp here! I imagine the temple filled with worshipers and a modern-day televangelist disguised as a Buddhist monk convincing all to sign over their bank accounts.

Flipping frantically through *Japanese Pilgrimage*, the book that inspired me to undertake this journey, I learn that over the past few decades Temple Sixty-one has become the richest of the eighty-eight temples due to the belief that prayers and a priest's blessing here enable a childless couple to conceive. Judging by the thousands of baby pictures—success stories—that line the hallways of the largest guest accommodations of any of the temples, I'd say that modern-day fertility techniques have nothing on this traditional prayer worship.

Outside on the temple grounds a car henro approaches and asks why Junko and I are stopping for the night when Temple Sixty-two is only a few kilometers further. "Because we're *tired*," Junko tells him succinctly.

What is only five minutes away for him, relaxing in the luxury of a car with the radio turned on, is more like half an hour for us, tripping over feet that have already walked eight hours' distance. I remind Junko, too, that Kobo Daishi is not likely to be hitching a ride in anyone's vehicle, whereas we feel his presence strongly on the henro michi. At that moment, a walking henro wielding *two* staffs windmills through the gate. He says he averages thirty-five kilometers per day on foot. Something to aspire to the next time I set out to hike a thousand miles in typhoon season.

I witness my first tea ceremony under an awning in the courtyard of Motoyama-ji, Temple Seventy. Carefully measured proportions of green tea to water are whisked together in a cup with no handle—more like a bowl—and presented to me by the bowing tea master. Junko shows me how to ceremoniously turn the cup a few times before sipping. I admire the mindful ritual required to drink this tea. How often have I hastily swallowed food and drink, unconscious of its taste? Junko is surprised that I like the warm green liquid—she says many Japanese find the flavor too bitter.

For a bedtime story, I tell Junko the legend surrounding tomorrow's afternoon climb to the cliff above Shusshaka-ji, Temple Seventy-three. At the very young age of seven, the child Daishi, then known simply as Kukai, scrambled to the peak of a 1600-foot mountain near his home. Up above the clouds, he threw himself off the cliff, imploring of the heavens, "If I am called to save the people—save me, O Buddha! If I am not, let me die!" At that moment, a band of angels appeared, caught the boy in their robes, and deposited him safely back on top of the mountain.* Junko says she's not crazy about heights but that she's willing to make the extra climb to the infamous site.

From the base of Temple Seventy-three we follow a steady incline to the prayer sanctuary just below the peak. I leave my staff resting on a stone wall to free both hands for the steeper rocks ahead. Junko holds on to hers,

---

* Oliver Statler, *Japanese Pilgrimage* (New York. William Morrow and Company, Inc., 1983), p. 36.

psychologically more secure with Kobo Daishi at her side. Navigating the next fifty yards is the closest I will come to actual rock climbing on the entire pilgrimage. Decisions have to be made about the best route to take, where to place hands and feet, and whether or not the strength in my arms and legs can pull up the weight of my body. Cooperation between my mental and physical capabilities enables me to reach the apex and the 360-degree view of the surrounding valley a few minutes before Junko. Exhilarated by my success, I feel tempted to throw my life in the hands of the angels as the young Daishi did.

I remember, as a child, conducting my own test of immortality in the neighborhood swimming pool. I thought that the only reason I couldn't breathe under water was because people *told* me I couldn't, and if I truly believed I could breathe under water, then I could. So one day, after what seemed like hours of mental preparation, I dropped down to the bottom of the pool. There, believing with all my might that I could breathe under water, I counted the magical One, Two, Three, and sucked in a deep breath of . . . water! Sputtering, coughing, choking, I surfaced, but gained composure quickly, so others would not witness my scientific setback. Stubborn and idealistic, I was not fazed. I simply told myself, "Clearly, you did not believe strong enough."

Here, twenty years later on the young Daishi's mountain, is the chance to test the strength of a more seasoned faith. I can see the headlines:

TALL AMERICAN FOREIGNER HURLS HERSELF FROM CLIFF
TO TEST WHETHER SHE IS THE NEXT BUDDHA . . .
SHE IS NOT!

Though dramatic, the suicide would not have gone over well with family and friends. Junko would have had to explain how, clinging to every rock and scared to death of falling herself, she watched the *henna gaijin* (crazy foreigner) scramble to the top as quickly as possible and fling herself over the edge. I'm sure it wasn't the descent Junko quite had in mind.

Instead, I thank Kobo Daishi for *his* faith in Buddhism, so I don't have to test my own, and offer to carry Junko's staff back down the cliff—she needs both hands free more than I do.

Tonight, Junko appears to be the anxious one. After all this time together, she's now worried about traveling alone. But we must separate, as my mother is coming to complete the last two weeks of the pilgrimage with me, and does not arrive in Takamatsu for a couple of days. I assure Junko she'll be fine—she speaks the language, after all.

On our last day together, Junko and I experience publicity to rival that of our idols, Madonna and Marlene, when we open the local Shikoku newspaper and discover a photograph of the two of us staring back from Zentsu-ji, Temple Seventy-five, the birthplace of Kobo Daishi. There, three days ago, a woman journalist requested an interview with us to understand how I had first learned about the pilgrimage and what brought Junko and I together as traveling companions. I don't realize the difference in our heights is so extreme until I see the image of us standing side by side. We used to joke that she required two steps to every one of mine, and this picture proves it to be true.

We cannot predict who will change our lives, nor whose lives we will change. I came to Shikoku believing I would learn about Japanese culture. But as much as I observed others, eyes cast equally inquiring looks back upon me. Where parents and bus henro stared curiously, honest schoolchildren called out *"gaijin!"* (foreigner) when I passed through their towns. It was less threatening to keep to myself, but certainly more limiting. And then I met Junko. With her, I traded isolation for companionship, independence for friendship, a one-way lens for a mirror.

Knowing we'll meet up in Osaka in two weeks (after I return my mother to the airport), Junko and I bid an easier goodbye at the hotel entrance, copies of the article about us tucked into each of our prayer books. As I watch Junko turn the corner on the road toward completion of her own pilgrimage, I call out the henro mantra: *"Ganbatte, neh!"* (Persevere!)

I whisper the refrain to myself as I pivot into the hotel lobby, alone for the first time in over a month. At the front desk, I try to act casual, asking the clerk if she has seen today's paper.

"Mmm, mimashita," she nods simply. (Yes, I saw it.)

It isn't the reaction I am hoping for. I point proudly to my picture to leave no doubt as to my fame. She laughs, amused by my bravado, but reiterates, *"Hai, mimashita."*

Yes, she has seen this wagamama.

Sisters

by Lisa Schnellinger

Two days into Senegal, I'm feeling ugly.

For one thing, my hair is a mess. Senegal's hot, windy December weather has turned it into a sweaty, straggly clump. I'm growing it out, and the odd ends won't tuck into a braid or a ponytail. Then there's my clothes—those sturdy pants and thrift-store shirts. I travel light, with just a couple of outfits, and though I wash them regularly in the sink, they were already bordering on shabby three weeks ago when I left Seattle. With all this dull practicality, I feel decidedly unfeminine.

In Morocco, my previous stop, I was actually trying to be unattractive because as a solo blond woman I endured constant harassment. Here, my grungy appearance creates a barrier I don't want.

Senegalese women wear swathes of brilliantly colored and patterned cloth in loose two-piece dresses, called *boubous,* that disguise both bulky and scrawny figures. They wrap headdresses in matching cloth, like turbans. And that's just the daily wear—when dressed up, as for an international flight, they wear heaps of jewelry in gold, beads and polished stone. Their filmy scarves drape over curving arms and shoulders. From under the boubous peeks more fabric in solid colors to accent the pattern. The women are so striking, it's hard not to stare at them. Even the old and the unbeautiful have allure and dynamism.

I want to know Senegalese women. I've come on this trip to write stories of ordinary African life; I can see that I'll have to fix myself up to fit in.

Especially on Gorée Island, a short ferry ride from Dakar, which serves as my home base for the three weeks I spend in Senegal. Gorée, a village of about 1,000 people, is filled with keen observers, and they are particular experts at observing white people. The first Europeans came here 500 years ago and began buying African slaves to ship to the Americas. Millions passed through this portal. Now the tide has shifted, as Western countries ship aid and loans, and tourists come to gawk at this historic port of misery.

In my first morning I walk most of the island. Its stone sidewalks push age against my soles. Goats wander in the sandy dirt, unmarked; their owners know them. Communal water pumps creak, drawing in women and children bearing buckets, who seem to drift in small formations like pools and streams. The female presence in public work is another sharp contrast to Morocco, where men dominate the visible workforce.

I buy a clump of necklaces from two bead sellers—an old woman and a teenage girl who quarrel over how I split my transaction—and lively print cotton pants from a third woman. For lunch I choose a beachfront table near the ferry, where an attractive, languorous young man waits on me with a smile that lingers long enough to be possibly flirtatious. After Morocco, I appreciate the subtle, laid-back attention.

As I finish my shrimp and rice, spiced just past naughtiness in a thick red hot sauce, a woman toting a bag approaches. In pantomime and French, she offers to braid my hair. Tiny braids, African braids, plaited against my head.

I hesitate. Growing up in the '60s, I learned to cower in ashamed awareness of what whites had stolen and appropriated. African hairstyles symbolized black pride, and so a white woman's hair braided this way carries, to me, the tinge of a politically incorrect affront. But I admire the look, and I need to tame my uncooperative hair. Braids will be comfortable in the heat, I tell myself; I won't have to brush my hair or fuss with it. If I feel too foolish, I'll just undo the braids. And, I rationalize, the Senegalese might forgive me if they see my hairstyle as a sign that I've spent money in the local economy.

Leading me over to sit on the ferry pier, Gunayba proceeds to pull and weave my hair. I become flustered at the prospect of being performance art, for the entertainment of all Gorée. In between squeezing my eyes shut from pain, I catch glimpses of the locals, staring. Some are smiling, especially the women. I can't interpret their smiles—are they mocking or encouraging?

Gunayba tugs at my hair with a comb as the breeze continues to ruffle it. Over the course of an hour she works her way across my head, weaving the hair in tight curves of fourteen rows that follow the lines of my skull. My pampered scalp is unaccustomed to scalding sun and pulling that seems to penetrate the roots. I flinch, at the pain and at my own guilty vanity, but absorb it in silence, with the deference of an initiate, wanting to belong.

My three older sisters would fuss over my long hair when I was still a preschooler, brushing it and tucking it into a bun, making me feel like a little princess. Then I learned, as a little girl, to sleep on hair curlers. The pink sponge rollers with flexible plastic clips were uncomfortable, but nothing compared to what my older sisters put up with. Maggie, newly a teenager, used full plastic curlers with bobby pins; Chris, an upperclassman in high school, clamped on rows of rollers as big around as a sapling; and Ann, the big-city college student, rolled her hair in orange juice cans with bobby pins the size of horseshoe nails. Hair was our lingua franca.

Now, as my hair disappears into braids around the back of my neck, I feel a twinge of anxiety. A few locals stop to voice their approval as the hairdo emerges. *Très bon!* I imagine deprecation from the ones who say nothing, and wonder if they see me as a stupid tourist trying to look like them.

Gunayba holds up a mirror so I can admire her work. I pat my head gingerly. It's a new head, my hair converted to a knit cap with macrame streamers. She demonstrates how tough the braids are, shows me that I can lather and rinse them. I give my head a stiff shake and the long braids fly. I feel lighter, cleaner. Almost pretty. The braids hang tight, durable enough for hot, dusty rides in crowded vans and buses, or hours walking with a loaded basket on top of them.

Later that day in a little corner store, as I struggle to buy something using my bad French, a woman with sharp, laughing eyes intercedes to translate for me.

"You're from the States," Sarita says, introducing herself and Nanu, the shopkeeper. Sarita is an African-American woman in her forties who, after years of occasional travel in Africa, has come to live on Gorée. I'm relieved to speak English with someone from home.

We have a beachside dinner and swap stories. We talk about our failed relationships with men, about the language difficulties and lack of good plumbing here. Sarita shares the hardships of her initiation into Senegalese life. I tell her about my encounters with hustlers in Marrakesh and Dakar.

I can relate to Sarita much more than I can to the average twenty-something backpacker—she left a career and a house and a car to come here, understands Africa in a larger global context from her graduate studies and views each day through the lens of her life's decades. It is like talking to one of my sisters, a familiarity that transcends the divergence in our paths. She offers me advice with the graciousness of a wise oldest sister, and the humor of a sibling's shared experience. I defer to her knowledge, seek her approval.

I confess my misgivings about my braids and how I might seem to the Senegalese.

She listens with indulgent nods, and says, "You know, there's this love-hate relationship with Senegal and America . . . but I think the Senegalese are pretty tolerant people."

"Yes," I say, "and I would hope they'd see this imitation as a kind of flattery."

Sarita concurs. I relax a little more, tipping my head to feel the woven hair tickle the back of my neck. We watch the twilight fall, ogle the waiters and passersby with low voices and giggles.

The next day, dressed in my Gorée-style pants and with braids wetted down, I wander down the back streets. I'm looking for signs of today's holiday, the feast of Abraham, whose obedience to God is emblematic of Muslim faith, and hoping I won't run into the slaughter of the bulls that I'd seen being led off the ferry.

In an open yard I encounter about two dozen women, their clothes a bright garden of color and pattern, as they cook the midday meal in great iron cauldrons. I greet them individually, *"As-salaam alaykum."* They reply automatically, *"Wa alaykum as-salaam." Peace be with you also.* Some eye me, taking in the clothes and hair; others ignore me. I linger, wanting to reach beyond our roles and histories, touch the familiar in them, let them know the part of me that is not ticketed by tourism.

One woman uses a jumbo wooden mortar and pestle to pound a red pepper mixture. She has to stand to heave the heavy club into the bowl, but her arms are strong and sure. I watch with curiosity and open admiration, and after a little while the women invite me to try. I fall to it with such gusto that the woman sitting closest to the bowl pulls back in alarm that her clothes will be splashed. I apologize and try to make my movements more coordinated—but with little success, so I relinquish the pestle.

The pounded pepper blends into a sauce with mustard and white vinegar. Endless trains of red sausages fry in oil. Meat, onions and green and red peppers sauté into a rich *roux*. All this melds with the cauldrons of rice as the women stir it with a shovel. My stomach is stirred, too, by the fragrance. I've been on the road for most of the previous four months, doing a fellowship in the South Pacific before I came to Africa, and I miss home cooking.

One of the seated women regards me, unsmiling, unblinking, for long moments. She is draped in a sky-blue cloth that, except for her tortoise-shell glasses and black skin, makes her look like the statues of the Virgin Mary that I grew up with. Her face is so pure and serene that she seems otherworldly. When she invites me to sit on a chair next to her, I feel blessed.

I smile a little, not too much, as I listen to the conversation, mostly in French but some in Wolof, the local language. I speak when spoken to. With my stammering French, I try to describe to them how much I like this place compared to Morocco. I manage to say that the clothes and faces of the women are beautiful, that I am relieved to be among women. They nod gravely. As I describe the hair-braiding, one woman points to a far corner of the yard and I'm happy to see Gunayba—and I win more points, for my local braids. My words are passed along to those out of earshot, and gradually the circle loosens and opens to encompass me.

The men gather for a meeting and sermon in a conference-type room nearby. They dress in elegant caftans in subdued colors, and float by with serious, yet placid bearing. One of them comes to take photos of the women. I ask the Virgin Mary whether it is possible the women will permit me to photograph them too. She nods.

I ask permission of each woman as I photograph them. They warm up as I position myself at their sides or at their feet, praising their beauty and thanking each one. A few of them even call me "sister." A word that moves under my skin.

Sisters: Ann, Chris, Maggie. My three sisters have been part of every day since I was born. When they talk and giggle, I hear myself in another voice. On the surface our lives are disassociated: Ann is a New York benefits analyst, Chris runs self-storage units near Cleveland, Maggie manages an animal hospital in Pittsburgh, I am a writer in Seattle. Yet each one carries facets of who I am. We can talk for hours. Whether I'm weeping over a disastrous affair or exhilarated about a new apartment, I can call a sister and she will understand me and love me.

For me sisterhood is the relationship with the purest motives, the least baggage. The thousands of hours spent playing in the same yard and eating the same cooking, the passing on of secrets about men and sex that our parents would not or could not divulge, the layers of understanding conveyed by our own language of words and gestures—all make the bond of sisterhood a fundamental part of who I am.

A sister will never leave me. Our connection outweighs all differences.

That is the intimate, tender strength I hear when African Americans call one another "sister" and "brother." But as an adult I learned that, no matter how close I am to my black friends and colleagues, the bond of being a "sister" eludes me. Whatever we share in values or interests, to them I can never really be a "sister."

Yet here, in Africa, there is room for me to be a sister. As I take photos of the women, looking at each face, each draped figure, each pattern of fabric, the uniformity of skin color puts their individual features into relief. More than anything else, I see them as women. Of a common mother, through some bloodline over millennia.

My camera, though, makes some of the women uncomfortable and they keep their expressions rigid; I'm literally re-creating them, and they don't know what shape I am giving them as I frame their images to take with me. I try to put some control back in their hands by being deferential and promising to give their images back to them. It seems to work, as they relax and their smiles come more easily. Several women make faces for me as they stuff food in their mouths. I make little jokes and pantomime about the size of the platters and the amount of hot pepper, and they laugh loudly. When the men come to take the serving platters for their separate dining, two of the women order the men to let me photograph them.

At last the women invite me to eat—first just a sample, which makes my eyes grow round with the dimensions of its long-simmering flavor. Pull up a chair, they say, and they draw me into one of the circles. Each group is seated around a communal bowl the size of a truck tire, filled with rice and the remnants of vegetables and meat that weren't arranged onto the men's platters. With the first spicy taste, its orchestra of flavors, I want to eat the entire bowlful. I try to hold back but the women monitor me, keep pushing me to eat more. They scoop up great handfuls of rice and squeeze out prodigious streams of the orange-tinged oil before popping each ball of food into their mouths. There is more than enough for the six of us in that one bowl.

We settle back after eating, and Niangua, who speaks a fair amount of English, pulls me to sit next to her. Her presence is commanding: great bulk swathed in burnt-orange clothes, smoldering eyes fully made-up, a cool countenance that sometimes breaks into folds with a huge laugh. She has taken a shine to me, partly because of my appetite, which matches hers. She finds it tremendously funny when I offer to do the dishes, and agrees I can help later.

A lone European man walks past. He gazes at the women as though they are part of the scenery. Niangua frowns and points to him and then her eyes, shaking her head. I nod and say, "He looks but he doesn't see." Niangua grins, and holds up her palm in "gimme five" fashion. I slap it and we grasp hands. Her eyes take me in, her warmth floods over me like perfume. "I like you!" she says. I sit pleased as a child.

My parents, who brought up their four girls to be independent, were born to two tough German mothers who raised large families virtually alone. As I watch the women, I'm struck by how much it feels like one of my own family gatherings—the collective cooking, the banter, the company of loud women who like to eat. Thanksgiving in Ohio: We'd be dressed up in our "company" clothes, trying not to get food on them when we helped stir pots or wash dishes, shrieking and laughing as much as we could get away with, exchanging "Yum!" or "Yuk!" expressions at the tastes we sneaked.

And the faces. There is a woman here whose forehead is just like Aunt Mary's; another who grins like my cousin Mary Kay; another who sits like Chris. I feel like I'm in my Aunt Bette's kitchen, where the women would assemble trays of cold cuts and vegetables and pull bowls of potato salad and cole slaw from the refrigerator, chatting, while the men turned the barbecued meat over the grill in the back yard, drinking beer and throwing horseshoes.

I have been away, on my own, for so long. Not just from the States, but away from family life, from the holiday gatherings where everyone present had seen me in diapers.

Tears come to my eyes, and in a jagged stream of words I describe for Niangua my family, and then the gauntlet of Moroccan men that had worn me thin. She hugs me, folding me against her large soft bosom, a maternal connection that means more to me at this moment than a hug from my own mother. Comforted, then embarrassed by my tears, I leap up to help with the dishes, as I would have at any family gathering. As I heft and wash the greasy platters, the women laugh with approval at my earnest labor. It is a delicious sound.

Dishes finished, we sit in the shade. A group of foreign day-trippers comes by, and some of the women stiffen under their indifferent eyes. Another tour group approaches a few minutes later with a guide. They stand and look at the women, waiting for the guide to describe the species, the behavior.

I thumb through my French phrase book and find *J'en ai marre*— "I'm fed up!" Not sure how to conjugate the verb, I try to ask Niangua if she is fed up with tourists.

She shouts in French, "I'm fed up with tourists!" as I try to shush her, and laughs so hard I think she'll fall out of her chair.

The tour group stops and the guide tells them, "These are some women celebrating the feast of Abraham." Niangua keeps laughing.

One tourist asks to take their photograph, but the women around me shake their heads no.

Sharing this holiday meal felt like a breakthrough, I tell Sarita over dinner—Niangua has invited me for tea at her home in Dakar, and another woman has told me about an upcoming women-only dance. Sarita joins in my delight. Still, her tales have made us both cautious about thinking I am "one of the girls."

Sarita has lived on Gorée for several months, and on the surface she fits in. She's got the build and hair of Senegalese women. She's had boubous made and she wears them well. Her French is decent, and she's starting to learn Wolof. I envy the stability she has, the routine of shopping and visiting she has begun to develop, the casual greetings she exchanges with some residents. She has a landlord and a neighborhood and is flirting with a potential boyfriend. Yet the slavery of her ancestors gives her no free passage here. Though she has made Gorée her home, she doesn't feel at home yet. We wonder if the residents see her as a privileged American before anything else.

For me, though, Sarita is my Gorée sister. We muse together about how to interpret double-entendres and snubs, we gossip about other Americans, we share our news from family and friends in the States. On the road it wearies me to go for weeks without seeing a single person I know. In just a few days, Sarita becomes that familiar face I long for. She is my bridge to home.

On Sunday afternoon, Sarita and I meet up at the *sabar,* a women-only dance. Words from the sponsor, a political party, interrupt the drumming and dancing. The women don't listen. They dance, by the hundreds. The men drum, but they might be a stereo playing prerecorded music for all the acknowledgment the women give them.

The women's bodies shimmy and shake like jelly. I studied African dance seven years ago from Senegalese teachers, but these women are improvising on nameless, uncopied patterns that I never learned. Watching closely I think I can identify what is moving, but realize it's not a matter of mere body parts. When the pelvis moves, it comes from the feet. When the head moves, it rises from the shoulders and chest. And all movement is propelled from some source that does not have an anatomical name.

Their dancing weaves a sequence that forms a whole cloth, just as a musical phrase carries a series of notes and shapes it into a piece. A few foreign women who are studying dance on Gorée are pulled into the circle, but their practiced movements seem a jerky patchwork in comparison to the Senegalese. Mere speed is not enough to turn notes into phrases.

The Senegalese women flaunt and lift their skirts, their hair and limbs going everywhere, their feet pounding and skimming the sand. Middle-aged women let loose and lose twenty years. Pre-adolescent girls take on the motions and confidence of courtesans. Together and apart, their bodies capture and release the beat of the drums. They dance for themselves, with a physicality that cannot help but be sexual. Sarita, always on the lookout for oversimplification by outsiders, points out that calling the dance provocative would be falsely judgmental, since girls here often stay virgins into their twenties. Yet any healthy woman's body that moves with such vibrancy projects her sexuality. The difference is that, in the safety of the circle, the sabar dancers don't have to worry about their moves being regarded as an open invitation.

The telegraphed passion of the Senegalese women moves me. I feel it flow in me, too; even though I'm not in the circle, I'm with them. If not sexual ecstasy, they're expressing something close to it.

I flash on a scene from Christmas at home, growing up. Ann, Chris, Maggie and me, dancing in a chorus line in the living room. Singing with utter abandon, we stick out our chests and fling our legs. We fall into each other, a wild heap of limbs and laughter.

In that memory I recognize the emotion of the sabar and of the feast, the one that braids us all together.

It is joy.

Dinner with Joyce

by Nan Watkins

Welcome, O life! I go to encounter for the millionth time the reality of experience.
—James Joyce, *A Portrait of the Artist as a Young Man*

I have come to this Swiss city for the first time, not because it is a famous financial center, not for the luxury shopping on the Bahnhofstrasse, but because of James Joyce. Here, in Zurich, in this neutral country, Joyce found safe haven in his self-imposed exile from his native Ireland, and here, by chance, he is buried. I have come to honor my favorite modern writer, the man whose torrent of words on paper so shocked his compatriots that they would not print his master work in their country during his lifetime. But I'm removed from all that. Joyce's words simply make me rejoice!

One of the benefits of traveling alone is having the freedom to make all decisions myself, without needing to compromise with companions about how to proceed. Today, despite the heavy November rain, I feel like walking rather than hiring a taxi from the train station to my hotel. Adjusting the wool hat I bought in Munich to protect me from the worst of the rain—I don't travel with umbrellas anymore—I cross the tram tracks and the bridge over the Limmat River, which originates in Lake Zurich and flows through the center of town. The rain is falling in sheets, and I'm just able to make out the ducks and swans moving about in the cold water below. The clouds are much too dense for me to see the Alps beyond.

I find my small, family-run hotel easily, and my first test is to figure out how to open the door. There's no handle in sight, and I'm unable to push the glass door open. I notice a button to the right of the entrance, and when I push it, the door folds open, accordion-style, just long enough for me to slip inside.

I am pleased to learn that the reservation I made on the Internet, a first for me, is in good order. I am given two keys, each of which requires figuring out, as neither is the simple variety of door key I am used to. I feel like the young girl in the fairy tale who must solve a riddle in order to advance to the next room. I climb the stairs, at each floor pushing a power-saving light switch that stays lit just long enough for me to walk through. I finally unlock the door to my room to find an inviting bed with a pristine white linen cover over a fluffy *Federbett* (goose-down comforter). My window overlooks the back street, and I can hear a man singing and women talking in the rain.

I want to make the most of my time here, so I collect my thoughts and, checking to see that my city map is close at hand, I set out in the pouring rain to buy two red roses to put on the graves of Joyce and his wife, Nora. With my roses carefully wrapped, I walk back through the rain to the nearest tram stop and take shelter under the small roof on the platform.

Unlike my student days in Munich years ago, there is no conductor to take fares and give tickets and directions on the tram. I find the automat, which people are stoking with Swiss francs, but even after studying the listed fares, I can't figure out what to do. So, in German, I ask an elderly woman where the zoo is. I once read that Joyce's wife had commented after his funeral that she thought he would like the cemetery because it was near the zoo, where he could hear his beloved lions roar.

"You must realize that this is not a good day to visit the zoo," the woman replies in the Zurich German dialect. I explain that I am really looking for the Fluntern Cemetery, and she nods understandingly when she sees the flowers. She patiently tells me that I need to go to the end of Line 6 and, with some juggling to get the right change for the fare, I purchase my round-trip ticket to the zoo.

With a feeling of relief, even comfort, I sit back in the warm, dry tram car slowly making its way around the curves and up the hill. I see the buildings of the University of Zurich and ride through the quiet middle-class neighborhood of tree-lined streets where James and Nora Joyce once lived. I enjoy the smooth, gliding ride, and listen to the rasping sound of the wheels making difficult turns in the track.

When we reach the top of the hill, I can see the entrance to the zoo across the street. I figure the cemetery must be close by and head for an area of tall trees on the left. I walk through the iron entrance gate of Friedhof Fluntern and notice signs saying that all flowers must be handed in at the administration building. I hesitate. I have not come these thousands of miles to honor Joyce by giving my roses to a cemetery administrator, so I walk on, not having any idea where his grave is in this huge place, and reluctant to ask because of my contraband roses. I am amazed at how beautiful everything is—it feels more like a park than a cemetery. I walk up the gentle slope that crosses avenue after avenue of neatly tended graves bordered by little hedges and tastefully planted bushes. I decide I will find the gravesite myself, even if I have to walk until dark.

I meander a long while over gravel pathways. At last I reach a cross-path at the top of the hill and a very small wooden sign that says Joyce and Canetti Graves. My heart leaps. With a few more turns I walk the last steps over glistening wet flagstones to find Joyce's grave in a green, grassy plot by itself. It is covered by a large rectangular piece of polished black marble lying flat upon the ground, with a miniature, trimmed hedge of boxwood surrounding the shining marble. Four names, outlined in white, are carved into the black stone: James Joyce and Nora Barnacle Joyce, and the names of their son and daughter-in-law. A family headed by the man whose masterpiece, *Ulysses,* changed the course of creative writing in our time, and next to him his wife, his helpmeet, who mastered the practical necessities of life so that her husband could write.

What captivates me is the setting of the grave with the near life-size statue of Joyce sitting on a bench, walking stick at rest, head cocked slightly to the side, observing the scene through his bronze spectacles. I am relieved to find Joyce's final resting place utterly peaceful, for in his unsettled life of exile he was constantly uprooted. Above the grave, large hemlocks sway gracefully in the wind and white birches stand guard on the hill. I unwrap my two red roses, stash the paper in my bag and lay the flowers along the right side of the stone. Offerings. To James Joyce for the unflagging spirit that kept him writing, and to Nora for her devotion and enduring love.

I stay here, ignoring the cold and the wet. The last time I visited my mother's grave, it was a rainy day, just like this. The gray marble of her small stone marker, nestled below the gravestone of her parents, was also adorned with wet leaves. I wonder what elixir of love kept James and Nora together through the thick and thin of life, whereas not only my parents but also my husband and I divorced.

"May we ever and ever be very divinely in love" were words I found in a letter my father wrote to my mother in the 1930s, before their marriage. A short time later my mother replied, "My last day of teaching tomorrow. I have fewer regrets than I expected. It's just one more proof of my love for you, dear heart, that I can renounce so lightly what has been life itself for me for almost ten years." Thirty years later their marriage split asunder, and now they lie alone in separate graves.

Unwittingly, I repeated the pattern of my parents and was divorced, also after thirty years. Like them, my husband and I had an auspicious beginning. We took a year-long honeymoon in Vienna. There my husband used his Fulbright grant to research his dissertation, and I studied piano at the Vienna Academy of Music, learning to play Mozart sonatas as Mozart once played them. Our happiest times together were spent sharing our love of travel, literature and music. We saw and heard von Karajan direct Richard Wagner's monumental cycle, *Der Ring des Nibelungen,* at the Vienna State Opera; we took a tram up into the Vienna Woods to drink the new harvest of wine; my husband drove our miniature Styer-Puch over the Alps to Venice, where we rode gondolas in the winding canals, and on to Ravenna, where we stood honoring the grave of Dante, who lies in exile from his native Florence.

I listen for the lions' roar in the zoo across the way, but all I hear is rain falling through the trees. I walk further down the flagstone path to discover the grave of Elias Canetti, Nobel laureate, another great writer, another exile. His grave is a rough slab of white marble with his signature carved into the stone; wet golden birch leaves, blown from the trees above, are its only decoration.

I am glad these two sorcerers of words, Joyce and Canetti, share this ancient Swiss hilltop in their eternal rest. I imagine their spirits in witty conversation in the dark nights on this quiet knoll, the same way I imagine my mother conversing happily with all of her Welsh relatives on the hillside above the coal mine in Pennsylvania. It is a comfort for our earthly minds to believe that we can still communicate with our beloved, in death, through the spirit.

It is six o'clock in the evening and I have just awoken from a deep sleep. It takes a moment for me to get my bearings under the warm down comforter, but I realize quickly that if I want to eat dinner at the famous Kronenhalle restaurant without a reservation, I had better get going.

With great determination, I set out into the Zurich night, the rain falling more heavily than ever. I walk along the river, whose moving waves sparkle with the reflections of city lights. The wind is whipping the Limmat into a froth and blowing so hard that I have to hold on to my hat. On the way to the restaurant I pass the Café Odéon, which had been a gathering place for artists and exiles like Joyce and Lenin, and I wonder if they ever met each other there. By now I have memorized the central portion of the Zurich map, and I know I have to walk all the way down to the Quai Bridge at the head of Lake Zurich, and at that intersection I will find the restaurant.

One miserably cold and wet January night in 1941, Joyce was feeling ill and depressed, and decided he wanted to leave his apartment and have dinner at the Kronenhalle. Nora tried her best to dissuade him from going out into the wintry night, but Joyce prevailed. The two ordered a taxi and drove through the blustery dark, then climbed the flight of stairs to this most hospitable of Swiss restaurants. After enjoying a splendid meal, the Joyces returned home. In the middle of the night, Joyce awoke in great pain and was taken to the hospital, where he died of a perforated ulcer. That night at the Kronenhalle, James Joyce ate his last meal.

I climb the same flight of stairs the Joyces mounted some sixty years before. Inside the dark wooden double doors, I am greeted with a concerned and questioning look from the maitre d'. It's just as well I can't see myself, because I must look a mess. The maitre d' inquires if I have a reservation, and in my best German I explain that I am visiting in town and hope very much that he has a free table for me. After a brief consultation with his charts, he beckons me forward and cordially leads me to a waiter standing by a cloakroom, ready to take my soaking coat and hat. I remove my steamed glasses and, after wiping them on my Swiss linen handkerchief, I replace them to see tall paneled walls filled profusely with paintings by Picasso, Chagall, Braque and many other twentieth-century artists. The dining room is humming softly with voices in conversation. My waiter, whom I take to be Swiss-Italian, shows me to a table with a white linen cloth set impeccably for one. The thought crosses my mind that perhaps he knew all along that I was coming.

Now I know why Joyce loved this place. He had been a friend of the owner, Frau Zumsteg, who hosted artists living in Zurich from 1921 until her death in 1985. She was an art collector and made her restaurant a gathering place for creative people from all parts of Europe. The maitre d' is her son.

The waiter exhibits all the traits of first-class European service. He brings the menu, which features a reproduction of a 1972 painting Chagall dedicated to Frau Zumsteg. He carefully takes my order for the house specialty, *Kalbfleisch Geschnezeltes nach Kronenhaller Art,* then asks what wine I would like. I choose a quarter-liter of Beaujolais and sit back to enjoy the ambience of this handsome place. The white roll arrives, as crusty as can be; the butter is sweet Swiss butter. The waiter brings a bottle of Swiss mineral water and pours the wine from a small glass pitcher with a mark delineating exactly a quarter of a liter. I raise the delicate goblet to my lips and drink. Just to the left of my table is a Chagall painting: In a snowy night, a grandfather clock is chasing a group of children through a village street, while the moon hovers above in the blue-black sky.

The art of dining alone is underrated. Without the need to converse with a companion, the single diner can be attentive to the fine food and surroundings and can allow her mind to wander where it will. The pumpkin soup—the perfect texture and temperature—warms my heart. The tender veal in a tasty cream sauce with succulent pan-fried potatoes, Swiss style, brings back intimate memories of wintry evenings: of green velvet curtains; of a grand piano; of watching, from a second-floor window at twilight, an old Viennese woman sweep snow from the pavement with a handmade broom of twigs.

I look at the paintings on the walls and eavesdrop on the conversations of the couples around me. I imagine James and Nora Joyce sitting at one of the tables, enjoying a meal like mine. Joyce would take a bottle of wine with his dinner and lean his head a bit to the side to listen to the talk around him. Nora would look fetching, the neckline of her dark dress low enough to reveal her smooth Irish skin. They would talk little to each other, not needing words for understanding, just a close and familiar silence. They would stay as long as they could in the warmth of the restaurant, before heading back out into the cold.

I think of the role of the artist in society, of how the artist stands outside of the mainstream, exiled as recorder of human experience, critic of human behavior, town crier, visionary. James Joyce was all of these. His masterpiece, *Ulysses,* is the story of a journey, a day in the life of a man in Dublin, told with such richness, such texture of memory, tradition, experience, forethought, that it is the modern retelling of *The Odyssey,* the Greek epic told thousands of years ago by Homer. No matter when, no matter where, each of us is on a journey, day by day, year by year, whether we are conscious of it or not. The artist's journey is purposeful; the artist may not be a tidy citizen, but the artist knows why he or she is here: to tell a story, to awaken our minds and hearts to the bigger story of the universe beyond. I admire the artist, who with heightened ability of expression is able to articulate the pain and joy of the human journey, whether through writing, painting, sculpture or music. James Joyce, whose earthly journey ended in this town, who once sat in this room, was a great artist. That's why I've come to honor him.

In this later stage of my life, I find that I, too, am striving to record the important moments of my journey in my music and my writing. My appetite for life has not diminished, and I enjoy as much as ever my interaction with the diverse people I meet along the way. Hobnobbing with the great artists who have gone before me by immersing myself in their works of literature, art and music inspires me to keep plying my own modest form of art.

I finish my dinner of veal and potatoes, and just as I put down my fork, the waiter, who has been watching me attentively from a distance, brings a second serving, identical to the first. He smiles sweetly as he removes the empty plate and sets the full plate before me. I still have a good glass of wine left. I decide that if I take my time, I can eat the second serving as well as the first. So I do. And the grandfather clock keeps chasing the children through the dark and snowy street, and the moon continues to light the way.

Cud, Sweat and Fears:
Confessions of a Desert Nomad Wannabe

by Holly Morris

"Time has been vacuumed out of this reality," I think to myself as I shove a needle through yet another set of blisters, on this, the third long day of walking through the sweltering central Sahara with Tuareg nomads on salt caravan. I never knew that nothingness could take up so much space. And since I can speak exactly one word of the Tuareg's native language, Tamashek—*"tamanmere"* ("thank you")—I pass the hours ruminating on the concept of ethereal nothingness; miming to my *cheched* (hooded), all-male comrades; or rolling over in my brain how I could know so little about Niger, a place five times the size of Great Britain.

The Historical Scoop
Being a fairly typical American (that is, passively isolationist and mildly ignorant) before coming here, I knew little about this West African country that sits just left of Chad. My crash education revealed that the Scottish explorer Mongo Park traipsed up through sub-Saharan Africa in search of the source of the Niger in the nineteenth century—although it was the French who played tribal powers off one another and jimmied themselves

into the position of colonialist power. Since the country wasn't worth much—that is, it had only a few natural resources to exploit—the French bowed to political resistance in the mid-1900s, and Niger won its independence in 1960. The French paw prints and its language remain (among the educated), and now, rebellion simmers in the populace.

Led by the Tuareg, a disenfranchised desert warrior tribe, the rebellion has gone on for two decades—ever since the droughts of the '70s, when the corrupt government is said to have failed to pass along its international aid resources to the desert people. Ongoing violence and banditry between the government and the Tuareg (who some say are armed by Khaddafi) and a few coup d'etats have made Niger destination non grata for travelers. A tenuous cease-fire between the government and rebels recently "opened up" the country, and that's where my unlikely gringa presence in this solitary place came in. I jumped at the chance provided by the cease-fire to experience a few of this country's legendary festivals and walk the Sahara with the Blue Men of the Desert—people with a proud, warlike stance, swords at their side, swathed in indigo and concerned mostly with transporting salt. I'm learning that political upheaval can sit right alongside magic, and that this long, long walk that has happened for thousands of years doesn't stop for mere rebellion.

Liberation
Strangely, even though I am not alone—as my comrades in caravan are constant companions—I'm beginning to feel all the scrumptious pleasure of the solo experience. What with the spare surroundings, the language barrier and my own sense of "otherness," the soul-scrubbed-clean feeling that usually comes with a week alone in the mountains might be downright accessible on this desert sojourn.

We are walking to the oasis town of Fachi to trade the dried tomatoes and onions that weigh down our camels for salt, and to join a celebration that marks the end of the rainy season. As far as I can tell, this "time of plenty" is relative—it is simply the season least likely to steal your life.

For days the salt caravan leader, Oumarou, leads us along an invisible path, navigating by wind and stars. The pace is constant for ten or twelve hours a day. Our lives are filled with utter silence and constant motion, in a place where small mistakes have big consequences.

The men's eyes have the eerie, slightly nondirected look of the blind; their eyes beam out a sliver of blue from behind their black cheches. A life of desert sun without Ray-Bans prompts a different sort of evolution. Their indigo garb is cinched with ornate leather belts, and each man carries a sword—a talisman of the Tuareg warrior tradition. Clearly my presence is strange, but the men seem to take it in stride, literally. My to-ing and fro-ing and as-yet-unsettled relationship with my camel seem to provide comic relief, given the laughter that slides from under their cheches.

The cheches, or *tagelmousts,* are scarves that cover the head and neck, leaving a slit for the eyes and mouth. I am not a fan of anything that remotely resembles a veil, and I firmly resisted adopting the cheche and all its attendant political baggage.

That was stupid.

An hour in the midday Sahara and anyone without sunstroke learns that the cheche is a savior from the punishing rays. I clue in late, but from then on Oumarou patiently wraps and rewraps my mustard-colored cheche as necessary, salvaging both my dignity and my frying skin.

A friendly banter of Tamashek peppers the early morning hours, but by noon the 120-degree heat rules and the group falls silent. I'm trying to stay true to the "amazing cultural experience" and not start a bitching loop in my brain about the increasing discomfort, but it's a losing battle. Oumarou veers my way and hands me a hollowed gourd filled with water. *"Aman iman,"* he says in Tamashek. *"Fishou."* ("Water is life and life is water. Drink.")

Only the pain from my blistered feet provides the edge that keeps me from succumbing to woozy, heat-induced delirium. Everything happens on the move. Water passes from goatskin sheath to gourd to man . . . the walking never stops. A pungent mix of millet, goat cheese and water is mashed together and run from man to man to me by the nimble twelve-year-old son of Oumarou, who is constantly trailed by a little white goat . . . the walking never stops. The flat, featureless landscape stretches into infinity. The desert is elegant in its simplicity, and liberating in its reduction of life to fundamental elements—simple lines, food, water, salt.

When the walking finally does stop and the moon rises, the camels are relieved of their three-hundred-pound loads and fed. Despite their pissy personalities, I'm coming to appreciate these efficiently built dromedaries that can survive seventeen days without water and regulate their own body temperature. Their slight squint and sexy eyelashes allow them to plod forth in any manner of sandstorm.

Camp is set in silence smattered with camel groans of relief. The hay that has been on their backs is arranged in what might be deemed in Silicon Valley as an "open space cubicle layout." Small fires are started. Meals of millet are prepared—a simple process compared to the effort that goes into tea. Tea prep is a ritual of high art. Thick, sweet liquid is poured three feet from a kettle to a shot glass to another glass, back to the kettle, then back in a glass in a confusing caffeine jig that would rattle even a Seattle barista.

A dappling of fires and the silhouettes of folded-up beasts against the horizon provide the only definition between earth, sky, desert, camp. I crawl behind some hay into my sleeping bag under the stars to the rhythmic serenade of Oumarou's boy pounding millet. Despite the tea, sleep comes fast.

Two weeks ago I witnessed the annual ceremony of another nomadic tribe, the Wodaabe, who number only forty thousand. They cover a thousand miles a year in their search for water and food to feed their zebu cattle and goats. Their gerewol festival was much more girl-centric than this trek with the Tuareg, but both are part of the region's many Cure Salée celebrations (salt festivals). The Wodaabe are impoverished materially, and therefore personal beauty—their bodies and how they are decorated—is a great status symbol. The gerewol features a dancing beauty contest of sorts—a *yaake*—for men. The men are judged, by the women, on their white eyes, teeth, quivering lips and sinewy hips. Romantic alliances flourish. The young Wodaabe men primp and preen and peddle their wares in hopes of being chosen by the female judges, thus gaining social standing. Wodaabe society is matriarchal. Women choose who they want to marry—but men waste no time in making their intentions known. A simple scratch of his index finger on her palm lets a lady know a boy's lookin' for some lovin'. Slightly unromantic, but refreshingly to the point.

The Wodaabe festivities feel like a lifetime ago, as every day that I walk across this stretch of the Sahara, leading an ornery camel with lovely eyelashes, feels epic. The Tuareg nomads have no word in their native Tamashek for tomorrow—the concept doesn't exist. Today is today and tomorrow is . . . not today. Talk about living in the present. Because survival is so primary, the Tuareg culture cuts to the chase, in almost every respect. Appropriately, the written Tamashek language is all consonants, no mealy-mouthed vowels.

Each morning we rise in the predawn light to cauterize the wounds on the animals and load up the camels with hundreds of pounds of blankets, millet, hay, dried tomatoes and onions. Each afternoon I pray for an oasis. When I finally see the lush oasis of Fachi, it hits me like a mainlined fruit smoothie, and I realize how starved I've been for color. I'm desperately happy to see this cliché come to life: palm trees in the desert sea and its mirror-image mirage, tantalizingly close. I want to sprint toward it, but the Blue Men of the Desert keep me at their steady pace as the light slides away for the night.

Cure Salée

Fachi is one of the oldest inhabited towns in the Sahara. There was once an enormous saltwater lake here, but it evaporated under the heat of the fierce Saharan sun, leaving behind an area rich with salt deposits. The Kanouri people, who control the salt deposits, are the descendants of slaves who have lived and mined near the cliffs of Fachi since the eighth century.

We set up camp on the outskirts of the oasis, and I collapse among sleeping camels only to wake eight hours later as hundreds of villagers arrive for the annual camel races that are part of the traditional end-of-the-rains celebration.

Dozens of women swathed in indigo garments, bangles and black veils sit in circles, drumming and bellowing out in what sounds like a cacophony of over-excited waterfowl. It's called ululating. Their tongues move really fast.

Contestants, who've walked days or weeks to get here, line up in ornate regalia, proud atop their camels. On most days, these one-humped domesticated animals are "work horses." Today, they are honorable steeds whose good looks and speed may bestow status, and a bit of prize money, upon their riders. I'm growing downright fond of the versatile dromedary. In addition to being able to carry half their weight, with their milk they can feed forty human babies in times of inevitable drought. But right now, wet nurses they're not—today each of these beasts is expected to behave like a thoroughbred. Frenetic drumming and ululating provides the backdrop to an inaugural ceremony led by the village's blacksmiths. The blacksmiths seem to be the grand pooh-bahs of most things ceremonial, probably because of their association with fire, the element of creation. They call out numbers, one by one, and steed and rider, both layered in colorful blankets and fringe, join a circle running around the blacksmiths. They are judged by their regalia and pedigree: White and leggy camels are considered the most beautiful. This is phase one of the competition. The drumming, ululating and throngs of onlookers keep the atmosphere at a heady pitch.

Genetically Possessed

The blacksmiths-cum-sorcerers bless the event, then drop the sword that sets ninety camels and riders off, in a hurricane of hollering and chaos, for the first of three races. As they speed past, I note a few significant differences between a horse race and a camel race. First of all, here there's the hump to deal with; second, there are no stirrups; and third, well, despite the beating they're getting, the camels never actually break into a gallop—it's more of a fuel-injected hyper-trot. Ouch. As I cross my legs, it occurs to me that perhaps this is a sport better suited for the ladies.

The racecourse wanders off into the distance, following what looks like a looping river bed. The race is twenty minutes long, give or take, and the riders quickly disappear into a cloud of dust and distance. After about ten minutes we hear that a rider has fallen off and been trampled—which is somewhat serious, as we are at least four days from any sort of medical care facility, and even then we're talking triage, not the Mayo clinic.

Because of the accident, half of the men drop out of the second race—preferring to wait to risk their necks for the last race, which has the biggest kitty. Attention turns to the injured rider, who is quite dazed, but luckily seems to have only broken an arm.

Adult Child Syndrome

In a matter of hours all the Zen equity built up on the long desert walk drains from my soul. I, the competitive Adult Child Of A Professional Athlete And Gambler, am secretly formulating a plan to get myself in race three. I humbly, and incorrectly, wrap a cheche around my head and walk up to the lead blacksmith.

"*Je voudrais monter sur le chameau.*" I say.

Blank stare . . . then bewildered grin.

I repeat my request again, knowing he understands French, as this is a former French colony. A frenzied discussion among the blacksmiths ensues. My head swings back and forth as if I'm at a tennis match. Clearly, there is concern.

"Your liver," he says to me in French, which I mostly understand, "may damage the delicate, pointy trifecta of horns at the front of the saddle."

"My impalement ranks second to the well-being of le saddle?" I say.

"*Mais oui,* saddles are our most valuable possessions," he replies.

It's true; in this, one of the poorest nations in the world, a saddle is gold—and who am I to make value judgments? I briefly weigh the chances of getting a liver transplant at the hospital, which is a week away . . . but continue to lobby nonetheless. No doubt benefiting from my traveler status, I'm eventually granted a place in race three.

I'm handed the reins to a ten-foot-tall white camel swathed in multi-colored blankets and layers of leather fringe, sporting an intricate saddle of silver, leather and lethal horns. "Shhh, shhh, shhh," I say to him, imitating my fellow jockeys, as he kneels with a cranky, homicidal shriek. I climb aboard my massive dromedary and line up with ninety or so others. And this is when it hits me like a tsunami that, this time, I've gone *too far.* I should not rip through the desert on a giant camel, competing against veiled men with sharp swords who've done this drill for thousands of years.

I hate this part of me.

Why can't I be content to learn a new pesto recipe (or any recipe), power-walk on Sunday mornings and send out birthday presents on time, just like my sensible midwestern sisters? The answer is more complex than a notch in ye olde adventure belt. I have a deep-seated, almost irrational worry that I will miss out on something—an experience within my grasp that I've passed up out of fear. I'll probably never know the calm of a deathbed, but if I do, I don't want to be lying there mumbling, "damn, I shoulda entered that race." And here, in the middle of the Sahara, as the sword is about to drop, the really sick thing is: *I want to win.*

Aaaaaand they're off . . .
The next fifteen minutes are a blurry heap of survival tactics, rapid-fire cussing and wholesale regret. My rusty horseback riding skills do not trans-

late, and my dream of winning (or at least placing) is trampled within moments.

I just want to live.

My camel runs at full-throttle trot, and I am shamefully gripping the saddle's horns in order not to be flung over the top of the seven-foot long curvy neck, or skewered like a holiday pig, or both in rapid succession. I *do* want to live, but my father's DNA sears through my blood: I don't want to come in last, so I try to do like the jockey just ahead of me, who has one leg wrapped around the camel's neck and the other foot quivering the camel's nape—a sort of Saharan accelerator. I wrap my leg accordingly, thumping the camel with my filthy, blistered bare foot. My giant white steed responds like Secretariat at the Belmont, determined to wear the Triple Crown. He lurches ahead several lengths, passing two contenders.

Rocky Revolution

My organs are being rearranged, but before I can mutter "kidney belt," I'm in the final stretch, eating dust. Two riders are behind me; one is gaining fast. Suddenly, the awkward rhythms click and I become Lawrence of Arabia—no hands, yelling to my camel, the power of an empire behind me. My bum and the camel's hump are in perfect sync and we're charging toward the finish, neck-and-very-long-neck with a taupe camel whose rider is a peripheral blur of indigo. With a final gasp, we place second (to last) by a nose, throttle past the finish line and are surrounded by group of ululating women, who smudge indigo on the camel's face.

The women seem particularly thrilled at our performance, which is mysterious to me since we finished nearly dead last. As I unsaddle my steed and watch the villagers peel off and return to their homes across the oasis, a blacksmith walks up.

"You are the first woman ever to enter a camel race in its 5000-year tradition. They can't believe you actually finished," the blacksmith says.

"This girl over here says she wants to race next year," he adds, pointing to a smiling young woman of about fourteen.

Who's to say: arrogant competitive traveler inappropriately messes with status quo? Or, an interesting spark toward a cheched feminist revolution?

You make the camel call.

The Best Seat
in the House

by Edith Pearlman

I'm an itinerant listener. What's playing where? I used to demand of the concierge as soon as I'd unpacked my toothbrush. And so I've heard famous performers in packed Civic Centers. I've attended the philharmonic in this city and the opera in that, climbing neoclassical steps and clinging to Rococo banisters. I've sometimes, with the luck of the arriviste or the help of the concierge's nephew, acquired a third-row seat. I've mingled, wearing my best clothes, with people wearing much better ones.

But a year in Jerusalem spoiled me forever for concerts in concert halls. A little museum off the Jaffa Road, once the residence of artist Anna Ticho, offers a recital every Friday at noon. In a second-floor windowed gallery, a few rows of folding chairs surround a makeshift stage. Elderly retirees sit in the chairs; the performers' families and friends clutch each other in excitement; an occasional office worker rushes in on her lunch break. The sad-faced proprietor of a nearby shop—I think of him as the Melancholy Man—is always in attendance.

The players, different each Friday, have much in common: youth, talent, nervousness, excellent training. Most were born in Russia or Eastern

Europe. During a year of Fridays I heard quartets, trios, duets and solos; strings, winds, pianos. Once I watched a brother clarinetist and sister flutist scowl at each other throughout a recital, continuing some breakfast spat; their ensemble playing, however, was flawless. At other times I enjoyed flashy violinists, somber cellists and a pianist from Budapest whose handspan was like Franz Liszt's: about two octaves, I'd say. He wore—who could blame him—a shoulder-length coiffure.

During the winter the windows of the Anna Ticho House are closed. In other seasons they are thrown open, and traffic supplies a brass accompaniment. After each concert I wandered through the fragrant city, convinced that the best time and place to listen to music is at noon on Friday, upstairs in a Jerusalem house, sitting on a folding chair, in the company of many tranquil pensioners and one Melancholy Man.

But those straight rows of chairs—perhaps they are a bit formal. This occurred to me during a summer in Paris. Near the Centre Pompidou is an old church, St. Merri. Across its stone floor, on an August afternoon, three men carried a piano to a cleared area and then lovingly set it down. They placed some chairs here and there. One by one Parisians wandered in, carrying net bags bulging with baguettes and melons. Their faces were uninformative. Perhaps they came to avoid the jugglers in the square outside, or to stare up at the flamboyant arches inside, or just to interrupt their Saturday shopping.

The chairs got taken. New arrivals stood behind the chairs, as unemotional as if they were waiting for a train. Then a fellow with a long face—the Melancholy Man, transported—placed a newspaper on the floor and seated himself upon it. Not far from him a woman in a very wide skirt did the same thing, though without a newspaper. The rest of us followed their example and sank onto the stones.

The pianist appeared—a tuxedoed South American with full, serious lips. He played only Chopin, and he played with authority. As he performed complicated expressive nocturnes the faces of the audience became complicated and expressive. As he played polonaises and mazurkas, our little crowd, now tensely excited, might have been Polish patriots surrounding their beloved Fryderyk, in Warsaw, about a hundred and seventy years ago. The recital had no intermission, and was rather long, and ended much too soon. We clapped and clapped. The gratified pianist took two encores but was too wrung out to perform a third. So my fellow listeners, their expressions again impassive, stood, picked up their shopping bags, and resumed their private lives; and I left too, having learned that the best time and place to listen to music is two o'clock on an August Saturday inside a sixteenth-century church in Paris, sitting on the floor, in the company of strangers.

Walls, though—they can be confining. This I noticed at an early music workshop in the village of Prokopi, Greece. I was a friend of a participant; I had dropped in for a week on my way to Athens.

Performers of early music are a dedicated lot. Singers practice much of the day. Recorder players practice most of the day. Viola da gamba players practice all day long, their bows drawing from the six strings of their instruments a quiet, unearthly sound.

Sunday afternoon, though, everybody took a break, to climb Prokopi's pine-covered mountain. I climbed too. A renowned countertenor was our leader. Up we went, the young among us prancing like young goats, the not-so-young like older goats. Real goats scampered in the grassy clearings, out for a snack. After a while we reached the bare summit. The group, except for me, formed a semicircle. I sat on a boulder. The countertenor led this gifted chorus in William Byrd's four-part Mass (he had brought the parts in his backpack). The voices soared toward Heaven, which didn't seem very far away. *Dona nobis pacem,* they sang; and I, a singularly privileged audience of one, concluded absolutely that the best time and place to listen to music is at four o'clock on an October Sunday, on a Greek mountaintop, seated on a rock, in the company of a few bold ruminants.

Then came a spring twilight, in Manhattan. I was ambling towards a restaurant. Somewhere within a second-floor apartment with a tall open window, a saxophone began a tune; four notes; the first four notes of "Our Love Is Here To Stay." I stopped—who wouldn't—and listened to the entire melody, rendered sweetly by the unseen musician. I remembered that this was Gershwin's last tune; the heartbroken Ira had written the words only after George's death, words that celebrate the love of two brothers. But the song celebrates all love, really, perhaps even love at first sight; and I thought that, should the saxophonist turn out to be a young and handsome man, why, then, I would forgive the vast difference in our ages and forgo my happy marriage to a tolerant stay-at-home, and forget my horrified children; the Rockies were tumbling and Gibraltar was crumbling, but Our Love . . .

The serenade ended. The musician appeared in the open window, loosely grasping his instrument. He was indeed young and handsome, and he answered my smile and wave with a smile and wave of his own. But he seemed to be expecting someone—someone else. I walked on, knowing once and for all that the best place to listen to music is under a linden tree in the east seventies, at six in the evening on a May Tuesday, standing, alone.

Contributors

Faith Adiele's essays about travel and culture have appeared in *Go Girl! The Black Women's Book of Travel and Adventure;* Travelers' Tales' *Indonesia; Life Notes: Personal Writings by Contemporary Black Women;* and *Testimony: Young African-Americans on Self Discovery & Black Identity,* among others. She is currently working on a full-length memoir of her experience as the first Black Buddhist nun in Thailand. She lives in Minneapolis, Minnesota.

Marybeth Bond is the award-winning author and editor of five Travelers' Tales books, including *A Woman's World,* winner of the Best Travel Book of the Year Award, and *Gutsy Women.* She has given travel advice on over 250 television and radio shows and is the travel expert for CBS Network Evening Magazine. When not traveling with her husband, daughters or friends, she hangs her hat in the San Francisco Bay Area.

Chelsea Cain is the author of *Dharma Girl: A Roadtrip Across the American Generations* and the editor of *Wild Child: Girlhoods in the Counterculture.* She lives in Portland, Oregon, where she is completing her first novel.

Joan Chatfield-Taylor is the author of several books, including *Visiting Eden: The Public Gardens of Northern California.* Her writing has appeared in the *New York Times* Travel section, *Travel and Leisure, Food and Wine, Architectural Digest* and other publications. She lives in San Francisco, California.

Robyn Davidson is the author of *Tracks: A Woman's Solo Trek Across 1700 Miles of Australian Outback*. She writes extensively for *National Geographic* and other magazines, and is the author of the novel *Ancestors*. She currently is at work on a book about living in Rajasthan, India. She divides her time between London, India and Australia.

Ingrid Emerick is the sales & rights director of Seal Press. She is the coeditor of *Gifts of the Wild: A Woman's Book of Adventure*. She lives in Seattle, Washington.

Ayun Halliday is the author and publisher of the alternative zine *East Village Inky*. Her essays have appeared in *BUST, Hip Mama, Moms Online, Breeder: Real-Life Stories from the New Generation of Mothers* and *The Unsavvy Traveler*. She is currently at work on a book about life with her kids, India and Milo. She lives in Brooklyn, New York.

Marianne Ilaw's writing has appeared in numerous publications, including the *New York Daily News, Black Enterprise*, the *Financial Times of London, Chocolate Singles* and *Go Girl! The Black Woman's Book of Travel and Adventure*. She lives in Queens, New York.

Pramila Jayapal is the author of the travel memoir *Pilgrimage to India: A Woman Revisits Her Homeland*. She is currently at work on a book of short fiction. She lives in Seattle, Washington.

Dawn Comer Jefferson is an Emmy-nominated television writer who wrote the animated movie *Our Friend, Martin* and an episode of the CBS drama *Judging Amy*. She has written and produced syndicated radio shows for National Public Radio and writes for magazines such as *HealthQuest* and *Fit Pregnancy*. She co-writes a monthly column about children, family and culture for the online magazine Africana.com. She lives in North Hollywood, California.

Michelle Kehm has written for many girls' magazines, including *BUST, W.I.G.* and *Girlyhead*. Her work also appears in *The Unsavvy Traveler: Women's Comic Tales of Catastrophe*. She is currently working on her first book about her travels around Asia and a photoessay book about her travels with her Polaroid 250 camera.

E. J. Levy's nonfiction has appeared in *Utne Reader, The Nation* and *Orion,* among others. She is the editor of *Tasting Life Twice,* which received the Lambda Literary Award for Best Fiction Anthology. She is currently completing a travel memoir titled *Amazons*. She lives in Taos, New Mexico.

Margaret McConnell is a regular contributor to *Nervy Girl!* magazine in Portland, Oregon. She is a happily and hopelessly addicted traveler who has made the majority of her trips solo, with only a journal for company. She is currently expecting a child, and looks forward to buying that first tiny travel backpack for family trips abroad.

Holly Morris is a former editorial director of Seal Press whose writing has appeared in books, magazines and online, in publications including the *New York Times Book Review, Outside* and ABCnews.com. She edited two literary collections about fishing, *Uncommon Waters* and *A Different Angle*, and has contributed to numerous anthologies. She hosts the Discovery Travel show *Treks in a Wild World* and writes, directs and presents the award-winning PBS travel-biography series *Adventure Divas* (www.adventuredivas.com). She'll never enter a camel race again. Unless, well, the stakes are high.

Mary Morris is the author of several award-winning travel books, including *Wall to Wall: From Beijing to Berlin by Rail* and *Nothing to Declare: Memoirs of a Woman Traveling Alone*. She is also the editor of *Maiden Voyages: Writings by Women Travelers*. She lives in the Bay Area.

Ginny NiCarthy's book *Getting Free* was the first self-help book for battered women and has sold nearly 200,000 copies. Her travel stories have been published in the English-language newspaper *Atencio'n, Maiden Voyages* and *Olympia Yarn,* among other periodicals. She is completing a memoir of her world-travel adventures and will soon go to Colombia as a Witness for Peace delegate.

Bernice Notenboom is the proprietor of an adventure-travel company in Moab, Uta, specializing in indigenous tourism, from Indian reservations in the United States to Aboriginal Australia and Greenland. She organizes ski and climbing expeditions, and stories about her adventures have appeared in *National Geographic Traveler* and on National Public Radio's "The Savvy Traveler." She lives in Moab, Utah.

Jennie Peabody was awarded the George P. Gardner Traveling Fellowship, which enabled her to hike and photograph the 1,000-mile Buddhist pilgrimage around the island of Shikoku, Japan. She is at work on a full-length book about her experience. She lives in Seattle, Washington.

Edith Pearlman's collection of short stories, *Vaquita,* won the Drue Heinz award for literature in 1996. Her recent work has appeared in various anthologies and literary reviews, including *Best American Short Stories of 1998, Best American Short Stories of 2000* and *Pushcart Prize XXV.* She recently received the Antioch Review Award for Distinguished Prose. She lives in Brookline, Massachusetts.

Lisa Schnellinger has been a journalist for more than twenty years; she has worked for newspapers in Ohio, Seattle and China. She currently is a freelance writer, editor and teacher, and is working on a book about her six-month solo trip through Africa and the Middle East. Her travel writing frequently appears in the *Seattle Times.*

Ena Singh works with the United Nations in India on issues of population stabilization, reproductive health and women's empowerment. She lives in Delhi, India.

Barbara Sjoholm (Wilson) is the author of the award-winning memoir *Blue Windows: A Christian Science Childhood* and numerous works of fiction. Her novel *Gaudí Afternoon*, set in Barcelona, was made into a major motion picture starring Judy Davis as the globetrotting sleuth Cassandra Reilly. She recently completed a travel memoir, *Raising the Wind: Northern Voyages in Search of Seafaring Women*. She lives in Seattle, Washington.

Holly Smith has worked in the bookselling industry for many years and is currently a book buyer at World Wide Books and Maps. She is the coeditor of *500 Great Books by Women* and *Let's Hear it For the Girls*. She lives in Seattle, Washington.

Susan Spano's column on women and travel appears weekly in the *Los Angeles Times*. Prior to that she wrote the *New York Times* weekly travel column "The Frugal Traveler." Her travel writing has been anthologized widely. She is also the coeditor of two books: *Women on Divorce: A Bedside Companion* and *Men on Divorce: The Other Side of the Story*. She lives in Los Angeles, California.

Wuanda M. T. Walls, an eighth-generation Pennsylvanian, has traveled extensively throughout the world. Her writing has appeared in numerous magazines and books, including *Hot Flashes from Abroad: Women's Travel Tales and Adventures, Go Girl: The Black Women's Book of Travel and Adventure* and *Gifts of the Wild*. She divides her time between Pennsylvania and Colorado.

Nan Watkins' writing has appeared in *Hot Flashes from Abroad: Women's Travel Tales and Adventures*. Her memoir of her round-the-world solo journey, *East Toward Dawn,* is forthcoming in 2002. She lives in Cullowhee, North Carolina.

Louise Wisechild is the author of two memoirs, *The Obsidian Mirror* and *The Mother I Carry*. Her work has appeared in several anthologies, including *The Sweet Breathing of Plants,* and in publications including *The Christian Science Monitor* and the *Seattle Times*. She is currently working on a collection of travel writing. She lives in Vashon, Washington.

Thalia Zepatos is the author of two award-winning travel books, *A Journey of One's Own: Uncommon Advice for the Independent Woman Traveler* and *Adventures in Good Company: The Complete Guide to Women's Tours and Outdoor Trips*. She authored *Women for a Change: A Grassroots Guide to Activism and Politics*. She lives in Portland, Oregon.

Jamie Zeppa's memoir of life in Bhutan, *Beyond the Sky and the Earth: A Journey into Bhutan,* was published in 2000. She currently divides her time between Toronto and Bhutan.

About the Editors

Avid travelers **Faith Conlon, Ingrid Emerick** and **Christina Henry de Tessan** work together at Seal Press where they have developed the Adventura series, a line of books devoted to women's travel and outdoor-adventure writing. **Faith Conlon,** the publisher of Seal Press, lives in Seattle with her husband and son and has worked in publishing for over twenty years. **Ingrid Emerick** coedited *Gifts of the Wild: A Woman's Book of Adventure* with Faith and has worked at Seal Press for a decade. She lives in Seattle with her husband and son. **Christina Henry de Tessan** has worked for book publishers in San Francisco, Paris and Seattle. She is currently editing an anthology titled *Expat: Women's True Tales of Life Abroad* and lives on an island off Seattle with her husband.

Suggested Reading

Beyond the Sky and the Earth:
A Journey into Bhutan
Jamie Zeppa
Riverhead Books, 2000

The Curve of Time
M. Wylie Blanchet
Seal Press, 1993

Desert Sojourn:
A Woman's Forty Days and Nights Alone
Debi Holmes-Binney
Seal Press, 2000

Dream of a Thousand Lives:
A Sojourn in Thailand
Karen Connelly
Seal Press, 2001

Drive:
Women's True Stories from the Open Road   4/3/06 released   5 ☆
Edited by Jennie Goode
Seal Press, 2002

Femme d'Adventure:
Travel Tales from Inner Montana to Outer Mongolia
Jessica Maxwell
Seal Press, 1997

A Foxy Old Woman's Guide to Traveling Alone
Around Town and Around the World
Jay Ben-Lesser
Crossing Press, 1995

Gifts of the Wild: 4/3/06   5 ☀
A Woman's Book of Adventure
Edited by Faith Conlon, Ingrid Emerick and Jennie Goode
Seal Press, 1998

Go Girl!:
The Black Woman's Guide to Travel and Adventure
Edited by Elaine Lee
Eighth Mountain Press, 1997

Gutsy Women:
More Travel Tips and Wisdom for the Road
Edited by Marybeth Bond
Travelers' Tales, 2001

Hot Flashes from Abroad:
Women's Travel Tales and Adventures
Edited by Jean Gould
Seal Press, 2000

Journey Across Tibet:
A Young Woman's Trek Across the Rooftop of the World
Sorrel Wilby
Seal Press, 2001

A Journey of One's Own:
Uncommon Advice for the Independent Woman Traveler
Thalia Zepatos
Eighth Mountain Press, 1996

The Last Wild Edge:
One Woman's Journey from the Arctic Circle to the Olympic Rain Forest
Susan Zwinger
Johnson Books, 1999

Maiden Voyages:
Writings of Women Travelers
Edited by Mary Morris and Larry O'Connor
Vintage Books, 1993

My Journey to Lhasa
Alexandra David-Neel
Beacon Press, 1993

No Hurry to Get Home:
The Memoir of the New Yorker *Writer Whose Unconventional Life and Adventures Spanned the Twentieth Century*
Emily Hahn
Seal Press, 2000

Nothing to Declare:
Memoirs of a Woman Traveling Alone
Mary Morris
Penguin Books, 1988

Pilgrimage to India:
A Woman Revisits Her Homeland
Pramila Jayapal
Seal Press, 2001

Safety and Security for Women Who Travel
Sheila Swan and Peter Laufer
Travelers' Tales, 1998

Solo:
On Her Own Adventure
Edited by Susan Fox Rogers
Seal Press, 1996

South from Limpopo:
Travels Through South Africa
Dervla Murphy
Penguin, 2001

A Taste for Adventure:
A Culinary Odyssey Around the World
Anik See
Seal Press, 2001

Tracks: SA 4/2/06
A Woman's Solo Trek Across 1,700 Miles of Australian Outback
Robyn Davidson
Vintage, 1995

Transylvania and Beyond
Dervla Murphy
Penguin, 1995

Traveling Solo
Eleanor Berman
Globe Pequot Press, 1999

Unbeaten Tracks in Japan
Isabella L. Bird
Travelers' Tales, 2000

The Unsavvy Traveler
Women's Comic Tales of Catastrophe
Edited by Rosemary Caperton, Anne Mathews and Lucie Ocenas
Seal Press, 2001

The Violet Shyness of Their Eyes
Barbara Scot
Calyx Press, 1993

Wall to Wall:
From Beijing to Berlin by Rail
Mary Morris
Penguin, 1992

West with the Night own ☆
Beryl Markham
North Point Press, 1985

A Woman's Passion for Travel:
More True Stories from a Woman's World
Edited by Marybeth Bond and Pamela Michael
Travelers' Tales, 1999

A Woman's Path:
Women's Best Spiritual Travel Writing
Edited by Lucy McCauley, Amy G. Carlson and Jennifer Leo
Travelers' Tales, 2000

A Woman's World:
True Stories of Life on the Road
Edited by Marybeth Bond
Travelers' Tales, 1995